Lester Venter is a renowned political journalist and broadcaster.

His early reputation as a commentator on South African affairs was established as the political correspondent of *The Sunday Times.* He became a familiar face on television to most South Africans – first as a presenter of the current affairs programme, *Agenda*, then as anchorman for the TV coverage of the landmark 1994 elections.

He has travelled widely on political assignments in more than 40 countries throughout the world and has been invited by the governments of the United States, Germany and Finland to undertake extensive studies of their political systems.

As a foreign correspondent, he was based for a time in London's Fleet Street and has also served as an editor on the Overseas Service of the Swiss Broadcasting Corporation. Apart from his journalism and broadcasting work, Lester is the author of a history of Namibia.

ALSO BY LESTER VENTER

History Makers

WHEN MANDELA GOES

THE COMING OF SOUTH AFRICA'S SECOND REVOLUTION

Lester Venter

Doubleday

TRANSWORLD PUBLISHERS LTD
61–63 Uxbridge Road, London W5 5SA

TRANSWORLD PUBLISHERS (AUSTRALIA) PTY LTD
15–25 Helles Avenue, Moorebank, NSW 2170

TRANSWORLD PUBLISHERS (NZ) LTD
3 William Pickering Drive, Albany, Auckland

TRANSWORLD PUBLISHERS (PTY) LTD
P.O. Box 9380, Johannesburg 2000

Published 1997 in South Africa by Doubleday
a division of Transworld Publishers Ltd

A catalogue record for this book is available from the British Library.

ISBN 0385 408846

Printed and bound in Great Britain by
Mackays of Chatham plc, Chatham, Kent.

CONTENTS

AUTHOR'S NOTE

Any project of this nature faces a nearly-insurmountable, start-up problem. Facts and situations that are discussed, or on which projections are based, may change in the necessary interval between writing and publication. Equally, forecasts of the outcome of events may materialize before the book does. This is a composite problem that has dissuaded wiser writers from predictions on a subject as volatile, as changeable, and as changing as South Africa. I'm afraid I have ignored such sensible reservations and have spelled out what seems to be the most likely course of events. In doing so I have courted certain risks, even some potential embarrassment. Yet I feel that the exercise is of greater worth than individual concerns. So this is a request to you, reader, to take on some of those risks with me. Accept, as I do, that by the time you read this some details may have changed – but that it is the flow and direction of events that matters, not the events themselves. With this proviso, I have no doubt at all that the argument will remain intact.

PART ONE

RISING ANGER

CHAPTER ONE

THE MEANING OF CHANGE

Learning from the past, facing the future

If South Africa is to continue moving along the same tracks as in the past and in the present, then, it is submitted, the future can be fairly easily predicted; it will be found in the following pages.

ARTHUR KEPPEL-JONES, 1947

The title of this book may have a familiar ring. That's because it is an echo of Professor Arthur Keppel-Jones's remarkable work of political prophecy, *When Smuts Goes*. The book created a sensation when it was published in South Africa in 1947, and remains an under-recognized classic in the quicksands of political forecasting. Its title has survived as a familiar expression. It appears often, in many variations. And here it is again.

I'm not going to suggest that history is about to repeat itself. But I do think the far-seeing professor's undertaking is worth emulating now, fifty years later, and on the same basis. Like he did, I believe the future is contained in the present, which itself is a product of the past. Accordingly, the future, as promised by the present, will be found in the following pages.

A MATTER OF TIME

When Keppel-Jones was writing his book in 1946, it was not uncommon to find references in the country's newspapers to 'South Africa's racial problem'. Believe it or not, the phrase then meant the tensions between English and Afrikaans-speaking whites. In that year my parents, one an Afrikaner, the other an English-speaker, were newly married and being shunned by their families for having crossed what was then a relatively strict ethnic divide.

Today you need only turn to the comic section of the Afrikaans newspaper *Rapport* to find the ghost of that tension surviving as parody in the cartoon family Ben, Babsie en Familie. Ben is long suffering and has to put up with the antics of a ridiculously pompous neighbour, an Englishman whose upper lip is so stiff it is pulled into a permanent sneer. The sneer underlines the disdain with which the Englishman looks upon his inferior Boer neighbour.

The afterwash of the Second World War, during which there was a distinct sympathy for Germany among many Afrikaners, was high tide for English–Afrikaans tensions. This was the social mood Keppel-Jones wrote in. It was also the social context in which Jan Christiaan Smuts appeared as an outstanding cultural hybrid. As an Afrikaner by birth and upbringing, his roots were in a disadvantaged socio-economic class. As an individual, though, he was sought after and admired in international society. Very much like Nelson Mandela.

Smuts was South Africa's first statesman of international rank. Mandela is the first since then. When Smuts stood at the brink of his career's sudden end, Keppel-Jones said so and spelled out the consequences. At the time, his vivid prophecies were greeted by a mixture of anxiety and disbelief. As South Africa faces its future in the closing years of the brief Mandela era, those feelings will return.

WHAT ARTHUR SAW

In *When Smuts Goes* Keppel-Jones laid out an accurate prognosis of South Africa's future under the Afrikaners' National Party.

He began with two fundamental assumptions – that the Nationalists would come to power, and that the course they would embark on would be ruinous. At the time, not everyone believed the Nationalists would wrest government from Smuts's United Party. Even fewer believed they were serious about implementing the fanciful notion of apartheid whereby the races would be statutorily and, ultimately, geographically separated. Keppel-Jones believed them.

From there it was not too great a leap to foresee a rising tide of black discontent, and anticipate the long years of national agony while oppression and revolt fed off one another, each making a necessity of the other. Keppel-Jones predicted the main elements of the unhappy time that would constitute the reign of white nationalism in South Africa. He also foresaw that the white state would eventually collapse.

He saw that, to begin with, two things would happen in tandem: blacks would be legally and even physically cauterized from white society and the new government would set about entrenching Afrikaner hegemony in all facets of social life. Specifically, he depicted the denial of passports to persons planning to protest outside the country, the disenfranchisement of the coloured people and the stripping of South African citizenship from the country's black population. He anticipated the introduction of Christian National Education and pervasive censorship. Both would be needed to coach the thinking of the white voters essential to sustain Nationalism's aims.

That an aggregation of these actions would lead to international isolation, emigration and a flight of foreign capital was a deduction that probably didn't tax the professor's prognostic powers. He saw a growing scourge of corruption as the state fell into moral bankruptcy.

WHAT ARTHUR DIDN'T SEE

Looking back over the fifty years that have passed, one might marvel that Keppel-Jones was wrong in only two major predictions.

The first was that Britain would eventually become so outraged by its wayward former colony that it would invade the republic. In this Britain was to be supported by other nations. The United States would contribute troops. No doubt Keppel-Jones's thinking was influenced by the post-war mood in which Britain and her American ally – the leading liberal democracies – had triumphed over German fascism . . . a version of which the Nationalists were clearly steering towards in South Africa.

It was in this way that Keppel-Jones foresaw the end of the white state, a major conflagration with foreign intervention. In the years that followed his prediction, many governments, organizations and individuals in the world joined him in that vision or some variation of it.

In the end, of course, South Africa escaped that fate. To my mind, though, history's jury is still out on the difficult question of the extent to which violence was, or was not, a factor in the decline and demise of white nationalism.

No, Keppel-Jones's second conceptual stumble was the fatal one: he could not imagine the way black nationalism would assert itself over its white equivalent. Keppel-Jones envisaged the rise of two black, or substantially black parties. One he called the African National Party, the other the South African Progressive Party. The ANP was drawn in radical terms that would soon become familiar in African politics. It propounded undiluted African nationalism; it demanded the withdrawal of foreign troops and the immediate granting of independence. The second party, the SAPP, was much more moderate, very much like the cross-over parties that tried to bridge the competing nationalisms in South West Africa and Rhodesia when they were on their way to becoming Namibia and Zimbabwe. The SAPP, Keppel-Jones tells us, stood for 'education, submission to the influence of civilized countries, suppression of the witch doctors'.

Alas, his Eurocentric thought prison allowed him to envisage only the victory of this party, the SAPP. Once it was in power with a black prime minister, Keppel-Jones saw the SAPP electing a white president. Such a figure 'would be the best channel for the Republic's relations with foreign powers'.

A 220-WORD HISTORY OF SOUTH AFRICA

We have just witnessed the closing of the second epoch of South Africa's history, and the beginning of the third.

The first epoch ended with 200 years of tentative exploration by Portuguese, Dutch and English mariners.

The second epoch opened in the mid-seventeenth century as colonists from first one, then other, European countries arrived at the Cape. Initially, the colonists' energies were spent in establishing their hold on the new land, and in settling their rivalries for control of it. Once this was done, they fell into a protracted argument about what best to do with the native inhabitants.

Eventually this argument overshadowed all else in white politics in the black land. For the last fifty years of the 350-year second epoch, power was held by a group of the settlers' descendants that advocated segregation and domination.

This was the final chapter of the second epoch because the country's black inhabitants came to the unsurprising conclusion that their fate was not for their white countrymen to decide. So they set about prising the power to decide from the grip of white hands. In due course they succeeded, bringing the second epoch to a close.

The third epoch opened as South Africans, for the first time in their history, prepared to be governed – not by a minority, but by themselves.

THE FUTURE ISN'T WHAT IT USED TO BE

The future, seen from the murky perspective of the present, is more difficult to divine than it was from the relative clarity that pertained fifty years ago. Then, the fateful final chapter of the second epoch was about to begin. The Nationalists had an unconcealed political programme. Keppel-Jones made the calculated assumption that they would come to power before long and that they would implement their programme. Once he had done that, the rest followed. In fact, it followed more quickly than he himself anticipated: he expected the National Party victory in 1952; it came in 1948.

Once the sequence of events began to play itself out in the way Keppel-Jones had predicted, a calamitous end for South Africa became the prediction of all except the Nationalists. When white nationalism collapsed, it was only the Nationalists themselves who were surprised.

The task that confronts anyone trying to look into the future today is a very different one. The reason for this is a cliché favoured by every generation and, as ever, it is now more applicable than before: we live in a very different world to the one occupied by Keppel-Jones fifty years ago. The dynamics that make up the present day differ in principle from those that applied in 1947. Not for us the relative luxury of taking the governing party's programme of principles, and then imagining the consequences that might flow from implementing them. For one thing, South Africa's first democratic government has been characterized by an absence of policy.

Leave aside for the moment the fact that it was probably a good thing that a government with no experience of governing didn't launch precipitously into a programme of far-reaching change. But do register that it was two years before the new government began to develop an economic policy, before it developed an approach to education, policing, housing, agriculture and land distribution. By the time the new South Africa's first government was halfway through its term of office, it had still not declared itself on population development, health, the environment, arts, culture and taxation; and it was still fumbling privatization, labour relations, foreign policy, technology and the public media.

The absence of a clear-cut policy and the political will to implement it is not the only way in which Mandela's present day differs from Smuts's. There is a more fundamental difference between the end of the second epoch and the beginning of the third. It is that government and government policies are meaningful only up to a point. After that, they are overwhelmed by the realities that make up the present, and that are defining the future.

Moreover, these realities are not a prominent part of the public debate in South Africa. They get limited coverage in the media, and they are certainly not the main stuff of parliamentary debates. That's why, in this book, they are called the silent dynamics.

So, seen from this perspective, this is not an anti-government book.

This is not even an anti-ANC book. In fact, a note of tragedy permeates the discussion that will follow. Despite South Africa now having a government that is governing more or less in good faith, and which can be measured by accepted norms, that government will probably be ineffective against the underlying realities impelling South Africa towards a future containing great perils, and threatening great hardships.

A SINKING FEELING

The chapters that follow are about change. They are about changes taking place in the world today, and how they are affecting the people of Africa, and the people of South Africa in particular.

Change demands special qualities from those who live through it. The highveld town I grew up in, Carletonville, was plagued by subsiding ground. Houses would tilt, crack and collapse. In one sad case, a family was simply swallowed up by a sinkhole that appeared in the night. I remember the Gregory family. Their kitchen was so badly angled that the table they ate off was pushed against a wall. Otherwise, things would simply roll or slide off it. For my sister and me it was a special thrill to climb through a window to go to school on mornings when the subsiding walls of our block of flats had pinned the doors closed.

Visitors from elsewhere were dumbfounded when they found us in our sinking predicament. 'How can you live like this?' they would cry. 'Aren't you terrified?' Well, we weren't terrified, and we simply went about our normal lives.

Our condition was abnormal to people who visited Carletonville, but normal to us who lived in it. The situation we were in hadn't sprung itself upon us. The Gregory family's house hadn't lurched suddenly one night. The process of change had been gradual. We had adjusted to it along the way, making all the little allowances necessary. What was clearly an abnormal situation seemed normal to us because we had grown accustomed to it. This ability to think of the abnormal as normal is known – not widely, I concede – as the Carletonville Sinkholes Syndrome.

Although he didn't grow up in Carletonville, a similar perception caused the poet T. S. Eliot to remark on this curiosity of life. He said that change can be perceived, but not experienced. It is difficult, usually impossible, to be aware of change while it is happening – but it is easy to see it has happened when one looks back.

So it is with South Africa. If you had been told fifteen years ago that by the mid-1990s most middle-class whites would be deeply fearful of venturing into downtown Johannesburg, you would have thought it either preposterous or a future symptom of a city in deep decay. Today, that reality is an accepted condition of the present. Most businesses that cater to middle-class white consumers have migrated from the city centre. Middle-class whites now consider it quite normal to restrict their business and social lives to the suburbs.

This surreptitious nature of change has a sobering implication for us today. For it means that the processes of change that are currently sweeping us along are not readily perceptible to us. If we don't understand the change that is happening, we can't know where it will take us.

The chapters that follow are a bid to evade the change trap. They will take each of the primary elements that make up our lives in South African society, identify within them their main characteristics, seek to understand those and the change they are undergoing, and then project those processes into the future.

WHEN DOES THE FUTURE HAPPEN?

The desire to know the future, and the temptation to foretell it, is a seduction as old as humankind's imagination. Yet the science of futurology is an infant one. It does not have a long track record, and that's a good thing because it's not an illustrious one.

One of the earliest futurists to see his stars, so to speak, was the eighteenth-century British demographer Thomas Malthus, whose name in its adjectival form, Malthusian, has become synonymous with predictions of doom. The doom Malthus had in mind in 1798 was his famous observation that the population of Britain was growing faster than the country's ability to provide it with food and other resources.

Happily, Malthus's envisioned catastrophe never happened. The reason it didn't was that there was a process of change underway that Malthus, like everyone else at the time, had not noticed . . . or, at least, had not taken the full measure of. The Industrial Revolution had begun and it brought the growing nation the ability to provide for itself.

Two hundred years later, in the present day, the Cambridge philosopher Isaiah Berlin surveyed the twentieth century, noting 'the great ideological storms that have altered the lives of virtually all mankind . . . [the] totalitarian tyrannies of both right and left and the explosions of nationalism, racism, and, in places, of religious bigotry, which, interestingly enough,' Berlin added tellingly, 'not one of the most perceptive social thinkers of the nineteenth century had ever predicted'.

In my own career of writing and broadcasting on politics, I have frequently seen that it is the unforeseen and unintended consequences of the acts of politicians that shape the events that follow.

So it is not my purpose in this book to make a vain attempt to foresee the unforeseen. Imagination and speculation have a very restricted role in what follows. My aim is to identify, understand and demonstrate the processes of change already under way in South African society.

There would be, however, little point – and certainly very little excitement – in looking at processes of change without looking ahead to see where they are leading. Every journey has a destination, and every process has a conclusion. What's more, the destination is an outcome of the direction the journey has taken, and the conclusion is a result of the nature of the process. It follows, then, that there are inescapable elements of South Africa's future contained in its present, and this investigation will unfold a vision of the future.

I have chosen two points in the future to tether that vision. Neither is meant to be exact, nor is the vision meant to be complete. The first is about five years from the present. President Mandela would have handed over to a successor, and that successor would be about halfway through a new administration, the second of the democratic republic. The second point in the future is about twenty years from now.

The reason for the first is simply that we all share a common desire to know what the near future holds. Regarding the second, we all want to know what the world and our lives will be like when we reach future landmarks.

You might be in your twenties now, starting or about to start a career and a family. You would want to know, when you reach the peak of your career in your forties, whether the twenty years of effort will bring you the rewards you want. When the children you have raised begin their adult lives, will they be doing so in a safe and fruitful environment?

You may be in your forties now. You would want to know whether, when your career matures, you, your investments, family and lifestyle will be secure and in a stable environment.

You may be either or neither of these. You may be elsewhere in the world and have instead a material interest, or merely a curiosity, about the fate of South Africa. In addressing these needs, this investigation of South Africa's future has been based on three fundamental ideas.

The first idea: Two Worlds in One

Until recently the primary engine of conflict in international politics was the East–West split. Since the disintegration of the Soviet Union and the liberalization of the communist economies, this is no longer so. The primary engine of international tension is now the North–South split, the division between the First World and the Third World, the yawning chasm between the developed countries and the developing nations. The terminology differs according to the finesses of political correctness. The reality remains starkly the same.

South Africa is, within the boundaries of one country, a microcosm of this global reality. South Africa contains within itself a first world and a third world. The points of conflict between the two, and the tensions between them, are the same in principle as those on the global stage. Hence, the course of the conflict in the world at large is likely to be mirrored in South Africa.

Globally, the tensions created by the development gap are escalating. They are steering towards a day of reckoning. The origins, elements, and fate of this conflict are the subjects of an important, emerging field of study. Much that is relevant to South Africa can be learned from the work being done in this field. Many of the findings of this work can be translated down from the global level and applied as a socio-political template to this country.

The second idea: A Political Decapitation

South Africa has recently been through a breathtaking burst of change. Indeed, it has been a revolution, albeit a relatively peaceful one. The change from a race-based oligarchy to a non-racial democracy came not through the barrel of a gun, as many had come to fear, but via negotiation and, ultimately, the ballot box.

However, the process of change has turned out to be greater than the change itself. The very fact of change, and the way it happened, momentarily stunned the world and enthralled South Africans. The results of the change, however, have been far less auspicious. In fact, viewed from the perspective of the average South African – whether black or white – the change in the country has amounted to little more than a political decapitation. One head, a white one, was removed and another, a mainly black one, was put in its place. One government was replaced by another. It has been a change of government more than a change in society.

The third idea: The Silent Dynamics

The change has still to come. And come it will. Moreover, change will not come primarily through the actions and policies of government. It will come from underlying forces to which governmental action will usually be a confused response.

Expectations have been aroused. Those in whom they have been aroused will not tolerate the frustration of unfulfilment for ever. Even if a present, older, generation is – to some degree – resigned to the immutability of life and acceptant of a pitiable fate, the sons and daughters of this generation are not. Expectations are self-fulfilling, at least partially. A process of change is already in motion. Change in South Africa didn't end when the results of the 1994 election were announced, as many people seem to think. In truth, that's when change began.

Affirmative action, empowerment, unionism, the redistribution of land and wealth and some other, limited, government initiatives are all contributing to a degree of change in South Africa. But these high-profile, much discussed issues are not the real agents of change.

The real motive energies of change lurk behind the visible props and sets of the daily political drama. They are not part of the public debate. They get only limited coverage in the media. They are seldom deliberated in parliament. When they are, most members slip out to do something they regard as either more interesting or more important. Yet these are the irresistible, nigh-unchangeable forces that are really deciding the way we live today, and the way we will live tomorrow. Before long, they will dictate virtually the entire political agenda of the society and government itself.

They are the silent dynamics, and part two of this book is an investigation of them and their effects.

WHAT'S THIS ABOUT A REVOLUTION?

The great impact that the French Revolution made on the psyche of modern humanity has left us with an enduring image of revolution. The word conjures pictures of a downtrodden proletariat, abused past the point of humble tolerance, storming the ramparts of power in an eruption of fury, seizing the battlements, and then putting the be-wigged gentry to the guillotine.

The twentieth century has given us an image of a doughty bush-fighter rising in the name of the peasants to rid them of a dictator, and bringing independence and dignity to their simple lives.

Significant as these may be as political events, they haven't had as much effect on the way we live as processes like the Agricultural Revolution, the Industrial Revolution, the cultural revolution of the baby boomers, and the information revolution currently under way.

South Africa has now experienced a political revolution, and is confronting the early stages of a social revolution. The first has prepared the way for the second. The three fundamental ideas set out above, taken together, spell out the inevitability of a social revolution. By the middle of the next administration, the one that will follow

President Mandela's, it will be well under way. By the time your children go to work, your career peaks, or you retire, it will have happened.

By the time you have read this book, you may know what it will be like.

CHAPTER TWO

PUBLIC ENEMY NUMBER 2

South Africa in the post-Cold War world

I and the public know
What all schoolchildren learn
Those to whom evil is done
Do evil in return

W.H. AUDEN

The Berlin Wall was a sullen symbol of the bipolar world of the Cold War, the world most of us spent most of our lives in. The Wall divided West from East, good from evil, prosperity from stagnation, liberty from bondage. It focused our minds. It gave a meaning and method to politics. It provided a ready moral handhold by which we could understand the purpose and worth of our secular lives, and the societies we lived in. Then it fell. In the aftershock of the fall, the world was left to re-order itself. That new order is only now taking shape. Our understanding of it, along with an ability to relate to it usefully, is a step behind. The new world disorder moved an acting American secretary of state, Lawrence Eagleburger, to despair: 'We are living in a world of random acts,' he wrote in an assessment of the modern world for the *International Economy*. While Mr Eagleburger is undoubtedly correct, we may not all share his indignation and despair. What he is bemoaning, of course, is the disappearance of an international order dominated by two superpowers that divided the rest of us into two sets of client states. No more. The bipolar world has given way to a multipolar world, and the Eagleburgers of many capitals are floundering.

ABOUT TURN

One of the happy results of the global shakedown has been a decline in militarism. This is an event of such deep import that it is affecting the present-day world not only politically and economically, but psychologically. When the superpowers and their surrogates were driven by the hidden hands of massively expensive military establishments, the globe's public enemy number 1 was the ever-looming threat of nuclear holocaust. The world hovered on the brink of it in 1962 during the Cuban Missiles Crisis, and brushed with it on many little-publicized occasions recounted by Bertrand Russell and other scientists in *Has Man a Future?* The threat became part of Western culture, and the ban-the-bomb emblem became the sign of the main social movement of the Sixties, the hippies.

That threat no longer sits like a modern Mephistopheles in evil lordship over our fate. Not gone, it is substantially reduced. And since the rest of us are no longer divided into one or other of the global surrogate armies, we have a commensurately reduced need for armies at all. Wars and violent conflicts in the world fell by more than a third between 1989 and 1995. Global military spending has fallen almost to half of what it used to be. According to the International Monetary Fund, it is down from 4.9 per cent of world GDP in 1985 to 2.5 per cent today. Translated into monetary terms, that is an amount of liberated funds equal to the operating budgets of several medium-sized countries – a sum that could be used to make a staggering impact on human development. Theoretically.

These have been heady days. South Africa, to the surprised delight of the world and the country's own citizens, became part of the good story. Where democracy had not triumphed, it was on the march. Laissez-faire economies had irrefutably proved their superiority as engines of human prosperity. An American political scientist, Francis Fukuyama, wrote the book that captured the ethos of the age. He called it *The End of History and the Last Man*, and in it he explained that the great ideological disputes of modern history had now been settled. For good. Mr Fukuyama seemed to be going a bit far. But no-one could say exactly why and, besides, no-one wanted to be seen to be the spoilsport at the dawn of the golden age.

In short, the entire experience has been similar to the one that played itself out in South Africa. Here, as in the world at large, when the darkness seemed deepest, unexpected rays of hope broke the gloom. Our mood lifted, and we looked to the future with buoyant anticipation.

As the launch party of the new age dribbled to a close, however, so there rose a dawning awareness of another presence. A sombre figure had been standing in the shadows at the edges of the jollity, not part of the merry-making. That dark and ominous presence, it turns out, is roughly half of the world's population. It is a little more than 2 billion people who are today posing the greatest threat to world progress and security. They are doing so not because they are bad, but because they are desperate. It would be serious enough if they were merely poor and lagging behind. But that is not the case. The really disturbing thing is that they are getting poorer at an accelerating rate – and they are multiplying in frightening proportions.

The ever-widening gap between the rich nations of the North and the poor of the South and the consequences of this rending of the planet are the focal reality of today and tomorrow.

The development gap will create a new duality in the world and drive the politics of the future. It will be the central theme of international politics simply because it will be the single greatest threat to peace and progress in the twenty-first century. The axis has turned.

The East–West conflict is being replaced by a growing North–South febrility. Public enemy number 1 has made way for public enemy number 2.

Once more, South Africa is, and will be, part of the story. The course of the coming conflict will be played out in South Africa, and other countries like it, as a microcosm of the whole.

FOR BETTER AND WORSE

The word civilization is of relatively recent origin, in linguistic terms, and was taking a foothold in English as the Industrial Revolution began in England. Shortly thereafter, the revolution moved to France, from where the word had come. It was to be expected that those who first began using the term applied it to themselves and the industrializing, technological societies they were creating. For a long time, the rise of technology and the rise of civilization were taken to be more or less the same thing.

In the world boom of the 1950s and 1960s there was a widespread belief in the industrialized nations that the prosperity they were creating would spread to the poor countries. Those poor countries would use the economic sparks to ignite their own industrial revolutions, and set off their own wealth explosions. Besides, the first effective quasi-world government had been set up in the form of the United Nations. It was spearheaded by a number of agencies specifically aimed at promoting development in the poorer nations. Everything would soon come right. Not to worry.

Well, before long, it became apparent that things weren't coming right. But how could this be, we asked ourselves? And having asked that, our minds turned to a deeper question: bearing in mind the advances we have made in sciences and social institutions on the one hand, and the wholesale slaughter of human beings this century, abetted by science, and the continuance of desperate need on the other hand; must we conclude that the world is becoming more, or less, civilized?

By now we have the answer. The answer is, ha-ha, a paradox: things can get better and worse at the same time, and they have.

I trust the South African parallel is making itself clear?

GOING DOWN

The United Nations' 1996 Human Development Report reveals that roughly two-thirds of the world's countries – 100 out of 160 – are worse off now than they were in the 1980s. The predicament of the poorest fifteen of those countries is worsening at an alarming pace: the worth of the average output of each of their citizens fell by 1 per cent a year through the 1980s. In the first three years of the 1990s the rate of decline accelerated to 5.7 per cent a year.

A survey of UN data shows developing countries lagging ever further behind the industrial nations in real GDP per capita, the number of pupils enrolled in schools, and the number of years they spend in school once they get there.

Researchers at the UN have devised a method that takes the availability of telephones as a yardstick of the functioning level of a national economy. Measured on an index where the industrial countries are 100, the developing countries stood at 12 in 1980. By 1992, however, the availability index had fallen by 50 per cent to 6. In the least developed countries it fell over the same period from 7 to 1, and in sub-Saharan Africa from 10 to 3.

This slump has left the world's poor in a pernicious state. A World Bank report in 1996 said about 20 per cent of the world's population was living on less than US$1 a day. In 1987 there were 1.23 billion people suffering this fate; by 1993 another 80 million had joined them.

In the developing world as a whole, the average per capita income is below $100 a month, compared to about $2,000 a month in the twenty-five most developed countries. Manfred Woehlcke, a researcher at the Institute for Politics and Economics at Ebenhausen in Germany, has suggested the following rule of thumb for the distribution of wealth: when the millennium ends in a few years, there will be about 6 billion people on the planet – of those 1 billion will be wealthy, 1 billion will be well provided for, 1 billion will be poor, and 3 billion will be desperately poor.

With ever-increasing speed, the shadow of the desperate ones is falling over the conscience of the privileged. Outside Jerusalem stands Yad Vashem, the world's saddest and most moving memorial. Among others, it commemorates the 1 million children who were murdered in the Holocaust. Yet in the present, the same number are dying every year. According to the World Health Organization, most of these children are being killed by neglect, their deaths arising from an absence of preventive measures that would cost a few cents per child. In fact, one of those children will die before you reach the end of this sentence. There will be no memorial for this child, nor, at twenty-three deaths a minute, for the many who will follow before you turn this page, and forget.

THE COMING OF THE UN-PEOPLE

The terrible poverty of the world's desperate ones is an ugly story, but not a complete one. We have already seen how their plight is getting worse, not better. The real crunch is that the poor are getting poorer while the rich are getting richer. The gap between the people of the world is widening, not closing. And it's happening all over, not just at the interface between the rich and the poor nations. The same dynamic is at work within countries, even developed and industrialized societies. Even though the national average income in the United States is increasing, the number of poor people is growing, and the income gap between them and the rich is greater now than it was in the depression of the 1930s. In an assessment of the are-things-getting-better-or-are-they-getting-worse debate in Britain, *The Economist* concluded 'the poor are both poorer and more numerous'. The facts back it up. In 1979, 5 million Britons lived in households with less than the average net income of their countrymen. In 1993 there were 14 million.

Thirty years ago, using the techniques of the World Bank, the wealthiest 20 per cent of the world's population was about thirty times better off than the poorest 20 per cent. Today the top bracket is sixty times better off. By a slightly different measure, one-sixth of the world's population now owns five-sixths of its wealth.

There is as yet no adequate model for this reality that is emerging as the primary characteristic of the world economy – but someone in some ivy-leagued academy is undoubtedly working on one. Once that model arrives, it will probably be something along the lines of concentric circles, because that which is happening in the macrocosm of the globe is happening in microcosm within the borders of individual lands, and even within sub-societies within those. The smaller circles have the same properties as the larger ones that encompass them, and vice versa.

This state of affairs was not created in the night. It has been growing around us for decades. The Carletonville Sinkholes Syndrome of change applies here. We take the situation to be a given, and as something that is a sad but unavoidable reality of life; something, nevertheless, quite normal. So it would be left to a visitor from another planet to see the frightening abnormality of how we are living.

The visitor would see a world where a small band of us, the privileged, are entering a universe of, truly, virtual reality; one where some of us are speeding giddily along information highways in pursuit of cyberthrills, interconnecting our minds through microchip extensions in the World Wide Web; yet where, the visitor would see, more than half the population of the planet has never used a telephone.

The visitor would see a planet dominated by an amazingly tiny elite, surrounded by growing seas of desperation and want; where 358 individuals (the number of billionaires in the world, according to UN figures) have assets exceeding the combined incomes of countries that account for half the world's population.

The visitor would see the lifestyle of the rich being imposed on the poor as the paradigm of progress. The visitor would see that our planet is spawning in its societies – and particularly in our own in South Africa – sub-societies in which people are unemployed, uneducated, unskilled, unhoused, unfed, unwell . . . and unsatisfied. They are the un-people.

THE REVENGE OF THE UN-PEOPLE

The historians, writers, futurists and social scientists occupied with this problem all agree on at least one thing besides that the development gap is now a crisis and it's growing – and that is that international society is heading for some kind of a great reckoning.

Still, one might ask why nothing has happened yet, and why comparatively little is heard about the crisis? The answer lies in the nature of poverty. It is a grinding, debilitating condition that suffers in silence just below your line of sight. How many residents of Johannesburg have been to Soweto? How many residents of Rio de Janeiro have been into the favelas? How many residents of Delhi have been into the sprawling slums? The self-perpetuating predicament of the poor is this: to have your voice heard, to initiate social action, you need social institutions to promote your cause; you need an education to conceive and organize those institutions; you need means of communication and the knowledge to use them; you need leaders who will represent you because your support is valuable to them in some way. None of these things is affordable to those who need them most, for the very reason that they need them in the first place – their poverty.

This view is part of the orthodoxy of social science and, of course, it is true. But it is also short-sighted, one-dimensional, and dangerously incomplete. The world's poor are not entirely voiceless and powerless. The voice they are acquiring will be harsh and bewildering to the privileged, and the power they wield is starting to hurt.

The problem is reaching a critical mass, and is now entering a quantum state: it is possible to predict that events of a certain nature are going to take place, although it is not possible to say exactly where or when.

MY HUNGER, YOUR PAIN

One of the first and most obvious manifestations of the crisis is crime. Around the world, a pandemic escalation of crime is being experienced. With the rise in lawlessness, the nature of crime is changing. It is becoming more than an aberration practised by misfits on the fringes of society. For many, it has become the only alternative. For the underclass of the un-people, it has become their economy – the only one available to them in the fight to sustain life. 'My son puts food on the table. We don't ask where he gets the money for it,' an unemployed Soweto father tells a television documentary filmmaker after police come to take the provident son away for his many crimes.

I know this is an excessively indulgent explanation of crime. It is Dickensian in tone and recalls the dictum of 'give me not hunger lest I steal'. Obviously there is a lot more to crime than this. But for a vital aspect of how crime affects our future, this is the explanation that matters.

Take another example. South Africa's First World component is, as elsewhere, communications dependent. Telephone cables, and the computers that use them to exchange business information, orders and even money, are the circulatory system of the economy. The un-people are denied formal access to this sophisticated economy – but they can live off it by stealing its cables. In South Africa this a substantial sub-industry in a sub-economy: about R12 million of cabling is stolen annually. Telkom and Transnet, the state-owned telecommunications and transport networks, estimate the costs in production downtime at about R300 million a year. That excludes the labour costs of crews almost permanently replacing stolen cable.

Let's return to the global picture, but take another South African example to illustrate it. During the night of 28 January 1996 a seemingly inexplicable event of random terror took place in the industrial district of Alrode, in eastern Gauteng. On that day word had begun to spread that a die-casting factory had 200 jobs to offer. As night fell, many hundreds of anxious people gathered at the factory gates, planning to wait through the night in order to be at the head of the queue in the morning. By 2 a.m. the crowd of desperate job-seekers had swelled dramatically. Then a car drove up. Men in it sprayed the crowd with gunfire. The crowd stampeded. In the aftermath, the bodies of eight dead and twenty-three injured lay in the dusty street. Despite a police reward of R250,000, no arrests were made, and no reason for the attack came forward.

This is a deeply portentous event. Think about it. Since terrorism made its appearance as a political tool, one of its classic functions has been to goad the oppressed into action. Blind terror has been the instrument. Now suppose someone, some unscrupulous group, saw political profit for itself in agitating the un-people to the point that they started doing something – preferably something violent – about their condition. Then, as a means of achieving that aim, the Alrode incident could have been lifted straight out of the textbook on terrorism. After all, it's been done before. It's called politicizing the masses, and several members of South Africa's parliament, on both sides, have their mastery of this dark art of politics to thank for their present positions.

I'm not suggesting that's what really happened at Alrode, or that the world is necessarily poised on the brink of a new genre of terrorism. But can the day be far off? According to our quantum theory of politics, it's already scripted in the book of political extremism. The ground has been prepared. All that is awaited are the committed practitioners.

MR CHAIRMAN, I MOVE . . .

Let's range similarly into the future on the political terrain. Imagine that in the United Nations General Assembly a bloc of the most desperate developing countries pushes into debate a joint proposal. It demands that all industrial countries above a certain floor index of per capita income must be compelled to apportion a certain minimum percentage of their GDP to foreign aid. The minimum percentage is so high it shocks the rich nations of the North and causes widespread alarm and outrage. The bloc of developing countries argues it's the only way to stave off a planet-wide human disaster.

Once again, I'm not suggesting such a move is politically practicable in present conditions. But can the day be far off? Is it really, against the background of the picture sketched so far, such a far-fetched notion? If such a move took place in the near future, the industrial countries would probably find a way to squash the resolution. But it would send the international debate, and international politics and diplomacy with it, off in a new, scary direction, wouldn't it?

No, it's probably not going to happen soon; but the facts, and the quantum interpretation of the facts, say that it is inevitable. In this case we also know where it will happen. It's simply when that we don't know.

Mr Woehlcke of the Ebenhauser institute sees similar outcomes in his investigation of the ramifications of the development crisis. He speaks of the 'chaos power' of the desperate nations, and writes:

> The distributional struggles not only intensify because scarce goods and services have to be distributed between a growing

> number of individuals, groups and institutions, but also against the background of the growing expectations, greater mobility and improved organizational ability of the underprivileged social strata. This often takes place in a framework of unsuitable political structures, which tend to serve as an instrument ensuring the privileges of elites and the enforcement of anti-developmental ideologies rather than a sensible and far-sighted development strategy. This encourages domestic and regional conflicts.

Dumped in this condition, Mr Woehlcke says, states would be distinctly inclined to use their chaos power in the flow of international politics and in deliberate disruptions of international trade. The banding together of the oil producers in 1974 to hold the industrial nations to ransom over oil supplies is an uncomfortable reminder that if this should happen, it wouldn't be the first time.

The German institute sees the international arms build-up taking on a new perspective in the development crisis. The arms race, remember, has slowed dramatically, but it hasn't stopped. Now that many states, particularly in the developing world, are no longer vassals of a superpower, they need no longer pursue their military agendas within a framework imposed by a superpower . . . nor do they need a superpower's consent to pursue military adventures. This is a very worrying prospect – and not only in the cases of hot-head states like Libya and Iraq. In southern Africa, one of the continent's rare success stories, Botswana, a neighbour to South Africa, is suddenly pursuing an arms build-up that is grossly out of proportion to the country's defence needs, and is puzzling military analysts. For radical states, the temptation to use their chaos power will sooner or later mean an escalation of attacks on aircraft and shipping, industrial installations and other acts of terrorism.

Lawrence Eagleburger spells out a similar vision. Only, he has a more direct word for it: blackmail. His vision is of a ship moored in New York Harbour with a nuclear weapon in the hold, ready to detonate. 'Someone like Qadaffi', he says, 'then reads off a list of demands to the United States.'

Another outcome of the development crisis that is causing deep rivers of anxiety in industrial countries is the possibility of great population displacements. Driven by overcrowding and hunger, populations may go on the move. Catastrophic refugee movements already follow the conflicts that arise from retarded development, particularly in Africa. The next step – tens of millions of migrants and refugees desperate to escape the poverty trap and eager to reside among the prosperous – is something the industrial nations are trying not to think about. Already the dynamic is at work in the flow of the needy from the rural districts of developing countries to the cities. The number of mega-cities (more than 10 million inhabitants) in the Third World is expected to grow from eight to eighteen by the time the century ends. How long before these cities begin to export their problems to the First World?

Despite the fact that the consumption of energy resources is thirteen times greater in the United States than it is in China, and 348 times greater than in Mali, environmental damage in developing countries is widespread and has global implications. Third World countries cannot, and will not in the foreseeable future, aspire to the same environmental protection standards as the industrial countries, because they lack the political will to do so. Faced with a cornucopia of lethal social problems, developing countries generally consider environmental programmes – which are usually expensive – to be unnecessary luxuries. So, as Third World populations burgeon, so do their flocks of domestic animals that graze ever more planetary flora, so those populations clear more of the forests to make way for man and beast, and so do they upset the delicate ecological balances of the planet . . . affecting us all.

The hothouses of overcrowded populations, most of them in the tropical belt, are incubators for diseases that are exported across the planet. Aids is the most outstanding, but by no means the only, example. In the cyclical nature of the poverty trap, the declining financial resources to fight disease, the breakdown of infrastructure, the weakening of government, all combine to make the growing populations ever more impenetrable to preventive-medicine schemes.

The last in this overview of development crisis implications brings us to where we began – the growth of crime. As the world's economy internationalizes, so does its attendant sub-economy of crime. This is particularly true of the drugs trade. Mr Woehlcke points out that while the major drugs consumption takes place in the industrial countries, the major drugs production happens in developing countries. Some estimates say that the turnover of drug cartels in producing countries, like those in South America, exceeds the budgets of the countries they operate from. Recent scandals have implicated Latin American governments in the drugs trade. The line between political leaders and leading criminals blurs and, again, a symbiotic relationship is formed between a formal economy and a sub-economy.

To understand the threat to security that the development gap brings with it, we need to expand the way we think about security. In the days of the supremacy of nation states, national armies would go to war, usually over territorial disputes. We don't really do that sort of thing anymore. The second half of this century saw the rise of terrorism to promote political causes; now, in addition, we have the random acts that worry Mr Eagleburger. Also, as will be discussed shortly, the nation state has been declining in importance relative to the multinational company. Our well-being today is increasingly dependent on the giant companies that straddle the globe. By comparison, our reliance on government to supply the good things of life is declining. In fact, one of the primary responsibilities of national government is becoming simply to see that there is a favourable environment for the mega-companies. The sum of this is that war, threats to security and the potential for destabilizing societies are all taking on more of an economic definition than ever before.

That's why a criminal stealing telephone cables, or a drug baron of the inner city, is as much our enemy today as a soldier in uniform was yesterday.

OK, SO WHO'S TO BLAME FOR ALL THIS?

The post-Cold War shakedown has brought the development crisis to the foreground – but it didn't cause it. The development gap is the result of a series of events, evolutions and revolutions, none of which was intended to have this outcome. The Carletonville Sinkholes Syndrome of Change joined up with the Law of Unintended Consequences to shepherd us to the place we find ourselves today. Accordingly, detection of the causes of change has been slow and often absent.

Now, however, the indictment sheet is clear. The perpetrators are: the population explosion; the knowledge revolution; and an interactive chain comprising the globalization of economic activity, the liberalization of the world economy, and the decline of government in the face of these two.

It's (another) boy!

Let's illuminate another of the fundamental laws that underpin the discussion in this book: things are invariably less complicated than they are made out to be . . . particularly by people who earn a living by being an expert in the field in question. Hence, a college degree is not necessary to understand the relationship between population and economics: the more people that a given number of goods and resources have to be divided among, the fewer of those goods each will get and the less each will benefit from those resources.

The simplicity of this equation is matched only by the frequency with which it is overlooked by governments. The importance of the formula really kicks in, though, when one measures the pace at which the population and the economy grow. So, if you have an economy growing at a respectable rate of, say, 3 per cent, and its fruits are to be apportioned among a population that is growing at, say, 1 per cent, then everyone will likely be getting a fair slice. Not only that, it means that everyone will be getting an ever-bigger slice.

This is the fulcrum of prosperity in the elite group of rich nations. For the rest of the world, the opposite is true. Populations are growing faster than the economies they live in. For the great majority of these countries, it means that not only have things reached the point now where everyone is getting less than a fair slice – they are getting an ever-smaller slice.

This all seems perfectly plain. Nevertheless, there has been a debate in the last two decades wherein an opposing camp argued that more people create more economic activity, hence more wealth. What this camp failed to take into account was the changing nature of the world economy, and that within many countries many millions of people would enter their economies unequipped to contribute anything significant, and unable to derive much benefit at all. There would be more takers than makers.

Commensurately, the rate of unemployment in the world has grown dramatically. Population Concern, an international population-monitoring agency, projects that, at current rates, in twenty years from now there will five times more unemployed people than there are today.

Countries caught in the population *vs* development dilemma have only two options for salvation: slow the population growth down, or speed the economic growth up, until the one passes the other. So far, there is no sign of this happening, nor of the likelihood that it may happen in the near future.

The fact that the world, at 5.8 billion, already has too many people hardly needs emphasis. What carries mind-addling implications for the future, though, is the rate at which it is growing. It took humankind many thousands of years to reach 2.5 billion – which it did in 1950. Then, it took only until 1987, a mere thirty-seven years, for the same growth to happen again. According to present UN projections, the next 2.5 billion will take little more than twenty years.

Yet again, the overwhelming weight of the problem, and the suffering that will come with it, lies in the developing world. The Central African Republic will take 35 years to double its population; by contrast, Japan will take 277 years and Sweden 990 years.

Some relief is provided by the fact that the overall rate of population growth is slowing. The statistical picture given here, however, takes that into account. Mention is often made, too, of the Aids epidemic. Here, even the most extreme predictions of the spread of the disease mean a slowing of population growth in most-affected areas, not a halt to it.

One more observation about population needs to be made, relevant to understanding the global context within which South Africa's future is going to happen, and which South Africa's future will reflect. The growing populations of the world are on the move. And it's the cities they are moving to.

The world is on the cusp of an important change in principle – from a planet on which the greater part of the population is rural, to one on which the majority of its people live in great, teeming cities. In a *Newsweek* compilation on the eve of 1996's UN Cities Summit in Istanbul, it was reported that the world's twelve mega-cities (10 million inhabitants or more) will grow to twenty-five before the century ends. Ten of the thirteen newcomers will be in the Third World and, incidentally, Johannesburg will be one of them.

Peasants stream to the cities to seek there the livelihood they cannot sustain in their villages and fields. To a degree, they do find improved conditions and opportunities, and the rate at which they multiply slows down. But that degree is a small one, and is dwarfed by the new problems that arise.

In *Preparing for the Twenty-first Century* Paul Kennedy looks into the near future of these urban centres:

> Consider, for example, the burdens that will be placed on such cities' already inadequate (or non-existent) housing, sanitation, transportation, food distribution, and communications systems if their populations double or treble in size. In many of these countries a disproportionate amount of the nation's limited wealth is owned by the governing elites, who will find it difficult to buy off the discontents of the fast-growing urban masses.

Now it's what you know

The world is undergoing a knowledge revolution. It's a post-industrial development, and it's sweeping some of us along into a radically new and different future . . . and leaving others of us behind. Before long a tourist will be able to visit three distinct worlds on one planet: there will be an agrarian world whose inhabitants work the land and tend flocks to sustain lives which are bound in time-entrenched customs; there will be industrial societies with mainly urbanized populations who work in manufacturing and commerce, and struggle with the effects that the social rupture of changing lifestyles has brought; and there will be a world in which a new reality will have been grafted on to the industrial society, a world where microchips process everything from home entertainment to advanced medical diagnostics, with economies based more on services than on goods.

The futurist Alvin Toffler calls this last, emerging reality the third wave. The first wave, or great tidal change in civilization, according to Toffler's metaphor, was the Agricultural Revolution. In this period, roughly 10,000 years ago, a rudimentary science of working the soil emerged. This allowed clans and groups to settle in one place and plan their harvests so that they could be sustained through the barren months of winters. The settled societies learned to organize themselves and manage their resources. That was politics. They applied themselves to production and trade. That was economics.

People lived in societies such as these until the age of the machine – the Industrial Revolution that transformed England in the second half of the eighteenth century. This was the second wave. It transferred political power from landowners to capitalists, and created an urban working class. England then exported its revolution – curiously, at roughly fifty-year intervals – first to France, then the rest of Europe, then the United States of America and then Japan. After that it penetrated – with varying degrees of depth and permanence, Eastern Europe and the Third World.

This era lasted until the coming of the silicon chip, the microscopic labyrinth that altered the way we do just about everything. This is the third wave and Toffler describes its replacement of the second by calling it the end of the 'smokestack' industries – where the great foundries and bustling factories of yesterday are giving way to quiet, knowledge-intensive places of production run by technicians and computers. Toffler illustrates the point with a typical product of the recent past, a frying pan. This product, he says, is 90 per cent material and 10 per cent know-how. A typical contemporary consumer product would be a video cassette recorder. This product is 10 per cent material and 90 per cent know-how. The inverted ratio reflects the change in skills and methods needed to work and live in the new age.

Other futurists may not be as vivid in their descriptions as Toffler. But on the central theme – that knowledge is the fulcrum of future prosperity – they are unanimous. Kennedy spells out in academic detail how societies that invest in education, that invest in automation of production facilities, that unfetter technology, will be the winning nations of the new era.

Until a generation ago, it was accepted that the classic formula for economic activity was land, labour and capital. Now there is similar consensus that knowledge and technology have to be added to the mix.

The awful implication of the knowledge revolution for the development gap is this: knowledge, as a product of education, costs money – but it takes knowledge to make money. The development chicken and the poverty egg; which, oh which, shall be first?

The market rules, OK?

The new kingdom of knowledge does not respect borders. Ideas and know-how are becoming a universal economic currency, and the rules and practices of trade are becoming standardized world-wide. The standard is a liberal one, and the institutions that organize trade, and the companies that trade, are becoming global. More than before, the success of countries is being determined not so much by what they can produce, but by how they respond to international trade and the global market place.

All over the world the same economic theme is playing itself out. Eastern Europe's centrally planned economies have been replaced by free markets, in East and South-East Asia the export-driven economic miracle continues, some Latin American countries have jumped on the bandwagon, and in Western Europe governments have quietly set aside their visions of mixed economies. Only Africa lags behind.

The new trading ethos is not merely a fleeting mood. The fifty-year-old General Agreement on Tariffs and Trade, GATT, has been pronounced dead. In 1986 the international rule makers of trade got together in Uruguay. Six years later they had formulated a new consensus, and in 1994 the World Trade Organization came into being as the new arbiter of the international economy – with a free world market as its leitmotif.

The phasing out of tariffs is hurting some countries. Unsurprisingly, it is again the poor, many of whom were overly dependent on artificially maintained commodity prices, who are feeling the pain. But their wails are being drowned by the din of the new order. It may be a liberal order, but it is unforgiving towards those who do not, or cannot, play by its rules and meet its exacting standards.

It goes almost without saying that the prominence of national government has declined in the face of economic globalization. Many of the large multinational companies have a larger asset base than some of the countries they operate in. They fulfil universal desires that governments cannot. The corporations and their customers look to government only to make it easy for the companies to operate where they want, and where they are wanted.

Once again, the world has arrived at a point of turning. Big government, and growing government, has been accepted as a fact of life most of this century. Public spending for public good has generally been regarded as a desirable thing. A 1995 IMF study showed that government spending as a percentage of GDP in industrialized countries rose from under 10 per cent at the beginning of the century to around 40 per cent by the 1980s. The same study showed, though, that the countries with the lowest rise were the most efficient. They got into a cycle of lower taxes, therefore more money for consumption and investment, hence more jobs, hence more money. With more money, people educate themselves, heal themselves, house themselves and save.

From now on national governments will be measured by the extent to which they absorb the new truth, and the degree to which they facilitate their countries' participation in it. They are expected to open the door, then step out of the way. Those that hang around the economic thoroughfare are going to get bruised, and will only interrupt the prosperity traffic.

Farewell to alms

There is one significant respect in which internationalism is declining rather than rising, and that is foreign aid. A joint report in mid-1996 by a group of international aid agencies showed that aid levels had declined rapidly in the 1990s. They are now at the lowest level for twenty years. Rich countries presently apportion only 0.27 per cent of their GDP to overseas assistance, the report said. The richest are cutting back the fastest – the United States's cutbacks are as great as 30 per cent.

That's not all. There's a peculiarity in the way in which aid is assigned: the flow of funds favours the winners among the recipient nations. According to one UN official two-thirds of the world's poorest people get only one-third of the total overseas development assistance. This is a reflection of the way international money behaves – aid and investment travel hand in hand. So, according to figures of the UN Conference of Trade and Development, UNCTAD, 34 per cent of foreign direct investment goes to developing countries . . . but 84 per cent of that goes to the fifteen most dynamic of those countries.

One of the reasons for the change in aid patterns is, of course, the end of the bipolar world and the superpower and client state relationship. But it is not the only reason. In industrial countries there has been a growing popular resistance to aid, much of which is seen to be wasteful – and wasted. That view is captured in the disparaging wisecrack: foreign aid is the poor of the North giving to the rich of the South. Years of reports of corrupt politicians in the Third World enriching themselves from funds that come from wage earners and taxpayers in the industrial countries have taken their toll. Public pressure is mounting on First World governments, and diplomats now speak circuitously, in forums such as UNCTAD, of 'donor fatigue'.

YES, THERE IS GOOD NEWS

The overall picture drawn up to now of the galloping gap between the world's rich and its poor is just that, an overall picture. In the gloom there are bursts of hope and light. They show us that the poverty cycle can be broken and that individual nations can escape a wretched destiny. Although they are a minority, they are beacons.

Their success is well known and often cited: the 'Asian tigers' – South Korea, Taiwan, Hong Kong and Singapore; latter-day tigers – Malaysia, Thailand and Indonesia; some Latin American countries showing promising signs – Chile and Argentina; and, lately, the rousing giants of India and China.

What is less well known, however, is what made them successful. Much energy is expended in a search for the Holy Grail of modern economics – the secret of the success of the Pacific Rim countries. The answers vary and, usually, the more dogmatic they are, the less convincing they are. The reason is simply that there isn't a common thread that runs through the economic success stories of those developing countries – such as there is for the established industrial nations.

It seems, then, that the most profitable search for explanations is in what the successful new nations did not do. Most striking in that area is that the winners did not pursue political emancipation at the price of economic emancipation. The pursuit of political freedom was placed second to the pursuit of economic freedom. This has proved to be a teensy embarrassment to free-market liberals (like this one). The Asian winners were stable and well ordered, irrespective of how that stability and order was achieved. And it stayed like that during their growth bursts. They waited until everyone had a television set before they demanded the right to see and hear what they wanted on them; they waited until everyone was educated before everyone was consulted on public policy.

There was another important thing the winners did not have, probably as a result of what they didn't do, described above. They didn't have a powerful component of the social pact in conflict with its partners. That's econo-speak for they didn't have union trouble. Where labour was organized, it was organized not as an antidote to capital, but as its instrument.

When governments intervened in their economies, they did so not as something permanent, or as a way of life. There was government intervention all right, but when government entered certain industries or industrial sectors, it was highly specific. Government went in as an economic SWAT team with a declared programme and goal. When those were achieved, government withdrew. Government did not park itself in the economy, or in industrial sectors, creating top-heavy bureaucracies with civil servants who would set about stealing, mismanaging and obstructing.

Additionally, the winners have not been particularly inward-looking. They have cared less about what they can build for themselves and sell to themselves than they have about what they can build for foreign buyers and sell in world markets. That meant they eradicated every obstacle they could find to export on the one hand, and foreign investment on the other. Put another way, while they may have been politically illiberal, they were economically very liberal. At the same time, those governments recognized that they needed healthy and educated workers to achieve their economic goals, and so great emphasis was placed on social programmes to that effect.

Lastly, the people as a whole did not misdirect their energy into unproductive avenues. They acknowledged that there were injustices and imbalances, that they had inherited a legacy of obstacles and disadvantage, and that they were entitled to a better life. Then, having acknowledged that, they set about clambering to a forward position where those impediments would be left behind, and their ambitions and entitlements would be materialized. They leapfrogged over their problems.

OH, AFRICA

With India and China awakening, Africa is the last continental space on earth that shows no signs of entering an industrial revolution. In fact, as a collection of agrarian societies it is not doing too wonderfully, either. The colonial period was undoubtedly sinful and wrought lasting damage; but when it ended, it left Africa not only self-sufficient in food, but a net exporter. Today, according to the Washington-based Food Policy Research Institute, a quarter of the continent's people are hungry and malnourished. Many of those are actually starving.

Africa has stolidly failed to modernize. For more than thirty years manufacturing has remained static at about 10 per cent of economic activity. The great boom of the 1950s in world demand for commodities hooked Africa on a dead-end economic dependency. The UN says a majority of African countries depend on one or two commodities for more than 90 per cent of their export revenue, and more than 75 per cent of the continent's working people are in the commodity sector.

In this age where well-intended political correctness tends to reorder reality, it has become fashionable to argue that Africa is the next – last, yes, but next – continent where growth will blossom. These arguments, however, are of the if and should variety. If African countries do such-and-such, then . . . African governments should . . . then . . .

Alas, the odds are stacked against these good intentions and exhortations. With 12 per cent of the world's population, Africa's economic activity remains stuck at about 1 per cent of the world's GDP, and it receives only 2 per cent of foreign direct investment.

While the global economy and developing countries are plagued by the development gap whereby the poor are improving their lot marginally, but are getting poorer relative to the rate at which the rich are getting richer, Africa is the only place that is in reverse in absolute terms. In the last fifteen years, output per head has fallen steadily.

Sadly, Africa excels only in the rate at which it produces people. According to most projections, Africa will add the equivalent of another Algeria to the continent every year for the next thirty years. Even the most conservative projections have the current population of 650 million doubling in the next twenty years. As Paul Kennedy points out, that's without a corresponding increase in resources – in fact, a decline in resources. Worse, by that time the majority of the population would have migrated to the continent's cities, hoping to make a living without marketable skills.

Many of the continent's woes are blamed on the colonial era. To be sure, colonialism imposed a First World component on Africa, denied the indigenous people access to it, stuck a bleedline into the natural resources, then precipitously pulled out and dumped the whole shooting match on the luckless locals, leaving them to sort themselves out as best they could. Yet Africans have failed to fill the post-colonial vacuum with anything of indigenous value.

Democracy has not been kind to Africa. A brief flowering of multi-party systems in the 1980s quickly careened out of control. Countries like Zaire and Zambia now have literally dozens of political parties, most with an imperfect interpretation of the democratic way. There is, as a result, an emerging consensus among Africans and others that a simplistic imposition of Western politics on African societies is not as automatically beneficial as was imagined. International agencies are quietly backing away from their insistence on Western-style multi-party systems as a prerequisite for financial assistance.

Thus there is a gathering tendency to political systems that are more African in flavour. These are unitary systems that internalize their democracy – single-party states, either by law or by practice, that create extended lines of consultation within the party . . . and cut out external opposition. You can differ with us, as long as you can demonstrate that you are with us.

Whether this development constitutes the first steps to a new stability and order that will lay a foundation for growth remains to be seen.

* * *

This is the world, and the continent, that South Africa has become part of. It has always been there, of course. But for reasons that we know very well, South Africa has only now emerged from half a century of looking inwards. In that time it acted as if its peculiar problems somehow removed it from the road the rest of humanity was on. To a large degree that was true.

Now, it is not merely that South Africa has become part of the world. The world has become part of it. The realities that shape the world today, and will shape it tomorrow, will shape South Africa in the same way.

CHAPTER THREE

TWO WORLDS IN ONE

Global trends intersect in South Africa

When the poor rise up, they'll rise up against us all.

THABO MBEKI

Apartheid was South Africa's Berlin Wall. It was the great divider. It was that which loomed largest in anyone's perception – no matter which side of the divide one was looking from. It was the way in which life in South Africa was understood, and it was the issue that drove all politics. Birth, school, love, work, home, sex and death were all governed in some way by apartheid. Whatever trivialities escaped its ambit were obscured by its shadow.

When apartheid fell, as part of the chain reaction set off by the fall of the Berlin Wall, a new vision of South Africa emerged from the settling dust. It was a South Africa that had always been there, of course. It's just that, without the obstacle of the wall, it now stood more clearly revealed. It was seen that many ills that had been blamed on apartheid had only been exaggerated by it, and that many of the effects of apartheid, direct or indirect, would not disappear just because apartheid had.

When the dust settled after the fall, there it was – a South Africa without the ugly blemish that had set it apart. The South Africa that was revealed resembled, more than anything else, the larger world of which it had become a part.

And that's just the problem. As with the world as a whole, things in South Africa had got better and worse at the same time. The yoke of oppression had been removed from the land's people, and they had elected a government of their choosing. They were free at last. As far as progress was concerned, the stage was now set. That was the good part.

But what kind of a show would the players on that stage put on? That was the question that arose after the setting of the stage. That question remains without an answer, and that's the bad part.

The paradox of getting worse and better at the same time would bring South Africa into line with the mainstream of social and political development in the world as a whole. That, in turn, would mean a new set of forces would get to work in South Africa to shape its future, as in the rest of the world. Those forces have become the silent dynamics of South Africa's present-day politics.

In South Africa, they mirror those at work in the world: widespread poverty, getting worse in relation to the forward leaps being made by the rich; population growth outstripping economic growth, and the slumming of the cities as unstemmable waves of migrants arrive there; the rise in crime and the development of an illicit sub-economy feeding off its formal partner; the promise of dramatic political instability and the wielding of chaos power; and the deterioration of the environment and its resources.

If South Africa's ugly blemish caused it to be shunned by the world, then it was set at an even greater distance from its fellow African nations. Now that South Africa has become part of Africa once again, another question has opened, and it's a question that South Africans are going to great lengths to avoid asking themselves: will we, the African nation at the southern tip of the continent, become like, or unlike, our fellow nations in Central Africa, in East Africa and West Africa? Will we join the trend to declining output, shrinking food and natural resources, ballooning populations and stagnant economies? Or will we buck the trend and become the noted exception?

The answer, as before, is both. The paradox shall be with us. South Africa will become ever more like a prism. Like a prism, it will bend light, truth and perception depending on the angle from which you look at it. Part of South Africa has already achieved the self-sustaining cycle of success and will remain on it; and part of South Africa hasn't achieved it, and never will. The gap between the two parts will get bigger, not smaller.

As an embodiment of the deep contradictions of our age, South Africa will therefore resemble the world, more than it will resemble Africa. It's just that South Africa is unluckier than the world – because South Africa will embody those contradictions, intensely focused, within the confines of one country. And that means that South Africa will remain among the most conflict-driven societies for a long time to come.

Before we look to the conflict and its outcome, we need to take a closer look at the elements that make it up. We need to see how the elements of the conflict that will beset the world in the twenty-first century will manifest in South Africa.

LAND OF THE POOR

South Africa's First World component – the high-rises and highways, the expensive cars and shopping malls – has always masked a land of extensive poverty. Statistics vary and each new report draws a slightly different picture. But a central theme of extreme want, largely hidden from the privileged, remains constant. The privileged, whether residents or visitors, are usually astounded to learn that about half of South Africa's people exist in extreme poverty, with an average of about R300 a month to live on. Nearly a quarter of black households has an income of that amount or less per month.

Half of the population accounts for less than 10 per cent of consumption in the country's economic life, and the poorest 15 per cent buy only about 1 per cent of the goods. Almost two-thirds of the country's children, about 60 per cent, live below the breadline.

Behind the bland statistics lies the squalid reality of people's lives.

A 1995 study by the Community Agency for Social Enquiry, CASE, found that water is available from an indoor tap in only 20 per cent of black households. There is no toilet of any kind in nearly 20 per cent of homes and nearly 60 per cent have no electricity.

Taking R900 a month as a minimum living level for a household, the CASE study found that two-thirds of black homes didn't make it.

IT'S THE GAP THAT MATTERS

There's no way to measure resentment and envy in a society. So there's no way to tell what effect it has. But you won't need that degree in politics to figure that where two worlds, one rich and one poor, live side by side, the politics of envy is going to be a significant motivator in parliament, in the workplace and in the underworld of crime.

A Palestinian protester once told a *Newsweek* reporter in Tel Aviv: 'No man can accept that he doesn't have water to drink, while his neighbour has a pool to swim in.' The Palestinian's anger could not have been framed more aptly for South Africa, where there are more black people without houses than there are white people; where a domestic swimming pool is fairly common to those white people, while about 12 million black South Africans do not have access to safe water for washing, cooking and drinking.

The UN's 1994 Human Development Index measured 174 countries and found that if white South Africa were one country, it would rank 24th in the world, with Spain, Hong Kong and Greece; if black South Africa were one country, it would rank 123rd in the world, with Congo and Cameroon. South African society is riven with disparities. The richest 20 per cent of the population earns about twenty times more than the poorest 20 per cent, according to the UN's 1996 HDI. Even in society's middle brackets, the gap is there: about 60 per cent of black household incomes are in the R250–R1,250 a month bracket; 60 per cent of white household incomes are in the R2,500–R8,300 bracket. (These findings, from a study by the SA Labour and Development Research Unit, backed by the World Bank, differ slightly from those of the CASE study referred to above – but they tell the same story.)

WHAT'S WORSE, IT'S GETTING WORSE

Two apparently contradictory things are happening in South Africa: the income gap between blacks and whites is slowly narrowing, yet the gap between the rich and the poor is widening. How come? It's because most of the thinking on the income gap, along with most of the information on it, like that quoted above, is trapped in the racial idiom entrenched by apartheid.

A new black elite is emerging, and it is pulling away from the black poor. Even in apartheid's last decade, according to political scientist Heribert Adam, the top 20 per cent of black households experienced a 40 per cent growth in income, while the buying power of the bottom 40 per cent declined by about 40 per cent. This is the new, and disturbing, reality that is being grafted on to the old racial paradigm. This is the gap that matters. This is the gap that's drawing the battle lines of a new class conflict.

While the elite is redefining itself from a purely white one to a new, multiracial upper class, the poor continue to get more numerous. There are more poor people in South Africa now than there ever were before. And tomorrow there will be more.

That's not all. The poor are multiplying in an environment where the country is ever less capable of caring for them. On the UN's HDI index, real GDP per capita in South Africa fell from 47 points in 1960 as measured against the industrial North's 100, to 25 in 1990. In a society where 6 per cent of the population accounts for 40 per cent of consumption, and where the first figure is getting smaller and the second figure is getting bigger, that shrinking 6 per cent of people better watch out.

THE POPULATION BOOM

In terms of population growth, South Africa is adding to itself the equivalent of another Bloemfontein roughly every six months.

This is the central issue. All else flows from it. It goes without saying that this government cannot – nor could any government or private economy – build schools, provide medical services and create jobs for that many people multiplying that fast.

Depending on whose figure you want to accept, the South African population is growing at around 2.5 per cent a year. Demographers say the rate of growth is declining, but against a world average of about 1.7 per cent, that's like a doctor telling a patient he has a little longer to live than at first thought. The course and consequences of the disease remain unchanged.

This multiplying population lives in an economy that must supply it with shelter, food, work and, c'mon, a little pleasure. That economy didn't grow at all for the ten years leading up to the democratic revolution, and since then has shown signs that it will settle in at about 3 per cent growth. That's the growth rate of the First World economies such as those of the USA and Western Europe. But those populations grow at much less than the world average. Some in Europe have reached zero, and even minus. Consequently, their economic growth has made them rich. The same economic growth will make us poor.

As a rule of thumb, an economy needs to grow at double the population rate to maintain an even balance between the two. To start creating and spreading wealth, and to start creating jobs, the South African economy must grow at a rate of about 6 per cent – and then hold it there. The Pacific Rim countries that escaped the poverty trap have grown at rates between 6 per cent and 11 per cent.

The problems caused by the growth of the population will be multiplied, as elsewhere in the world, by its movement – the migration to the cities. In the next eight years, the four main metropolitan areas of the country, the Durban–Pinetown–Pietermaritzburg complex, the Pretoria–Witwatersrand–Vereeniging triangle, greater Cape Town and Port Elizabeth, will grow by the equivalent of two of them – the Durban and Cape Town complexes.

Already the cities are breaking down. They cannot provide essential services to all the people who live in and around them. In the near future, millions more will arrive, to live in the cities' cores and peripheries without proper housing, sanitation or water supplies.

Pressure on the suburbs housing the privileged will increase. At present they are sandwiched between decaying central-city hubs and an outer band of shanty slums. Ever more, they will become islands of plenty, shrinking in relation to the sea of want that surround them.

The inner-city cores and the outer band of slums will be depots of crime and disease. Politically speaking, though, they will spawn the most harmful disease of all – unmanageable discontent.

PAY DAY

The population's growth and instability are the fundamental problems of developing societies, such as this one. They are such big and intractable problems, that politicians pretend that they aren't really there. They are relegated to the outer edges of public policy, and are not considered part of the exciting hard core of politics.

Traditionally, in South Africa at any rate, they are assigned to a junior cabinet minister holding a low-profile portfolio.

For the political establishment to take runaway population growth seriously would be to accept failure and hopelessness, and therefore ruin all the rest of the game. What's the point of getting enthusiastic over a new policy, project or programme, if things are going to be worse afterwards . . . even if it's successful?

Does this sound unnecessarily pessimistic and doom-laden? Take the example of housing. Everyone agrees that this is the root measure of a stable society; namely, that it has somewhere to live. Consequently, a central plank of the new government's main platform, the Reconstruction and Development Programme, was a promise to build 1 million houses in its five-year term of office. At the halfway mark of its tenure, the government reached about 6 per cent of its target. That means reaching half its target, or even a quarter thereof, in the five-year period will not happen.

But even if the government met its full target of 1 million houses over five years, it would have fallen just short of the rate at which the need for houses would have grown in that time. So, even if the policy were successfully implemented, there would be slightly more people without houses at the end of it than there were to begin with.

That is why, shortly before he died, the new government's first housing minister, Joe Slovo, began to talk quietly of hoping, at best, to 'freeze the backlog'.

If the housing crisis doesn't work for you, let's take the second fundamental of social stability: jobs. A peculiarity of the modest growth that the South African economy is experiencing is that it is not creating jobs. In fact, over 1995 and 1996, a *Finance Week* investigation found, the economy shrunk by 40,000 jobs. Place that against this backdrop: every year the population's growth injects about 350,000 people into the job market, by virtue of their coming of age, leaving school, or getting a qualification; of those, an average of about six out of every hundred find a job.

In the face of these grave realities, politicians nod in the direction of the Minister of Health and encourage her to encourage birth-control programmes . . . and then they get on with something more interesting. So, while they ignore it, population growth forms an unholy alliance with a slack economy, and becomes the primary influence on crime, health, politics, education, the environment and the social mood – the silent dynamics that are moulding our lives.

We have left them silent and unattended for too long. They are now approaching a critical mass. They will tip the scales and we will have to pay the price of neglect. There is a day of reckoning.

REACTIONARY POLITICS

It is too late for politics to master the silent dynamics. From now, they will be the masters of change, and politics will follow. What will masquerade as political leadership will be reaction disguised as initiative. The neglect has gone on too long. This is the true legacy of apartheid. It obscured the real work and diverted attention, time and money into a doomed venture.

The new government will not shake itself out of the torpor it has slumped into. There wouldn't really be much point even if it did, or could. A fine new macro-economic policy notwithstanding, there is little the government can do to kick-start the economy until South African workers themselves decide to. And South African workers won't decide that until they get what they believe they are entitled to – from the reasonable, like jobs, to the unreasonable, like pay-packets grossly disproportionate to productivity.

The main effect of government impotence will be the rise of a chaotic new political force in the country. It will rise to the left of the

ANC. It will be born from the ANC's failure to deliver on its promises, and to satisfy, even partly, the hopes of the broad mass of voters for a new society. It will be nurtured by frustration and radicalism and it will throw up a new cadre of activist leaders who are now in gestation.

There will be a brief *danse macabre* to the ANC's right, as some partner swapping takes place there. The partners will be those who presently occupy that political floor space. It will not be an edifying spectacle. The National Party is, and will remain, crippled by four decades of moral decrepitude. The Democratic Party is crippled by its hopeless sense of decency, which will be as inappropriate to the politics of the future as it was to the politics of the past. The Inkatha Freedom Party learned too many lessons from the National Party in the past, now occupies a position far to its mentor's right, and will remain a home mainly for Zulu jingoists. That is, only if it outlives Mangosuthu Buthelezi. A new party or alliance may arise, made up of fragments of the foregoing, joined by a few fugitives from the ANC who will be frightened by what is happening to their left, and dismayed by the inactivity at the centre.

The clash of political swordplay between parties, and within them, will increasingly obscure public policy, which will in itself become an ever-extending exercise in crisis management.

YOUR MONEY AND YOUR LIFE

South Africa's crime problem is more than a crime problem. It's a class war, and it's going to get worse. To call it a class war conjures a picture of an upper class being attacked by an underclass using crime as a weapon to hurt it, weaken it, and to exact a form of punishment or revenge. In South Africa's case, this explains an important dimension of the crime wave, just as it does to a lesser degree elsewhere in the world where crime is burgeoning.

But there's more to it than that. Crime is now a class war because there are enough criminals to be considered a distinct social class. They have numbers, a characteristic way of life, occupational organizations and their own sub-economy. The social class that lives outside of society's laws, and the class that lives within them have such clashing goals and interests that they can be said, without exaggeration, to be at war.

The statistics of crime are extensively measured and catalogued. But what cannot be measured is what motivates the criminal. There is enough circumstantial and anecdotal evidence in this country, however, to make it quite clear that a substantial portion of criminal deeds has its roots in the country's politics – past and present.

That's individual crime. Something similar holds true for organized crime. The opening of South Africa to the world also meant opening the country to international crime. There are now more national crime syndicates and branches of international syndicates at work in South Africa than there are detectives to assign to the cases.

Those syndicates and the criminals they are made up of now constitute a more formalized element of society than is generally credited: they have institutions and hierarchies; they import and export – cars, jewellery, electronic goods and drugs; they deal in foreign currencies, laundering enormous sums for illegal transactions; they understand and exploit the complexities of the monetary system; they have economic and political clout; they are not only on the streets but in banks, elected office and public institutions.

Between the criminals and the class that lives within the law is a police force ill-prepared and ill-equipped to deal with its task. Not only is the force significantly seduced and corrupted by the growing evil it is facing, it is sluggish in transforming itself from a political instrument to a social agency. Long focused on maintaining political order, the police service is adapting slowly to being an institution purely for the detection and prevention of crime.

HEALTH AND EDUCATION

Alongside housing and jobs, health and education make up the 'big four' development issues in young societies. In South Africa they will evolve along roughly the same lines.

When seen from a broad perspective of benefits to the population as a whole, both health and education suffered markedly under apartheid. In certain key yardsticks of health management, like life expectancy and containment of diseases of poverty like tuberculosis,

South Africa lagged behind the average for developing countries; its infant mortality rate was merely average. Bantu education was specifically designed to ensure the inferiority of the black pupils who would pass through it.

The new government has no choice but to focus its resources on the bottom ends of the health and education spectra, leaving the middle and upper ends to fend for themselves . . . for at least a decade or two. This means privatized medicine and education for the middle and upper echelons in the society.

In medicine, privatization is not so unusual a concept. The privileged have long since accepted that they will buy their medical services themselves, whether directly or through medical aid or insurance schemes.

Not so education, where the opposite has been true. Education has been regarded a state obligation and a benefit to be extracted from paying tax. That will change, and so will middle- and upper-class spending patterns to accommodate that change.

GRAVE NEW WORLD

In these ways South Africa has shaken off the obscuring mantle of its past and become part of world trends. And in these ways those trends will begin to shape a new-found future for the country, and the lives of those who live in it.

There was little debate and discussion about South Africa's future before the fall of apartheid. On the contrary, apartheid's dwindling band of proponents couldn't admit to a post-apartheid future at all, and the realists among apartheid's opponents couldn't drain away the dynamism of the struggle by disclosing it had goals of hollow promise.

Now the full irony is upon us, and it is unlikely that South Africa will escape a difficult and dangerous future. Unlikely, but not impossible.

The responsibility for a hazardous future has shifted from the previous government to the present government. In the process, the fundamental realities of South African society have been revealed, but not changed.

If South Africa is to defy the odds and join the small band of nations that has jumped the development gap, it will do so only by understanding, first, where it is presently going and what that destination looks like. That discussion makes up Part Two of this book.

PART TWO

SILENT DYNAMICS

CHAPTER FOUR

POWER PLAY

The future of politics

From progressive organizations, from quarterlies
Devoted to daring verse, from membership of
Committees, from letters of various protest
I shall withdraw forthwith.

CINNA, CIRCA 85 BC

At the heart of present-day South African politics lies a mystery: why is there no opposition to the ANC from its left? The sheer logic of politics demands that there should be. After all, the ANC is a centrist party. It has to be, to keep its divergent elements under one political roof. Besides, disciples of Reagan or Thatcher would be perfectly at home with its economic policy. So why shouldn't there be something to its left? Politics, like nature, abhors a vacuum. Where one exists, something soon appears to fill it. There is a political vacuum to the left of the ANC and it will not be long before something fills it.

BROKEN ACCORD

In April 1994 a little more than 12 million South African voters, about 63 per cent of the total, entered a social contract with the ANC. They would give the ANC their vote and, in return, the ANC would deliver a new South Africa. The 12 million kept their side of the bargain, the ANC didn't keep its. It's not difficult, then, to imagine an opportunistic voice calling to those so betrayed: 'Follow me, I'll resurrect your dashed hopes.'

But wait. That voice is already heard. It belongs to a swelling band of ANC mavericks, ominously known as the 'populists'. Most prominent in their number is Winnie Madikizela-Mandela (she hyphened her name after the divorce from Nelson Mandela). Others in this group are less prominent. Most are entirely unknown; at least, to us. In the depressed communities where their political activism is based, though, they are heroes. The populists are a political iceberg. Eight-ninths of their mass is under the surface of establishment politics. They don't have structures or formal organizations, they don't have flags or emblems designed by PR firms and they don't have congresses and policy bodies. They don't put out press releases or make formal statements on issues of the day. They don't have flunkies that ensure their events are on news editors' diaries. But they are bound, the mighty and the lowly, by an ideological umbilical. It unites them in a shared sense of disillusion, betrayal and resentment. Their meetings take place in the squatter camps that make up the frayed edges of the metropolises of South Africa. They take place in small groups at night around paraffin lamps and in larger groups on weekend afternoons. The crowds produce their own speakers. Frequently, they invite the prominent mavericks. Winnie Madikizela-Mandela and Bantu Holomisa are their favourites. Every now and again, when SABC television genuflects in the direction of inclusive coverage, and there's a speaker of sufficient weight to attract the cameras, you'll catch a glimpse of an idolizing crowd amid the shanties. The message on these occasions is clear, potent and repetitive: this is not what lives were given for in the struggle.

ALL ABOARD

Adding to the mounting disaffection with the government is an entrenched perception that it is riding a gravy train. The degree to which this is true or untrue, fair or unfair, accurate in comparison to the previous government or not, no longer matters. It is in the popular idiom. In Archbishop Desmond Tutu's ringing phrase – they stopped the gravy train just long enough to get on.

Popular perceptions share an irksome characteristic. They take hold easily and sometimes even inexplicably. Once they have, they are difficult and often impossible to dispel. This one is no exception. If the ministers and officials who have their noses in the trough could look up to the horizon, they would see an enemy of their own making gathering there. As far as political vulnerability goes, in a society where voters are impoverished and frustrated, the government might as well have painted a bull's eye on its collective forehead.

It's hard to imagine a peace-time government in a more precarious position – with an unprotected flank facing on to a political no man's land where there is only simmering discontent. The failure of the social accord, the rise of populism and the tarnishing of the government's image are not the only reasons why a new political force will rise to the ANC's left, but they are decisive.

FUTURE TRIGGERS

On closer inspection, the mystery has rephrased itself: if political action is going to take place on the terrain to the left of the government, who will the political actors be? What will be the nature of the action? And when will it happen?

To get to the answers, we must weigh up the three most important catalysts that will spark off the series of events we want to know about. The first of these is the departure of Nelson Mandela. When he goes, Mandela will take with him an aura, an era, and a set of national priorities that made South Africa's transition possible. The second will be that which emerges in Mandela's wake – the coming of his successor and the circumstances that his time and political personality will create. The third catalyst will be what happens to the ANC. The vehicle that would have carried both Mandela and his successor to their political destinies will not remain what it is today. Both have acknowledged it. In the afterglow of the South African miracle, no-one has wanted to contemplate that change, but we will have to live with its impact when it comes.

OLD-FASHIONED VALUES

The telephone rang in the office of F.W. de Klerk. It was back in the days when South Africa's reform-minded president and the man he had released from twenty-seven years of martyrdom, Nelson Mandela, had an affable, easy-going relationship.

The telephone was answered by a boyish man in his late twenties, F.W.'s private secretary, known to everyone as the PS. It was Nelson Mandela on the other end of the line. He was just wondering if they had any suggestions for him. He had to pay a visit to a squatter camp on the Cape Flats and didn't have anything appropriate to wear, having brought only suits with him to Cape Town.

Well, ventured the PS tentatively, why didn't he simply buy something . . .

That was just it, responded Mandela in his deliberate, slightly nasal way: he also didn't bring any cash, cheque book, that sort of thing.

The PS said he would get back to him. F.W. was consulted on this minor, yet delicate, matter of state.

Mandela was called back. Why didn't he go to an outfitter in the town that F.W. favoured, get what he needed, and simply send the money afterwards or arrange payment for when next he returned to Cape Town?

Well, no, that wouldn't really work either, Mandela mused. He felt he couldn't impose because, you see, he had never bought at that shop before and they couldn't be expected to give him 'an account'.

The exact response of the PS is not recorded, but you can fill in something like: sweet suffering mackerel, you're Nelson Mandela.

You're the single most trusted person in the world today. The World Bank would give you a *fiscus* of credit without even a handshake.

In the end F.W.'s office explained the sensitivities of the matter to the shopkeeper. With F.W. expressly standing good for the proposed purchase, the venerated Mandela went along for his squatter camp outfit.

This was not a turning point in the triumph of liberal democracy. But it illustrates better than any of the grand moments the qualities that made Mandela its most outstanding figure. In an age when politicians consult opinion polls and PR men before they decide what they think, when promises are scorned and expediency is a virtue, Mandela reminded the world of values it thought it had lost. His saint-like humility and rock-fast adherence to old-fashioned notions of honour and loyalty elevated him from the ranks of politicians and made him an icon.

Yet he was an icon with a job. His job, with a fixed salary drawn from the public payroll, was to head up the management team that would remodel South Africa into a going concern. The two roles, that of icon and working political leader, didn't always mesh perfectly. South Africans had an uncomfortable illustration of this when Mandela drew two international outcasts, Cuba's Castro and Libya's Qadaffi, into his political embrace. Mandela was acting out of the most honourable of motives and the most old-fashioned of values – you stick by people who stuck by you when you needed them. You don't pretend you don't know them when you no longer need them, just because it's not fashionable to be seen in their company. Fine. But it meant that South Africa's foreign minister later issued a statement siding South Africa with Libya and against the United States in the dispute over the extradition of terrorists wanted for the bombing of the Pan Am flight over Lockerbie. It is an observation hardly worth making that South Africa should avoid cosying up to people who can only do it harm, and avoid antagonizing those who can only do it good. The observation does become worth making, though, when hindsight reveals that this was one of the events that triggered the slide of the Rand in early 1996.

So it was that in spite of some of his impracticalities, Mandela became a beacon of enduring virtues in a world awash in cynicism. At home in South Africa, Mandela became more prominent in his embodiment of the spirit of leadership than a practitioner of its mechanics. He became a symbol of the new order rather than its architect. True enough, the new society needed its architects and mechanics, and it didn't need an icon so dominant and pervasive that all others became impotent before it. At the moment of its birth, however, the new society needed something more than it needed architects and mechanics of change. It needed a unifying symbol, and Mandela was that symbol.

BEYOND THE SHADOWS

There was a moment in South Africa, in 1994, when history held its breath. The forces that had driven South African politics and society up to that point had never been more precariously poised. White nationalism and black nationalism had clashed for decades. Now they touched for the first time. The aim was the forming of one South African nationalism. Would the bond hold or would it break? Blacks faced the awesome task of taking on their own destiny. In many whites, a long-buried fear surfaced: would blacks take revenge for years of oppression?

With history on hold, Mandela stepped into the moment with an unerring sense of what it needed. He brought to South Africa, in its most precarious moment, the prospect of a society beyond division and beyond retribution. He made reconciliation the theme of his presidency. He became the medium through which South Africans glimpsed a future that worked. It was a future in which the qualities of citizens transcended their race, and in which life had a new dignity.

There was an aspect of Mandela, leader of the liberation and of the ANC, that was above politics. In an important way, he seemed to South Africans to be involved in the issues of the time, but above the matters of the day. In this role he became a standard around which a new concept of society could form. To blacks and whites alike, his manner embodied a healing message: the great virtues of dignity, fortitude, wisdom and courage would transcend the petty vulgarities of race that had until then divided them. New vistas of hope were opened.

Mandela's actions illustrated his beliefs. His credentials as the great liberator were unassailable. Now he embraced his tormentors. Where they had already gone to their graves, he had tea with their widows.

At his official home, he entertained the state's advocate who had urged and won a life's sentence against him at his trial in 1964. Defusing the symbol – revered by some, reviled by others – of South Africa's crude chauvinism, Mandela donned the Springbok rugby captain's jersey at the World Cup.

When Mandela goes the era of active reconciliation will come to an end. Racial reconciliation, engineered by Mandela, will then be the foundation on which others will come to build the new society. What would have been achieved under Mandela, the opportunities that will have been seized by the time he goes, will stand the new order in good stead. The possibilities overlooked will remain overlooked, and the reconciliation not undertaken will remain undone.

A new leader will have a new political persona and a new agenda. New urgencies will press on him and a new era will begin.

MANDELA RULES, OK?

There are, broadly speaking, two kinds of leadership: one is hands-on, day-to-day; in the other the spirit of the leader permeates the organization under him or her. The rest of the organization knows what the leader would want and not want, approve or disapprove of. The leader isn't always present, but the spirit of his leadership is. The first kind of leadership is the leadership of the warrior and the second is the leadership of the king. The warrior leads his troops on the field of battle. The king doesn't enter the battlefield but the battle is fought in his name and on his behalf. Mandela, clearly, practises the leadership of the king. He embodies the spirit of the party he leads, and that spirit infuses its organs.

Just as the nation did, the ANC faced a precarious moment in 1994 when it had to transform, literally overnight, from a liberation movement into a government. Ordinarily, it would have been a time for such an organization's disparate internal forces to factionalize and split. The pressures of the conversion from liberation rhetoric to practical public policy are frequently, in such a case, too much for unity to bear. But it didn't happen, and one of the main reasons it didn't happen was the binding power of the spirit of Mandela.

Because the ANC is made up of so many different elements, it practises a reasonably vigorous form of internal democracy. It must, to stay intact. But there is a point where the debate, the dissension and the argument stops. That point is Mandela, who presides over the party as its patriarch.

The ANC is like a home in which the siblings squabble over their rights, obligations, possessions and territories. This is allowed as part of their development. Then the stern father intervenes, and pronounces a ruling that goes unchallenged. Mandela's rigid patriarchy over the ANC has provoked resentment and criticism, but never even the hint of rebellion. Disobeying Mandela and the ANC orthodoxy he embodies is unthinkable. It carries a connotation of a betrayal of the legacy of the comrades who gave their lives in the struggle and a shameful disrespect of the world's greatest liberator.

Or, at least, it used to. The changing mood within the ANC towards its leader and its organization was perfectly illustrated in the affair of Bantu Holomisa, the boyish homeland general. When he was summoned to the president's office to be fired from his deputy minister's post, he didn't even dare to ask why. But his humble deference in the leader's office didn't prevent him from rattling the bear's cage afterwards – nor thousands of ANC supporters from gleefully egging him on.

When Mandela goes the ANC will not again have a leader like him. The era of patriarchy will be over. The organization will revert to a formula more recognizably normal for a large political movement – a balance of forces, interests, camps, and personalities and their ambitions. The new leader, and the leadership elite around him, will head up the dominant faction, or be the most capable of neutralizing competing factions . . . or, more probably, a combination of both. The new leader will be buffeted by factionalism, not untouched by it as Mandela has been. Leadership by symbolism, the leadership of the king, will be over. The new leader will be a warrior. He will not sit in the throne room of politics, he will have to survive on its battlefields.

I SAY, MR PRESIDENT . . .

When Nelson Mandela met the president of the United States, it was an unusual experience for the American. It would be the only time in his term of office that he would meet a political leader more widely known than himself and who, as an individual, wielded greater political authority.

Mandela was given a ticker-tape parade in New York, became the only foreigner in decades to address a joint sitting of the British parliament, dined with the Queen and was fêted in France. While it has become common wisdom to observe that very little of this translated into foreign investment or stepped-up aid, Mandela's stature went a long way towards giving South Africa a special status in the world. When bankers, investors and politicians met Mandela they were not dealing with just another supplicant in the long queue of needy nations. They were very aware of it, and they responded accordingly.

It's not possible to quantify in rands what Mandela meant to South Africa as its super-salesman and conduit for foreign funds, and it's useless to try. But it is instructive to imagine for a moment what canvassing would have been like without Mandela. You needn't spend more than a moment imagining it, though, because we'll soon be in the position of doing it without the Mandela magnetism. And if hard-nosed donors and investors have placed merit above sentiment up to now, wait until it's that nice Mr What's-his-name asking for the money instead of Mandela.

When Mandela goes South Africa will lose a figure that history will, in time, treat as a Gandhi, a Joan of Arc or a Thomas à Becket. For South Africa, immediately, it will mean the end of the campaign for reconciliation at home, and the start of having to earn its place in the hierarchy of nations. For the party it will mean the going of its great patriarch, and its last enduring symbol of unity. He who comes after Mandela will have to do business more by the handbook of politics than by the textbook of history.

WHEN MBEKI COMES

It was way back in time and place, goes a story you could hear in politics not so long ago, back in the rural Transkei. Two aristocratic young Xhosa men, one a teacher, one a lawyer, made a pact. They would groom the teacher's young son to be president of South Africa one day. They did not expect that the day of liberation would come in their lifetimes, even less that one of them would precede the boy in what must have seemed a very far-off dream. The teacher, Govan Mbeki, had called the alert, open-faced lad Thabo and the yearnings of the father and his friend, Nelson Mandela, would be instilled in the boy.

No-one today is inclined to verify this story, for the obvious reasons. It would say all the wrong things about nepotism and survival of tribalism. Whether it really happened that way is not that important, because the trajectory of Thabo Mbeki's life has been as if it did.

It's not possible now to define the decisive moment when Thabo Mbeki was assured of the presidency. What is certain is that he now stands alone as the anointed one. In a process that unfolded slowly, and which didn't seem to have any greater purpose while it was happening, all other contenders for leadership of the party and the nation were eliminated. Winnie Madikizela-Mandela contributed as much to her own elimination as anyone else did. Although she was not, in recent time, mentioned seriously in connection with the leadership, it was very much within her reach if she had played her political cards differently. Her status as 'mother of the nation' and her great popularity and strong individualism, combined with her close association with Nelson and her role in keeping the name alive through his incarceration, meant that a Mandela dynasty was very close to materializing. She is sixteen years younger than her former husband and South Africa would merely have been following examples from Argentina, the Philippines, India and Pakistan if power had passed from Nelson to Winnie Mandela. As it was, the collapse of the Mandela marriage, Mrs Mandela's personal conduct and her conviction in a kidnapping case cancelled her prospects.

The elimination of a more serious contender, Cyril Ramaphosa, has been a vivid illustration of the precedence of power politics over merit politics. As a subtle and skilled political manoeuvrer, Ramaphosa was the man who ensured that the ANC's historic triumph over white nationalism was translated into a practical, constitutional victory at the negotiating table. Time and again it was he who outwitted the National Party during four years of talks about how a new South Africa would be structured and governed. When the new government sat down behind the controls of the new society, Ramaphosa was pointedly kept away from the levers of power he had been instrumental in creating. This despite his powerful party base as general secretary of the ANC.

Beyond these individuals who could have impeded Mbeki's ascendancy lay a more pervasive threat, a threat residing in a constituency within the ANC rather than in particular personalities. Mbeki is an ANC elitist and is seen as a moderate. A quick survey of fortunes that have declined in the ANC since the leadership issue came to the fore – roughly a year into the Mandela term of office – reveals that they all have at least one thing in common: their departure or decline benefited the Mbeki ascendancy.

There has been a low-intensity war in the ANC between moderates and populists. The populists, as their name suggests, have a charismatic appeal to the politically hungry masses, but the moderates are in firm control of the mechanisms of power within the party. The populists are personified by Winnie Madikizela-Mandela and Bantu Holomisa, who used to have high positions in the party and government. Used to, get it?

Jay Naidoo is another. His position as head of Cosatu, the trade union component of the tripartite alliance between the ANC, labour and the South African Communist Party, gave him direct access to the ANC's single biggest mass constituency. In the euphoric days of the formation of the new government he was given the Reconstruction and Development Programme portfolio the new administration's primary image and policy vehicle. In this he had a platform from which he could have developed a public persona second only to that of Nelson Mandela. Could have, if it hadn't been taken away from him.

Winnie, Bantu and Jay have been the public hangings. In the labyrinths of the party an invisible struggle has been conducted along the same lines, although factions and interests often overlap, obscuring those lines. Occasionally, those clashes have flared in the public eye, such as the protracted one between Mbeki and another leadership contender, Gauteng premier Tokyo Sexwale. Others have remained under party wraps, such as the events that led to the relegation of the articulate broadcasting and communications minister, Pallo Jordan.

MACHINATIONS OF POLITICS

Not all of these developments and movements were part of a premeditated path-clearing exercise to assure an Mbeki presidency. In many cases they have had causes that were peculiar to each. But in politics, like anything else, once the terrain is inclined in a certain direction, the river of events tends to flow accordingly. The net effect of this flow of events has been to leave Thabo Mbeki standing on the high ground, alone and unchallenged as Mandela's successor.

A common fallacy is to think of events culminating in what we see around us in the present, whereas events merely pause in the present as they journey from the past to the future. In this case it means that time will probably show that the manner in which the Mbeki succession was managed was far too ruthless. Mbeki would have got to the presidency without drawing the stiletto from its scabbard. But it has been done, and its effect has been to parcel a dark collection of grudges that will follow him into government and add to his burden there. When the time comes, he will regret the entrenched animosities, for the full drama of his burden will be to preside over the dissolution of the ANC.

THE MAKING OF MBEKI

Thabo Mvuyelwa Mbeki was born in the quiet of rural Transkei, ancestral home of South Africa's Xhosa people, at Idutywa on 8 June 1942. His grandfather was a chief who had been deposed in one of the government's campaigns to get rid of troublesome native rulers. His father Govan and his mother Epainette had the stoic dignity that is preserved by wronged aristocracy. In the rolling hills where pastoral Xhosa society practises its intricate and ancient ways, the young Thabo was steeped in the manners of African aristocracy and acquired the bearing of one born into position, and expected to lead.

The Transkei and surrounding areas of the Eastern Cape were home to many dissident families whose names are now part of South African history – Mandela, Mbeki, Hani (Chris Hani, assassinated head of the South African Communist Party), Makwetu (Clarence Makwetu, leader of the Pan Africanist Congress), Gomomo (John

Gomomo, president of the SACP) and many others. There reigned in the region an atmosphere in which the brightest and the best were determined to resist their oppression. The ANC was actively being organized and Mbeki and his peers were taking a strong role in its youth league. The young Thabo was sent to be educated at the Lovedale Institute in the town of Alice. It was a leading place of instruction for promising black pupils, which is one of the reasons the government closed it down when Thabo and friends organized a series of strikes in his senior years there.

This was, classically, the point at which a young black activist would go underground – and several of Thabo's peers did. But not Thabo himself. Not immediately, at any rate. He sat for his matriculation exam at St John's High School in Umtata, the Transkei's main town. Then, in a clear indication of the ambitions his elders harboured for him, he was exhorted to take his British university entrance A levels.

At this time, 1961, the greatest ambition of white nationalism was realized: the creation of a republic. The year before, the ANC had been banned and Mbeki had turned to underground organization. He was a leading activist in the stay-home by black South Africans at the formation of the republic. A year later the newly established ANC headquarters in London instructed the young Mbeki to leave South Africa. He knew he would not be given a passport, so, one day soon after, Mbeki slipped across South Africa's northern border. In present-day Zimbabwe he was caught and jailed. The Rhodesian authorities planned to hand him back to the South Africans. Many young political activists had their careers, and often their lives, come to an end in botched border crossings like this. In Mbeki's case, however, his special destiny was once again revealed. Family, position and connections played their role and his case was taken up in the British House of Commons by a Labour member. He was released and sought asylum in Tanzania. From there he went on to Britain, Sussex University, an MA in Economics in 1966, and spare-time devotion to ANC work.

There was never any thought that Thabo Mbeki would use his qualifications for a career in commerce, becoming merely a part-time politician. From university he went straight into full-time work with the ANC, rapidly being pressed into an apprenticeship under Oliver

Tambo, president of the ANC. At Tambo's side Mbeki began to learn the skills he would need to keep the ANC together. Tambo was a man of mild manners and appearance, but was a subtle political dealer. He needed to be, for the ANC was a difficult party to manage properly. From the remote comforts of London it had to inspire the masses it planned to liberate in a fatherland many thousands of kilometres away. There was no track record of strong internal organization when its banning splintered it into two components, one underground and one in exile. Both of these, in turn, were dispersed in many branches, cells and factions.

Mbeki's apprenticeship extended also into the important sphere of the ANC's international contacts. Here, too, the ANC was confronted with a difficult organizational problem. It was based in the West, supported mainly from the East, and trying to mobilize in Africa. Mbeki undertook a special brief to acquire allies and build support in the West, which he did mainly in Scandinavia. This was the start of the honing of his diplomatic skills. Fortunately for the ANC, Mbeki and Tambo were much aided in their campaign for Western support by the repeated outrages perpetrated on Western sensibilities by the South African government. With apartheid wrongs as a torch-lighter to the moral high ground, the ANC rose rapidly in Western esteem, and Mbeki along with it.

Mbeki undertook a number of missions that required a deft hand. With Western sentiment and support falling into place, he turned his attention to the organization of the patchy network of political activists and groups underground in South Africa. He met members of the ANC's rival black-consciousness movement in Botswana and had some measure of success in persuading them to throw their lot in with the ANC. Mbeki also persuaded the government of neighbouring Botswana to allow the ANC bases in that country.

His position in the upper structure of the ANC was secured. But it was only in 1984, when Mbeki was made director of the ANC's information and publicity department that he started to become known outside political circles. In his new role Mbeki was the ANC's official spokesman. To white South Africans, some curious, most apathetic, Mbeki's debonair figure became the acceptable face of the liberation movement. He was refined and erudite, and he seemed like someone you could talk to. And that's exactly what started to happen. Mbeki led an ANC delegation that met a group of South African businessmen led by the Anglo-American Corporation's Gavin Relly in Zambia in 1985. It was the first real touch-and-feel encounter between white capital and black liberation, and it was not a popular move in the ANC.

With the wave of defiant protest that swelled in 1984 after some years' hiatus following the upheavals of 1976, there were many in the ANC who believed the South African government was teetering. Those who thought this way believed it was not necessary to begin dialogue with a soon-to-be-vanquished enemy. But Mbeki knew there was a complex terrain that lay beyond the fall of apartheid. Exploration of its features had to begin. Mbeki was looking further into the future than his colleagues.

The Mbeki–Relly meeting proved to be merely the first of its kind. Two years later, in 1987, Mbeki again headed an ANC delegation that met white South Africans. This time the large group, put together by the Institute for a Democratic Alternative for South Africa, included prominent Afrikaners and a cross-section of business people and journalists. The South African president, P.W. Botha, was apoplectic. Pillars of the establishment were flouting his authority. They were doing what he had expressly decreed would be the downfall of the nation – negotiating with the ANC. The pattern of politics was shattering. From the kaleidoscope of events emerged the figure of Mbeki, smoking his pipe and in genial conversation with middle-of-the-road whites. The de-demonizing of the ANC was under way, and Mbeki was its mascot.

South African politics began a slow process of maturing and in due course the preliminary stage of talks about talks was reached. Thabo Mbeki was one of the figures in the Groote Schuur and Pretoria agreements of mid-1990, which cleared the way for the start of full negotiations at the end of 1991. The next two years of talks were known as Codesa, the Convention for a Democratic South Africa. In this time the ANC limelight was occupied by Mandela and the more charismatic liberation leaders. South Africans formed an impression of Mbeki, quite accurately, as someone who was prominent in the background. Within the confines of the party, however, Mbeki was consolidating his position. In 1993 he succeeded his former mentor, Oliver Tambo, as chairman of the ANC.

During this time of talks and the election campaign that followed, a telling aspect of Mbeki was revealed: he was not a magnetic politician. His strength lay not in his appeal to the crowds or his ability to sway them. He does not have the manner of a common man. He is aloof, and he is not a good orator. His public speech is calm, delivered in a subdued voice, and is stripped of the imagery and epigrams of podium oratory. In the election campaign that installed the ANC government, Mbeki spent little time on the hustings and was not one of the ANC's leading crowd pullers and vote catchers. This didn't count against him. The ANC's euphoria in its ascendance to power was not the time to measure the shortcomings of a favoured son.

Once the new government was in place, Mbeki was installed as a deputy president. The period of preparation for leadership had peaked. All that remained was for Mbeki to ensure, from his commanding position, that any potential usurpers of the throne were banished from the castle.

MEASURE OF THE MAN

By the foregoing means of cultivation – position, apprenticeship, exposure and natural gifts – was Thabo Mbeki made. There's one more thing, though. Behind the urbanity of the polished and amiable man you might meet today, you will sense a more opaque quality. If you liked him you would call this quality a steely pragmatism and a dextrous diplomacy. If you didn't like him, you would say this quality was a manipulative cunning and a ruthless expediency.

It is a curiosity worth noting, for example, that Mbeki has subtly contrived to let his communist background fade into obscurity. After completing his studies in England, he spent a year in the USSR undergoing military training. He joined the South African Communist Party and rose in its ranks to become a senior office bearer. In recent time, however, his ready perception of the way the political wind blows has led him to loosen his ties with the SACP. Nowadays the connection is seldom mentioned. The curriculum vitae put out by his office extols his political virtues and accomplishments, and details his rise to deputy president . . . but mentions nothing of the sojourn in the USSR and membership of the SACP.

The point is not that Mbeki is a closet commie. He is patently anything but, and there are reasons other than ideology that made the SACP a political stepping stone for many dissident South Africans. The point, rather, is that a dispassionately calculating politician resides alongside the familiar figure of intelligence, dash and affability to make up the dual persona of South Africa's next president.

THE NEXT ELECTION

After the next general election the second parliament of the democratic republic will convene in Cape Town to swear in its new members and elect a president. Thabo Mbeki will be the ANC's only candidate for president. The ANC's majority, which will have fallen by only 4 per cent, mainly because of a stay-home by some supporters, will make Mbeki's election a simple formality. According to the constitution, the next election must be held at the end of the present government's term of office, which will be in May 1999. In fact, the election falls due within six months of the end of the term of office . . . but it can be held any time before, and that is almost certain to happen.

South Africa's next election will probably be in September 1998. Mandela is scheduled to relinquish the leadership of the ANC at the end of 1997 in the final act of clearing the path to the presidency for Mbeki. The idea is that Mbeki should have an opportunity to consolidate his leadership of the party before taking on the leadership of government. That, however, is already a reality in all but execution – and Mbeki will be impatient to complete his long journey. Mbeki will have practical considerations, too. If the election is held, as scheduled, in the second quarter of 1999 it will follow shortly on the passing of the budget for the financial year 1999/2000. That, in turn, will mean that the first year of the Mbeki administration will be constrained by the previous government's financial allocations. If the election is held, rather, at the end of the third quarter of 1998, Mbeki will be able to supervise the preparation of the budget for the first year of his rule. Besides, the symbolism of steering the budget that takes South Africa into the new millennium would not escape one such as Mbeki.

It is not only Mbeki's ambitions that will give cause for an early election. The political environment in South Africa is beginning to change. Mandela's slackening hand on day-to-day affairs is allowing the cracks in the ANC to become visible. Strains are appearing not only in the party, but within its alliance with Cosatu and the SACP. There are manoeuvres to the left and to the right of the ANC. It needs to make a bold move of its own, and make it sooner rather than later. An early election will do just nicely.

The idea of an early election will find a powerful ally in Mandela himself. It is no secret that Mandela is looking forward, enthusiastically, to his retirement. He speaks of it often, revealing a vision of himself dispensing wisdom in equal measure to his grandchildren, to the party and to the government. He sees himself now as the wise father of the nation. He would rather be chairman of the board than managing director. It is not rash to say that Mandela probably believes that his best role now is that of the conscience of the nation. He would not be wrong if he does. As a leader, Mandela knows he has already seen his finest hour. His image has reached its zenith. He has lived his greatest moment and realized his highest hope. He can no longer add anything to his entry in the big book of history. Because the Mandela image cannot shine any more brightly, it can only tarnish. The slow grind of reality can only erode the myth. The hero-worship span of contemporary public opinion is brief. Ask Mikhail Gorbachev or F.W. de Klerk. Mandela's time to go, if only to save himself from disillusion, has come.

For these reasons, the election will be in 1998, not in 1999. Whichever way, it doesn't matter. The outcome will be the same. Simply for the sake of clarity, the next election will be referred to in this discussion as the 1999 election.

ROMANCING MBEKI

South African society, black and white, is deeply patriarchal and it craves leadership. Commensurately, it has a naive and optimistic disposition coupled with a belief that someone will come along and take care of everything. The media, generally speaking, is run by middle-class people with the same outlook. When Mbeki becomes president, there will be a flirtation with his novelty. The suppressed hope of the three or four years preceding his inauguration will bloom in new anticipation. The media will suspend critical judgement for an initial period and South Africans will wait to see if he does what his predecessor left undone. Mbeki will have a honeymoon.

He will be an impatient groom. He will want to make the mark of his leadership before the honeymoon ends – which he will have the insight to know will be a development not long in coming. His main reason, however, for moving quickly and firmly will not be readily detectable outside of the ANC. That reason will be the prevailing conditions within the party.

BEHIND CLOSED DOORS

Conditions in the party will not be as celebratory as in the country at large. It is normal for there to be wounds to heal after a leadership struggle within a party. The surprising ruthlessness with which the Mbeki succession has been conducted from the second half of 1994, however, will leave some mighty severe wounds indeed . . . and some ugly political scar tissue that will simply never go away. There will be the resentment of those who were despatched or neutered during the knife work of the struggle. In some, such as Winnie Madikizela-Mandela, the resentment will be an open, flaming furnace (tempered only by a belief that her ex-husband's absence might offer new opportunities, and that the Mbeki regime will be more radical than Mandela's). In others, like Ramaphosa, Jordan and Sexwale, it will be a more discreet sentiment. But it will build rapidly into an obstructing grudge, shared by the supporters and hangers-on of those personalities, as Mbeki surrounds himself with a buffer zone of loyalists.

The 1999 election itself will multiply the grudge quotient in the ANC, and for an unusual reason: some of the candidates will conduct their campaigns as if they were in opposition. Take Winnie Madikizela-Mandela, for example. In the run-up to the election, the ANC will be caught in an unpleasant fix: there is simply no way it can leave Winnie off its candidates list. To do so would send a signal to the increasingly impatient and increasingly radical masses that there is no home for them in the ANC. It would be tantamount to expelling her from the ANC – and would propel her into the political jungle to the ANC's left where there will already be disturbing signs of the chaotic forces there welding into a single party. No, as difficult as it will be for many in the upper ranks of the party to contemplate, and although it could be seen as courting disaster, Winnie will have to be on the list. And so will others of her brand. By the same logic that Peter Mokaba, hero of the township militants, was chosen to replace Holomisa as a deputy minister in order to hold the radical constituency, he will be on the candidates list. So will others, less prominent, perhaps, but with a distinct sympathy for the populists' argument.

So it will come about in the campaign that Madikizela-Mandela, Mokaba and others will conduct what amounts to anti-ANC campaigns on an ANC ticket. Their rhetoric will be familiar to those who had been hearing it since 1996 – the victorious struggle was not about replacing a white elite with a black elite; those who died in the struggle did not do so merely to see affirmative action favour a select few; the aspirations of the masses remained unfulfilled. The criticisms will be couched in generalizations. Artfully, they will stop short of direct attacks on the central ANC leadership.

That will become the speciality of ousted comrades. Direct, vicious and telling assaults will be made by populists like Holomisa and others of lower rank who will have been pushed out at arm's length in the regions in the last years of the Mandela government. Some of these populists will not officially be in the election, but they will find platforms nevertheless. It will be a time of wandering for ANC dissidents. Some will find welcoming new political homes in fringe parties such as the Azanian People's Organization (Azapo) and the Pan-Africanist Congress (PAC). Others may draw together in a new party that will be a party more in name than in practice, having been created for the election, and destined to be short-lived. Eyebrows will be raised, much comment will be excited, the press will fall into whirlpools of speculation, but, with an election on, the ANC couldn't afford a self-inflicted bloodletting, and nothing will be done about wayward members and candidates.

TRANSITION TO TRANSFORMATION

With a hurtful and, at times, embarrassing campaign behind it, the Mbeki government's opening days will be brittle with tension. Everyone will know that a settling of scores will not be put off for long. But before that happens, Mbeki will be moved by another reason to imprint his leadership quickly. He will know that the task facing him, of governing a country so much in need, is so daunting that he must be firmly established in leadership before inevitable disillusion sets in.

So Thabo Mbeki will move quickly once in office – and the way in which he will move, and the manner in which he will go about making his leadership mark, will hasten the end of the honeymoon. For he will begin to confront South Africa, particularly the corporate sector and the privileged classes, with some stark realities of the time. To open the policy door on the main agenda of his presidency, Mbeki will draw a distinction between two much-used and misused words – transition and transformation.

Transition, Mbeki will tell an audience that will increasingly begin to sit up and take anxious notice, is what happened between 1994 and 1999. In the Mandela presidency South Africa completed its transition from an apartheid state to a democracy. The government had changed. South Africa had changed from a country with a government obsessed by race, sectarianism and security to a country with a government chosen by its people and dedicated to universal norms. But the idea all along had not been merely for the government to change. The idea had been for South Africa itself to change.

The time has arrived, Mbeki will say, for the transformation of South African society to start. Now his audience will be listening very carefully, and very apprehensively. The glow of the honeymoon will begin to fade as the realities of a rapidly approaching future begin to reveal themselves.

BRING BACK THE PAST

As Mbeki spells out his agenda, his rhetoric of the past will come into focus, making its real meaning apparent to those who overlooked the message the first time it was heard. Looking back from the future, it will be seen that in the soporific Mandela days of sports prestige and smug 'I-told-you-so's as the new government slipped into the bureaucratic bad behaviour of the old, few understood that Mbeki's presidency would, necessarily, have to be very different to his predecessor's. Those that did understand didn't want to look too deeply into what that difference would be. They feared that what they would see would not be reassuring; and no-one wanted to disturb the comfort of a new South Africa that so mercifully – for the privileged, at least – so resembled the old.

Mbeki himself had been little heeded once he started to give form to his view of the future. This was around mid-1996 when Mbeki's ascendancy had become assured and the end of the Mandela era was in sight. He began to speak of the future task of government. An early platform he chose, apparently not accidentally, was an interview with *Millennium*, a magazine for the business elite:

> you cannot maintain the status quo of the economic situation. If you do, I think you are asking for trouble.

Clear enough. Even so, he expanded on the implications:

> We have been talking ever since the transition, we have been trying to say that we have to marry two things, that they have to go hand in hand. Reconciliation is very important, critical, to success but so also is transformation.

There should have been no doubt about Mbeki's vision. His first public moulding of his presidential image was his keynote speech during his budget vote in parliament on 17 May 1996. He left little room for ignorance about the South Africa he saw lying ahead of him and, by implication, his role as its head of government:

> Where our society cries out for fundamental transformation, the temptation to regress into average, routine and normal thinking and behaviour threatens the realization of the truly revolutionary imperatives still facing our country.

If Mbeki was making clear his vision of a South Africa that had initiated change, but had yet to undertake it, or undergo it, he was being equally clear about why. In a speech on 6 September 1996 he spelled it out: democracy in South Africa would not survive if the majority of the country's people remained impoverished. It would be his aim, he said, to transform the economy to eradicate that poverty.

WORDS INTO ACTION

In this way it will be possible in 1999 to look back on our present day and see what isn't seen clearly now – the Mbeki agenda. It's no great surprise, though, that not much notice is being taken at this time. This is a time of mere talk. Mbeki isn't in office, Mandela dominates the country, and the future is obscure.

Just as the opening months of the Mbeki term will be a time that will dispel that obscurity, it will also be a time to begin converting words into actions. And that's just where the trouble will come in. To do what Mbeki has in mind, he will need three things: the financial resources to tackle reconstruction and transformation, a slick team around him to execute the vision and manage its many facets, and an efficient and inventive civil service to deliver it to the intended beneficiaries.

Those are the three things he is not likely to have. First, the basic structure of government finance is not going to change between now and then and there is nothing that is going to happen that will make the government more cash rich by 1999 than it is now. Second, Mbeki is likely to pick a cabinet that is sharper and more switched on than its predecessor, but a criticism that has tagged him consistently is his inability to build a strong team around him, and to delegate effectively. Besides, he is unlikely to find talent that can pilot an innovative programme from the existing ranks of politician–bureaucrats. It is a group that has shown, at best, only average ability. Third, the civil service, currently mired in inertia and sinking, is not going to turn around just because somebody, even Mbeki, tells it to.

Of the three problems, only the question of team building and management style is amenable to short-term solution – but it won't help much if the other two remain stolidly in place, which they will. Changing the pattern of government financing and revitalizing the civil service are long-term undertakings. So there Mbeki will be, a new president in a hurry to get on with transformation, yet without the means at his disposal to do so. What to do?

There will be only two things he can do – one will be to keep talking, and the other will be to start badgering others, who do have resources, to undertake the tasks of transformation. The targets for Mbeki's badgering have already been lined up: the business community and the media. For some time now Mbeki has made no secret of his displeasure with both these sectors. In his *Millennium* interview he returned repeatedly to the theme of business's failure to line up with transformation: business was 'disinterested' in transformation; business produced plans for 'growth for all' – but it always omitted to say what business itself would do; business provided 'no sense of a direction' of where it was headed in terms of reconstruction; business merely criticized what the government tried to do; business exploited the social partnership with government and labour for its own interest; foreign business was more responsive to social needs in South Africa than local business was. And just in case the point wasn't clear enough, he reduced it to one, clear sentence: 'There isn't sufficient commitment on the part of business to do something.'

The depth of Mbeki's feelings on this subject have been overlooked because of the apparent ease with which he gets along with the business community, and it with him. Mbeki has a liking for sophisticated company, and people with commercial influence are abjectly eager to court those with political power. These social dynamics have obscured the ideological gulf between Mbeki and business.

The media will find itself in a familiar role as scapegoat. Here, as with business, Mbeki has long failed to disguise his displeasure. His view is that the media fails to join in the spirit of national reconstruction, is unnecessarily critical of the government, and fails to convey an appropriate picture of the government's plans, doings and achievements. He has been behind abortive moves . . . or so-far abortive moves . . . to compel the national broadcasters to devote a certain amount of air time to 'government news'. Mbeki says all the right things about freedom of the press, of course. But his unadorned views reflect the Margaret Thatcher maxim that 'people should be free to do what they ought to do'. Mbeki, like many, if not most, politicians believes the media should be independent – so that it may arrive at a position broadly supportive of the government without being forced into it by the government.

PASSING THE BUCK

When Mbeki begins to pile the pressure on business he will be doing something that is not of his own invention. He will be conforming to a world-wide trend. There is a growing readiness, in governments and international development agencies, to admit that governments have failed as instruments of development. The admission may be, and often is, refined in different ways: government has failed as the sole instrument of development . . . or, government has failed as an instrument to provide development sufficient to meet national needs. Whichever way, it comes to the same thing. Government alone cannot guarantee or provide a nation's development.

The outcome of this has been a search for a new model of development by the briefcased, conference-going elite that makes a living from evolving, tabling, discussing and workshopping new models of development. What they have come up with is 'entrepreneurial development'. It's a fancy way of saying: we, government and the international agencies, see that development is not something that arises from our models, our conferences, or even from our projects; we recognize that there is no greater agent for a people's development than the people themselves . . . more specifically, there is no greater engine for growth and development than a vigorous business community. Therefore, the bureaucratic elite is now saying, we are hereby shifting the onus for development from the public sector to the private sector.

Governments are following suit. All over the world, recent years have seen a wave in which free-enterprise systems have been embraced. The cause has not been pure ideological conversion. It's simply that everything else has failed. Mbeki will go with the flow.

STOP THE REVOLUTION

One of the laws of political analysis is that there is never only one reason for anything. Any circumstance you care to examine will usually be the result of a complex flow of events. So, here's one of those flows that will have a major role in shaping the circumstances of the next government.

The Mbeki vision that South Africa will become familiar with in the opening phases of the 1999 government will arise partly from altruism. It will be a vision of change that first became familiar as the guiding star of the liberation struggle. And it will be a vision that will arise from Mbeki's conviction that it is his historical task to bring about the change that was glimpsed, but not grasped, in the Mandela years.

For the main part, however, Mbeki will be moved by a realization that will resemble that of another predecessor – the last white president, F.W. de Klerk. When de Klerk contemplated his term of office as he stood at its doorstep in 1989, he could see that the South African revolution had already begun. Furthermore, numbers and history were on the side of his opponents. His own side was financially exhausted, had lost the propaganda war, and was without an ally in the world. The only sensible choice was to loose the tiger and attempt to ride it. He had to anticipate the result of the revolution. He had to make it look as if he brought about the changes that were inexorably on their way.

Mbeki's position will be similar; less overt, perhaps, but similar, and he will reach the same conclusion. Mbeki will know that if he doesn't elevate the teeming masses, if he doesn't bring some hope to the un-people of South Africa, he will lose the initiative. He will lose it to someone else, or something else. If he fails, as Mandela has, to bring about changes at ground level, the masses will elect someone whom they believe will not fail them. And if there isn't someone for them to elect, their chaos-power will cause the initiative for change to slip into their anarchic domain anyway. If Mbeki does not attempt to transform South Africa, South Africa will attempt to transform itself.

HOLLOW HOPES

Shifting the development burden from a declining public sector to a growing private sector, sharpened by a local need to anticipate a new revolution – that is the combination that will determine Mbeki's policy. And the business community will bear the brunt of it.

The question that it calls up, of course, is what success will the Mbeki policy have? The specific areas in which pressure on the private sector will be felt, and the focus points of the Mbeki doctrine, will be the familiar development nodes: affirmative action and black empowerment, infrastructural development, job creation, housing and the eradication of poverty. These issues will all be discussed in some detail in the next chapter, so now it might simply be observed that neither Mbeki nor the commercial surrogates on to whom the burden will shift will experience runaway success in any of these fields. The majority is predicated on general economic growth – that's the theory of entrepreneurial development. The more an economy grows the more trade and manufacturing there is. More business means more jobs. More jobs mean more people have more money to provide houses, education and health care for themselves. There is, though, a vital qualification – the economic growth must be substantial, pervasive . . . and greater than the population growth. South Africa's economic growth is around 3 per cent and, for reasons that will be discussed later, that is where it will hover for a long while yet.

Those factors that are not directly dependent on economic growth, like affirmative action and empowerment, will show some advance, as private-sector initiatives roll over, expand and bear fruit. But the capacity of business to undertake programmes with a social face is limited. This is particularly the case when slow economic growth strains business resources. Additionally, South African business believes it has been involved in social upliftment beyond the normal call of such obligation. There is only a limited degree to which business and government could still enter into partnership schemes on housing subsidies, training of workers and the like. By and large, business is extended to the maximum of its reach. Or, at least, it believes it is.

Mbeki will meet resistance from business. The resistance is there already and it will become firmer as the pressure escalates. Business believes it devoted time, resources and personnel to socio-political initiatives to help bring about the democratic revolution. That was clearly in business's interest even though it was outside its normal sphere of activity. The transition has now been accomplished. South Africa is a normal society at last, and government must simply get on with the business of governing. Business wants to go back to its business. Certainly, business has an on-going social responsibility to its employees, and to itself, to ensure workers are happy, secure and expanding their horizons – but business is content that it is meeting those obligations, and is well within the applicable international norms.

That is the view of business, and while there will be many cordial meetings, some vague initiatives and much posturing from both sides, that is how things will stay. At any rate, someone is bound to point out along the way, South Africa's crises of society lie not with people who have jobs, but with those who haven't. The workless are beyond the reach of business.

UNINTENDED CONSEQUENCES

The face-off between Mbeki and business will have a paradoxical effect. The rhetorical dust that will be kicked up in the course of it will deepen the crisis of expectations – the single greatest enemy of the present government, and of the next. As Mbeki berates business's failure to shoulder an upliftment burden, as he extols the entitlements of the poor, and the necessity of addressing their needs, the higher the stakes will be raised in the political battle that really matters: in South Africa as in other developing countries and, indeed, in the world of the new millennium, the primary point of conflict is between the rich and the poor.

The main effect of the Mbeki agenda will be to heighten the sense of entitlement the poor have harboured since the start of the revolution that toppled apartheid. More than they are now, the poor, the workless and organized labour will be emboldened. They will sense their hour approaching. But there is nothing to suggest that the crisis of delivery of the present day will improve in any meaningful way in the future. Frustration will multiply.

The net effect can be nothing other than to fertilize the terrain of political discontent to the ANC's left. It is a terrain on which there will be no shortage of persons willing to sow, in order that they may reap a harvest of changing political allegiances. Populism, already germinating, will by that time really be on its way. And it is there that Mbeki, like a tragic hero from Shakespeare, will find that the qualities that made his greatness will also bring about his downfall. His elitism, his sedate oratory, his discreet profile, even his intelligence, will leave him dramatically ill-equipped to combat populism. The result of that, in turn, is that Mbeki will be drawn ever more into a vortex of power politics, the politics of the corridors, and the politics of internecine battles – in place of the politics of national development.

In the discussion to here we have looked at the departure of Mandela, and the nature of the person and times that will follow him. There remains, then, the last of the three catalysts to future politics, the fate of the ANC.

THE BEAR OF POLITICS

When he was state president, the unloved P.W. Botha liked to tell a smug joke. A hunter entered a forest, he said, to hunt a bear. Unexpectedly, the hunter came face-to-face with the bear, too close to aim and shoot. The bear suggested they negotiate.

'What do you want from this situation?' the bear asked the hunter.

'I want a fur coat,' said the hunter. 'What do you want?'

'I want a square meal,' replied the bear.

So the bear grabbed the hunter, and swallowed him whole.

So they both got what they wanted.

And that, P.W. said, was why he would never negotiate with the ANC.

The funny thing is, of course, he was right. In the eight decades of its existence, the ANC has become the behemoth of South African politics, simply swallowing lesser creatures that impeded its progress.

In its journey to hegemony, the ANC was aided, more abundantly than by anything else, by apartheid itself. One of the many elementary principles of politics that escaped apartheid's rude apostles was that apartheid would create a united opposition. So, through the long years in which the ANC falteringly felt its way towards a cohesive liberation organization, it became the main home for anyone opposed to apartheid. As could be imagined even at the time, that would be very many people indeed.

ANC BUILDING BLOCKS

Communist ideology spread in popularity in the Western world and in Africa in the third, fourth and fifth decades of this century. The murderous excesses of communism's masters were then still hidden from Western ideologues. Communism's humanist notions of a brotherhood of man, in which both the lowly and the mighty in society worked for the common good, had a powerful appeal against the rise of fascism in Europe, the wars it caused, the rigours of capitalism and the cruelties of racism. In South Africa the effect of those circumstances was to funnel support into the ANC. A hard core of ideologues formed in the ANC. The South African Communist Party (SACP) worked closely with the ANC, soon became part of it, and rapidly the lines between the two blurred.

The ANC also became home to a large category of people who were not motivated by ideology, but moved by their opposition to racial discrimination. This amorphous group included various shades of political persuasion – social democrats, liberal democrats and even a smattering of pale blue conservatives.

The ANC became home to an aggrieved proletariat. The rise of the ANC coincided with the migration of millions of black South Africans from rural to urban life. From peasants engaged in a subsistence economy, they became a wage-earning proletariat. Like Marx's proles, they rapidly became unhappy at their impotence as captives of capital. Their lot in South Africa had an added sting, however: the absence of any political rights, therefore the absence of any hope of improving their lot. In the 1970s this segment of the ANC coalesced into the black trade unions, and the unions became part of the mother body. A tripartite alliance formed out of the ANC, the SACP and the union group Cosatu (Congress of South African Trade Unions). The union group remains the hard core of socialist thinking in the ANC.

The ANC's banning and exile created a fault line in the organization that would have ramifications for its future, unappreciated at the time. When the ANC was unbanned and returned home, the organization found it embraced two distinct groups of people, the exiles and the 'internals'. The ANC's experience was similar to one that occurred elsewhere in the world at the same time: when Germany was unified, the worldly West Germans were politically and culturally more sophisticated than their parochial East German cousins. The result was the westerners dominated the political scene. A similar dynamic played out within the ANC. In South Africa, though, the division was spiced by the resentment of the internals, who had borne the brunt of apartheid repression while the exiles had languished in relative ease abroad.

THE GLUE

These disparate elements in what the ANC itself likes to call its 'broad church' were held together by apartheid. It was the cause in which all the groups within the ANC were united. Their opposition to apartheid was greater than any differences between them. A political ideology for the ANC was not of great importance to the organization. To be united in opposition to apartheid and the white, racist government that applied it, was enough for the ANC and its domestic and international supporters.

The ANC was banned at home and never had to face an electorate, much less participate in government. There was no anvil on which ideology, and its practical off-shoot, policy, is traditionally formed. What ideology did exist arose from the fact that the brains trust of the movement was its communist segment – the most talented ANC members were usually members of the SACP or those who associated themselves with it. The rump of the ANC thus developed a loose adherence to socialist views.

The fact that the ANC had no coherent ideology – and glaringly lacked an economic policy – aroused much comment in the years before the ANC came to power. When the movement was unbanned and entered domestic politics in 1990, all it had was a creaky and comically outmoded policy of nationalizing mines and banks.

TODAY'S ANC

The point about all of this is that the ANC has changed. The circumstances that made the ANC what it is have changed. And the inner character of the organization has changed.

When he was first given the economics portfolio of the ANC early in the 1990s, Trevor Manuel was asked by a mischievous reporter, who knew the answer, what his qualifications for the portfolio were. The young activist Manuel glibly replied: 'I don't have to be an economist to know what the people want.' In one sentence he revealed the mentality underpinning the economics of dispensing wealth. Today, as minister of finance, he has been through a baptism of fire in the economics of creating wealth. Manuel's economic vocabulary now echoes the speech and thinking of free markets and the World Bank, and the ANC's long-awaited economic policy has been labelled 'Thatcherite' by critics within the alliance. This is one example of the bewildering process for the ANC of growing from a liberation movement to a government. There are many others.

Change is a difficult thing for a political party to live through, and many don't. A party garners support on the basis of a particular platform or image. When it changes it confuses supporters, loses some, and seldom compensates by gaining new support. This factor, combined with the many congregations within the broad church has always made the ANC a very difficult party to manage. At any given time, the fortunes of one faction or another may be in ascendancy or decline. Allegiances come and go.

The ANC's condition is more precarious today than it has ever been before. The great unifier – opposition to apartheid – is gone. The second great unifier – Mandela – is going. The unity that remains in today's ANC is in no small way due to the fact that there is no other political home for disaffected ANC supporters. This will not always be so.

LOOK LEFT, LOOK RIGHT

The recent departure of apartheid and the imminent departure of Mandela are not the only factors that will weaken ANC cohesion.

History bears a lesson for the ANC here. In the 1940s the South African Labour Party was eclipsed by the National Party because Labour vacillated between two constituencies with divergent interests – white workers and black workers. The Labour Party's power base was, essentially, white workers on the mines and in industry. But the party genuflected in the direction of international opinion and attempted to speak for disenfranchised black workers too. Arthur Keppel-Jones said: 'It looked both ways and was paralysed.' The Labour Party was no match for the tunnel-visioned National Party that clearly demonstrated its superior capability to look out for the white worker.

Similarly, the ANC today has to look to business and capital on the one hand, and labour and the jobless on the other, to the First World and the Third World simultaneously, to white fears and black aspirations . . . it doesn't matter which framework one casts it in, it comes out the same. It is no wonder that the ANC in government so often appears paralysed.

ALL ABOARD

Despite the absence of political alternatives for dissidents or, perhaps, because of it, the pressure in the ANC will continue to mount. The ethos of the struggle has drained from the party. With great – some would say alarming – speed the party's elite has slipped into the comfortable role of government. The gravy train has been boarded and all the seats are taken.

The last trench of anticipated resistance, resistance that might have galvanized the ANC, failed to materialize. The civil service, the police and the army might have been expected to provide varying degrees of sullen opposition to the new order. But the functionaries of these arms of government were stultified by years of unquestioning obedience to authority, and they embraced their new masters with embarrassing haste.

The ANC was left high and dry, dumped into government without an enemy. Even its nemesis, the National Party, was trying hard to please. For a movement that had been deeply committed to a single goal, that was bad psychology.

The ANC made a big mistake when it did not replace the sense of purpose that united it in the liberation struggle, with a new sense of purpose. That sense of purpose should have been a mission to transform South Africa into a cleansed, reconstructed society. The ANC's new members of parliament, including the nine regional governments, needed to be imbued with the zeal of a great undertaking, instead of merely replacing their predecessors at the helm of the ship of state. Sir Laurens van der Post, the South African-born author and philosopher, has observed that there is one 'frightfully important' element missing from the Mandela make-up – for all his resoluteness of character, and personification of high ideals, Nelson Mandela does not have a vision. As the world's most famous prisoner of conscience, Mandela became the repository of a myth, and the locus of a dream for millions. But he has never articulated that dream. He has inspired through his unyielding belief in the triumph of justice, but he has never spelled out a vision of a new society.

In this regard, what can be said of Mandela can be said of the ANC. Apart from mouthing the cliché of 'a non-racist, non-sexist, democratic society' it has not coloured in the detail of a new South Africa. This has left ANC followers without a clear idea of where the party hopes to take them. More importantly, it leaves the party's office bearers and its members of parliament without a clear idea of what they are working towards. Without an external goal to focus on, it is natural and inevitable that political energies will be directed inwards, to power plays within the party, and to the pursuit of personal agendas and ambitions.

DRIFTING TO THE FALLS

So there is the ANC of today – an incongruous alliance of parties, factions, unions and clashing philosophies, without a cause or an external foe to unite them, with an imperfect vision of its own future and that of the constituency it serves, facing a turbulent sea of unfulfilled expectations, and about to lose the transcendent spirit of the leader that embraces the ensemble. This is not a recipe for longevity.

That said, there is a final reason why the ANC faces an inevitable fragmentation: because its future leader says it does. Mbeki has said publicly on several occasions that the ANC as it is today will not remain that way indefinitely. Like everyone else, he does not know exactly how it will break up, what will trigger the process, or when it will happen. But he has made it quite clear that he is resigned to it. And although he hasn't said so, he must figure that there is a more than likely chance that it will happen in his tenure.

The *Millennium* profile of Mbeki recalled his words from an earlier interview:

> As South African society becomes more normal, and the further away it moves from the apartheid past, the closer you will get to the transformation of the ANC. How long this takes depends on the speed with which you transform South Africa. The faster you move to become a normal society, the sooner you will arrive at a situation where people in the ANC will say we have always recognized that this is a broad family that has done what it set out to do, and we can now go our separate ways.

No doubt Mbeki's expectation is that the break up will leave a dominant rump of social democrats who will simply carry on business as before, presumably with him still in the leader's chair. This would explain the apparent equanimity with which he views the future watershed. In turn, this would mean he probably hasn't taken into account that the surrounding circumstances in which the ANC will undergo this metamorphosis will be very different to what they are today. When the time comes, he will probably not be as serene about the ANC's fate as he is now.

GETTING TO 1999

The ANC is a party that maintains ruthless internal discipline. Members like Bantu Holomisa who displease the hierarchy by showing it up in a bad light can be harshly dealt with, even expelled. Others – like the former provincial premier Patrick Lekota and the deputy minister Carl Niehaus – who lose out in power jousts are forced from office and despatched to far-off ambassadorships. But that iron-fisted internal control cannot, and does not, extend beyond the party's formal structures to its rank and file supporters. For example, when the newly elected Speaker of Parliament, Dr Frene Ginwala, wanted to entertain visiting dignitaries from the European Parliament to lunch, she found she couldn't. Embarrassingly, the catering staff at parliament was on strike. When Holomisa was banished he was told not to hold meetings and the word was sent out to ignore him if he did. ANC supporters turned up in their thousands to the meetings he subsequently held. The point is simply that, increasingly, the supporters' disgruntlement at the lack of change is becoming greater than the fear or respect with which they view their leaders.

As the next election draws closer, ANC members of parliament will increasingly feel the tug of their constituents. Increasingly, they will have to reflect their feelings in order to hold their allegiance. The arrogant among them or, to put it another way, those among them that regard themselves as untouchable, like Winnie Madikizela-Mandela, will regard few holds barred. They will go all out to tell their followers that they believe with them that the new South Africa has been an illusion, and that the struggle has been betrayed. Others, the less bold among them, will be more circumspect in their criticism of the party on whose platform they will stand. But the message will be the same.

Members of the tripartite alliance whose point of allegiance is rather the labour federation or the Communist Party than the ANC will be in a particularly hot political spot. If they don't reflect their voters' disenchantment with the lack of progress in social change, they will risk dangerous alienation from their followers.

WHAT'S THE PARTY GONNA DO?

The ANC's rising sensitivity to criticism and its growing intolerance of internal dissent, more and more detectable in the present, are symptoms of its malady. The pressures of an election campaign will make things worse. But that's all they'll do. Despite the tensions and the spats, some public, some private, the party won't need to do anything. That's because the strains in the party pose no immediate danger.

Way back, at the negotiating tables of Codesa, the ANC portentously introduced a provision that any member of parliament who leaves the party on whose ticket he or she was elected automatically loses his or her seat. This provision is now part of the constitution, and it will preserve unity in the ANC beyond its natural expiry date.

In any event, there will be nowhere for ANC dissidents to go before the 1999 election. The parties that presently exist on the ANC's left flank will remain as small and weak as they are now. ANC dissidents who have already been expelled may, like Holomisa, try to get up a new party for the next election. But the sheer logistics of funding and structuring a nation-wide party that stands a decent chance in a general election will defeat them.

THE SECOND REVOLUTION

The 1994 election was the culmination of the political revolution in South Africa. The 1999 election will be the start of the social revolution. The Mandela government that was installed by the 1994 election consolidated the historical wrench from white minority rule to black majority government. Additionally, through Mandela's policy of reconciliation, the country was stabilized. With the task of consolidating democracy and reconciling old foes done, it will fall to the Mbeki government to initiate the far-reaching social changes that must necessarily flow from the political revolution.

The second revolution is not only inevitable, it is necessary. It must change the social order created by apartheid. The distinction between a white upper class and a black underclass must, and will, go. The country cannot, and will not, forever have two middle classes – one white, one black. The un-people will not forever use their vote as an instrument of their own oppression, which is the effect of voting for a government that fails to alleviate their misery.

The question about the second revolution is not if, nor is it really a question of when? The hard part is the question of how? Will the second revolution be brought about by President Thabo Mbeki's leadership and political agenda, or will it occur as a result of social and political forces beyond his control, and yours, and mine? The answer is likely to be: a little bit of the former, and a lot of the latter. The argument I have put forward up to now is that Thabo Mbeki has a clear perception of both the inevitability of deeper change and the necessity for it to ensure his political survival. However, because of a lack of funding, efficiencies and overall capacity, he will not be able to implement that change successfully. Still, like F.W. de Klerk before him, he will perceive the need to anticipate the revolution, to make a wave of inevitable change seem like his own doing, and so he will talk about it. He will extol the virtues of further social change, he will sound dire warnings about the consequences of failure to bring it about, and he will position himself as the champion of the downtrodden. I don't mean to impute purely utilitarian, or even cynical, motives to Thabo Mbeki. His background has instilled the soul of a committed ideologue behind the tailor-suited façade of the bon vivant. Thabo Mbeki will be motivated, at least partly, by long-held convictions.

The effect of all this will be not so much to bring about change, but to increase the temperature of the change debate and to set off a new cycle of heightened expectations.

CHANGE HITS THE PARTIES

The period of change, and talk about change, that will follow the 1999 election will not leave the political parties untouched.

The first to be affected will be the tripartite governing alliance, and the way in which it will change will be simply by a continuation and intensification of trends already under way. With the bindings of common purpose now dissolved, the ideological tensions between the alliance partners will multiply; the policy clashes will deepen and the factional rifts will widen.

Cosatu's position in the alliance will become increasingly untenable. To begin with, its very existence in a governing alliance contradicts an established pattern. Classically, Western societies are made up of three elements – capital, labour and government. The interplay among them creates politics. Capital and labour create the economy, and government acts as a sort of referee to the push and pull of their competing interests. It's not that labour in government is an unusual thing, it's that labour in a governing alliance with both its traditional foe and the referee is unusual. Moreover, the ideological distance between the ANC and Cosatu is growing, not shrinking.

The government's new economic policy looks like an MBA class's model of economic modernism. It inclines distinctly to wealth creation (a polite new euphemism for capitalism) rather than workers' interests.

One element, particularly, in the new policy will create a point of escalating conflict. It is privatization. It's an element that is destined to create much havoc in the alliance, despite the papering over of cracks that followed the initial furore over the publication of the economic policy. The ANC has decreed that privatization is 'fundamental policy' (a cash-hungry government has little alternative) and it cannot end its first term of office without any movement on this policy at all. Therefore, there will be significant privatization activity in the final months of the ANC's present term. Cosatu's objection to privatization will not be merely that it is ideologically alien to the public ownership ideals of the union movement. If privatization is to work there has to be at least an initial shedding of jobs. The clashes that will arise around the loss of jobs, Cosatu's efforts to resist the process and the media attention it will generate will all increase the temperature of public debate. The underlying question of whether the ANC is still the party of the masses will be notched up on the public agenda.

All that will be needed will be the circumstances conducive to a breakaway by Cosatu. Continued failure to deliver a new society combined with a further rise in expectations will provide those circumstances. So, sometime after the 1999 election – about eighteen months after is a good estimate – Cosatu will leave the alliance.

FELLOW TRAVELLERS

Cosatu's departure, which will be rightly greeted as an historic turning point, will focus attention on its ally, the SACP. What will become glaringly apparent then is something that is true even now: for a communist party to be in an alliance with a party that espouses free markets, privatization and decentralisation is simply preposterous. The policy of the ANC today presupposes a society that is the antithesis of the communist vision. The ANC and the SACP are going in opposite directions. They are headed for an ideological divorce.

In the past, of course, the two parties were closer. Their policies were never an exact overlap – the ANC's was more inclined to socialism than communism – but they were close enough for an alliance to make political sense. Besides, they shared the overriding joint imperative of liberation from apartheid. Even then, though, the SACP had to rationalize its partnership with the ANC. The explanation then was that, at first, it would participate with the ANC in the march to power. Once there, the ANC would lay the foundations for a socialist society. Finally, when that was done, the SACP would take over and install a fully communist system. A time frame of twenty years between steps one and three was often mentioned by senior SACP members.

Step one has now been completed but it has taken the SACP since April 1994 to absorb the fact – and its implications – that the major partner is moving away from the second step, not towards it. By now the incongruity is so enormous that the SACP will simply leave along with Cosatu . . . if it can wait that long. The SACP is preconditioned to move with Cosatu. The piggy-back stratagem it has employed up to now has worked well. By being part of the ANC, it has been able to survive the recent world-wide expiry of communism and communist parties. All it will have to do in the not-too distant future will be to switch hosts, from the ANC to Cosatu.

WHY OLD COMMIES DON'T DIE

One more observation about the future of South African communists needs to be made before we proceed with what will follow the break-up of the alliance. The SACP of the 1950s and 1960s was by far the most multiracial of all South African political organizations. Others, like the ANC, had non-racial constitutions, but in practice the SACP had the greatest racial spread of members. Consequently, the party became the political home for many whose motive was to experience non-racial politics. Additionally, the party's credo of a brotherhood of man and equality for all had an obvious appeal in one of the world's most unequal societies. The sum of this was that the SACP attracted persons motivated by laudable ideals and of high calibre, even though many were distinctly hazy on the actual meaning of communism.

This tradition survived and the SACP became the source of the liberation movement's best thinkers. When the alliance met its apartheid foes at the negotiating table in the 1990s, the opposing parties were frequently surprised at the innovative role played by SACP members. In fact, the concept for a government of national unity, which eventually became the subject of the 1994 election, was an SACP initiative. The tradition will endure after the break-up of the alliance. The post-break-up will be a renaissance for the SACP as its members once again become the leading theoreticians of new political directions – directions more conducive to their kind of thinking than the present circumstances are.

THE NEW PARTY ON THE LEFT

Cosatu and the SACP won't walk out of their alliance with the ANC precipitously, in a fit of pique. Discussions about such a move are already under way in the inner reaches of the two organizations. There are many defining battles yet to be fought over privatization, economic policy, housing, candidates for office and election, and similar. There are factions still to form, allegiances to betray, and political knife fights to be fought. The closer the 1999 election comes, the more intense these activities will become. There has still to be an acceleration in the early signs that the ANC's method of decay will be a fraying at the edges rather than a corruption of the centre – branches will defy central committees, regions will pursue their own agendas, and rural potentates will set up political fiefdoms. As these things occur, the ANC is set to become even more authoritarian and intolerant of dissent . . . thereby spurring further rebellion and hastening structural decay.

After the election of 1999, and after the Mbeki honeymoon, and in a new period of dissatisfaction with the ruling party, the calls that are already being heard at union congresses for a breakaway will become more strident. The debate currently being conducted deep within the SACP will break surface. There will also be many more casualties of domestic scraps in the ANC, leaving people like Bantu Holomisa, Winnie Madikizela-Mandela and Cyril Ramaphosa freelancing in the political environment. Gradually these elements will congregate around the idea of a new party.

LOCATING THE PARTY

Clearly, the new party would want to be to the ANC's left. It would pick up the constituency that got left behind in the ANC leadership cadres' rush for power and privilege. The new party will address itself to the throngs of unfortunates who were left standing when the gravy train departed, who were left to languish in tin shanties, in jobless despair, without meaningful education opportunities, without the amenities of life – both practical and symbolic – that would suggest a closing of the white–black gap entrenched by apartheid.

Cosatu will be the biggest structured force backing the formation of the new party because the new party will be speaking directly to and for Cosatu's own constituency, the workers. In this process a factor of decisive significance will come into play. While addressing initially a similar constituency, the party will be able to do something a union cannot do. The traditional brake on unions' political clout, particularly in Third World environments, is that they speak for those that have jobs – not those that don't. Typically, a union will negotiate a wage of R100 a head for fifty workers, rather than R50 a head for a hundred workers – because it's workers who vote for union office bearers. But a union-backed political party immediately extends the constituency to those who would like to be workers. A workers' party would be a ready point of aspiration for the unemployed. The same would be true for the non-unionized workforce. In this way Cosatu's quasi-metamorphosis into a political party will transfer a vital and, ultimately, decisive support base from the ANC to the new party.

WHAT ABOUT THE THINKERS

The new party will also attract a strata of intellectuals who will recognize the great political potential of the new party. They will be those who understand the simple dictum that democratic politics is mass politics. In the countries of the West that are the traditional home of democratic politics, the greatest voting majority is the middle class. In South Africa, like other countries in which democratic politics has only recently begun taking hold, the voting mass is a working class with modest educational levels, and an underclass of workless persons. That is one of the main reasons that democracy in Africa or Latin America, for example, is often so different a thing to what it is in, say, Canada or France. But that is another topic. The point here is that the new party will be tapping into the aorta of one-man-one-vote politics.

The new party will also attract a class of persons who are neither workers nor their educated fellow travellers. These will be persons who will find the party attractive simply because it is a viable alternative to the ANC – something that would not have existed until then. These persons will come from what will by then be a meaningful group of ANC dissidents and victims of power struggles. Their numbers will not be very great but their weight will be. It is entirely feasible, for example, that Jay Naidoo, the former chief of Cosatu, drafted into the ANC in 1994, given the critical Reconstruction and Development Programme (RDP) portfolio, then dispossessed of it and relegated to an obscure ministry, will see in the new party an opportunity to revive his fortunes. So might any of the several leading ANC figures whom Mbeki despatched with such unnecessary ruthlessness in his climb to the presidency.

All in all, and however the details work out, the new party will have a politically healthy vertical cross-section, from a mass base through populist leaders and opportunists of high calibre at the top. The new organization's overall positioning will be as a workers' party and it will lay claim to the spirit of the liberation movement and the true soul of the ANC. For these reasons its name will probably be the African National Labour Party – Anlap.

CHARISMA IS BETTER THAN POLICY

Anlap will bring the focus back from where the ANC has successfully located it – on the politics of wealth creation – to the politics of wealth distribution. And, like the ANC before it, it will be vague on policy and strong on rhetoric. Anlap will rely heavily on the personalities at its forefront, and will capitalize on the rolling torrent of publicity and speculation that will flood the months leading up to the split in the alliance, culminating in the formation of the new party. It will build its image by attacking the failures of the ANC and projecting itself as the enemy of the new South Africa that differed little from the old. The ANC will be portrayed as a captive of its policies of white appeasement; as a lap dog of international monetarism, World Bank strictures, capitalist agendas, liberals and free markets. By implication, this will send Anlap in the direction of state intervention for the creation of jobs, the redistribution of wealth and the provision of houses, education and medical services. But this will be a direction only. There will be – there are any number of examples in African political movements for this – no specific policy programme. The population dynamics that will pertain at the time will mean that Anlap's support base will be overwhelmingly youthful and of a low education level. Those supporters will not be looking for an opportunity to evaluate competing policies. They will be looking for a vehicle through which they can manifest the ambitions and frustrations engendered by South Africa's root political dynamic – the poor and the desperate living in explosive proximity to great wealth.

NEW GOVERNMENT

To say that the ANC will be dealt a staggering blow by these developments is to say the least. In the breakaway – and in a probable second wave of desertions shortly before the election in 2004 – Mbeki's government will lose about six cabinet ministers and dozens of senior MPs. (The second wave will occur because many ANC members will not want to lose their parliamentary seats at mid-term, when the main break happens.)

Mbeki's suave political persona will make it seem as if he is taking the historic shake-up in his stride. That would not be far from the truth for, if he is anticipating the coming split even now, then it will not arrive as a surprise when it actually happens. Even so, a privately worried Mbeki will have no choice but to go on the offensive after the split. He will try to spike the new party's guns by emphasizing the ANC's pedigree as the party of liberation in South Africa. He will extol its virtues and achievements. Along the way he will give the screws which he applied to the media during the build-up to the breakaway another tightening twist.

Ultimately, though, his argument will be a hollow one. His government's inability to deliver change up to that point would have been unaltered since the Mandela era, for the same reasons: lack of money, a culture of inefficiency, inexperience, failure to stimulate growth in the economy and the effect of social dynamics like population growth, crime, debilitating urbanization and loss of morale. Of course, these are the very things that will make it impossible for an ensuing government to do anything about the lot of the land's needy millions – but no-one will heed that at the time.

Anlap will hijack the aspirations of workers, the youth, the unemployed and the un-people – and, with this majority of the voting populace behind it, will win the election in 2004.

ON TRACK WITH WORLD TRENDS

This course of events may seem unlikely to many. But that will be because the types of people who might be reading this book don't want things to turn out that way. Cool powers of reason reveal a story different to the one we want to hear. It may be, too, that the course of events depicted here seems to buck world trends. After all, did Francis Fukuyama not encapsulate the spirit of our beliefs in *The End of History*? Is this not the age of the final triumph of liberalism? Is the rise of global markets not limiting the opportunities for governments to deviate from the new orthodoxies?

Alas, this not entirely the case. These world trends do not herald a homogeneous globe, and futurists like Kennedy and Toffler foresee that the sparks emanating from the shifting balances of power between the world's haves and have-nots will ignite the great crises of the new century. In global forums like the United Nations there is a clear shift in the power balance from the First World bloc to the Third World bloc. The political and economic dominance of the USA and

Europe is being eroded by China, India and other Asian countries. The end of the colonial era has amounted to a massive transfer of power from old world countries to the developing world.

This book is about how a South Africa that is once more part of the world will be picked up and carried along by world trends – and how those trends, because of South Africa's population and economic make-up, will be reflected in microcosm in South Africa. And so it is that power in South Africa will slip from the First World component of its society, as it has, through the ANC as an intermediate stage, to its populous masses.

UNLEARNED LESSONS

Anlap in power will play all the wrong policy cards. The global truism that wealth distribution is a by-product of wealth creation – not the other way round – will not have changed. And Anlap will not have learned the lesson. The new custodian of the will of the people will remain locked in the rhetoric that brought it to power. Its mind will be set on wresting the new kingdom from the hands of the avaricious and placing it in the hands of the needy. Consequently, the growth of state intervention will inhibit the application of private capital, the entrenchment of collectivism will erode individual responsibility and entrepreneurship, the introduction of protectionism will cause a loss of efficiency, and the fostering of entitlement will create a decline in initiative.

The economy will slide into accelerated decline and the rest of the world will be significantly less inclined to do anything about it. The international goodwill engendered towards South Africa by the Mandela era will have been exhausted. The Anlap government will find that, even more than the Mbeki administration that preceded it, it will not have the money to do the things it wants to do. It will sink into impotence and decay in the same way and for the same reasons that so many before it have.

Meanwhile, the silent dynamics of change – population growth, urbanization, joblessness, crime and the knowledge gap – will course and pulse through daily life with ever-greater impact.

F.W. WHO? . . . THE FUTURE OF THE NP

The course that South African politics will take from the present will leave the National Party in the position it is today – a spectator of national politics making unheeded cries on the sideline. Like the fat, awkward kid in glasses whose ball it was in the first place and who is now pushed out of the play, the NP will be irrelevant to the main event and will be ignored. Since the NP triggered the events that led to the new deal for South Africans, it has been in steady decline as a national force. Thus the question the NP faces is: will anything happen to change its steady slide to obscurity – and, if so, what could it be?

The National Party is a textbook illustration of the fact that there is, or should be, a moral base to politics; because without a defensible moral base, a party simply cannot have any long-term prospects. Despite this, for a long time it seemed as if the NP was inviolable. The immorality of its apartheid policy, and the violence and cynicism it bred, is well known. Apartheid so isolated its perpetrators and so concentrated its enemies that it doomed both itself and the society it sought to regulate. But, curiously, the NP remained strong. It sustained itself on its own propaganda that it was right and everyone else was wrong, and that it was fighting the advance of communist imperialism on behalf of an ungrateful world.

It was only when the party admitted it had been wrong all along – which was the net message of the unbanning of the ANC and the release of Mandela in February 1990 – that decay in the party began to mirror the decay that had already taken place in society. The decay set in for an abstract, but decisively important, reason: when the NP admitted that the policy on which it was founded was wrong, it conceded its legitimacy as a government. The consent of the governed is the source of a government's legitimacy, and the NP conceded that it was not governing with the consent of the people it governed. And when it lost its legitimacy, even in its own eyes, it lost not only the right to govern, but the will to govern. The only problem was, it still had four more years to govern.

GIVING UP THE SHIP

The first symptom of the NP's decay was the start of what would prove to be a steady bleeding away of leading party figures. Citing the usual transparent reasons, Barend du Plessis, the finance minister, then Stoffel van der Merwe, another cabinet member, went. They were followed by the cabinet academic, Dr Gerrit Viljoen, and eventually the party's popular icon, Pik Botha, and his acolytes Chris Fismer and Leon Wessels – all ministers. The problem for a political party about losses and resignations of this kind is that they are the tip of an iceberg of waning confidence and indecision – even though the resignations themselves may not be great in number. For every resignation, there are several members thinking about it; every resignation follows a period of introspection in which commitment declines . . . and there will be any number of members in this mood. Taken together, it amounts to a loss of will and energy in the party.

Thus hampered by a tacit admission that it was the party in the wrong, and with its human resources in decline, the NP entered negotiations. It put up a brave front of bargaining a new South Africa. In reality, though, it was negotiating the terms of its surrender – and merely going for the best deal it could get.

The NP viewed its major achievement in negotiations as the agreement to establish a government of national unity. Under this arrangement the NP, along with others, would govern the new South Africa with the ANC. While this co-operative government eventually played an important part in stabilizing the new society, the NP rapidly saw that it had gained a hollow victory. It had talked itself into a split personality. As a partner in government it had to implement and defend government – that is, ANC – policy. Yet it also wanted to be an opposition party, free to criticize the government and compete in the political market place for a constituency of its own. The duality could not be sustained for long and the NP pulled out of the national unity deal to go into opposition. Trouble is, it hasn't really become an opposition party either. The contrast between it and the tiny but spunky Democratic Party illustrates the point. The NP continues to founder.

The NP's window of opportunity to undergo a real transformation and emerge as a political contender in the new South Africa was the four-year period from 1991 to late 1994. In the beginning of this period the NP's standing was higher than it had ever been in the party's history. It enjoyed world acclaim for its part in the end of apartheid, it occupied the closest thing to a moral high ground it had ever seen, and its leader was to be awarded the Nobel Peace Prize. Its foe, the ANC, had been deftly wrong-footed by its sudden unbanning, had no regular structures in the country and no experience of conventional politics.

Looming ahead of the NP at the end of this period was the certain prospect of the ANC gaining power and getting its hands on the organs of state – which would enable it to dig into the human rights transgressions of the NP government. Additionally, a Truth and Reconciliation Commission was envisaged to probe those abuses. It did not take a clairvoyant to know the commission would shatter the halo over the NP's head. Nearly everyone knew the abuses were there. Colonel Eugene de Kock, the infamous police hit-squad commander who was later given two life sentences and 212 years' imprisonment for his crimes, was well known to reporters. So was the general nature, if not the details, of his activities. His colleague, Dirk Coetzee, was spilling all to the weekly *Vrye Weekblad.* Most damning of all, the NP's subsequent explanation of these events failed a simple credibility test. If the de Kocks, Coetzees and others (several thousand later applied to the Truth Commission for amnesty!) were rogue elements in the security establishment who had exceeded their briefs – as the NP leaders said – then those in the security and the intelligence establishment who remained within the brief would have stopped the violators and told the political chiefs some individuals were committing acts that jeopardized the political process. That's what they were there for, state security, wasn't it?

The Truth and Reconciliation Commission marked the end of the NP's window of opportunity to reconstitute itself – but it didn't take the gap, and now it's too late.

The National Party will retain a core of support from whites who have grown accustomed to politics without morality; who believe that the NP will – or should – be chosen as the sensible alternative to the ANC once voters sober up from the intoxicating emotionalism of black liberation. The party itself entertains delusory notions of attracting mass black support, perhaps even under a charismatic black leader, once ANC policies are seen to have failed. But while apartheid remains a living memory, nothing of the sort will happen. No persons of distinction or credibility in black society could join the NP and retain their status.

There is one other constituency that will never vote for the NP – the Afrikaans right-wing. An emotional blockade has been thrown up between Afrikaners at the perceived betrayal of the Afrikaner cause by the NP. For the aggrieved whites the betrayal of their kin has been a more heartfelt cut than any that could be inflicted by their mutual enemy.

The only area where the NP has meaningfully grown electoral support in recent years – and, therefore, its only area of potential – is within South Africa's mixed-race ethnic group, the coloureds. Afrikaans is the lingua franca in this group and its cultural profile is Afrikaans. Yet the slightly darker skin of its members was enough, for four decades, to make it disdained by the masters of apartheid. When apartheid ended, the coloured community split two ways, in a rough proportion of fifty–fifty. One group continued to side with the oppressed and the other, as unbelievable as it might seem, made a dash for the ranks of its former oppressors. This latter group was motivated by some specific anxieties, like a fear of losing out in black-focused affirmative action, and a fear of encroachment of a black working class into coloured residential areas. But mainly it was spurred by a status-seeking desire – with disquieting racial overtones – to be identified with the prosperous white elite rather than the largely poor black masses.

It is unavoidable that, while it is in its present form, the NP will remain tagged by ethnic politics. Its only growth potential is in the areas where coloured voters are numerous – the Western Cape and the Northern Cape provinces. And then it would have to be prepared to become predominantly a coloured party with a strong white element in it, rather than what it is today – the other way round. It would have to accept, too, that it will be primarily a provincial party.

The voting pattern that sustained the NP in the 1994 election, and has since, contains the potential for the party to lose support in future developments, rather than gain it. The voting imperative for the NP stemmed from coloureds and whites who, for a mixture of reasons, wanted a political bulwark against the ANC. This imperative was at its peak while the ANC was an unknown factor as a government. In the Mbeki administration, when Anlap is formed, this 'anxiety vote' will move leftwards across the spectrum, and come to rest with the ANC, for the ANC will become the bulwark against Anlap. Just as in South Africa's period of transition the NP was seen as a party of moderation against the feared extremism of the ANC, so the ANC will become the party of moderation against the extremism of the new force to its left.

All the above factors taken together spell out a clear message about the NP's future: its current national support of about 20 per cent is a ceiling it is not likely to see again. Therefore, the most sensible course for the NP to take would be to find the resolve to listen to its inner voice. That voice is telling it to dump its existing identity, and to change into something new, or become part of something new.

DEMOCRATS IN THE SUNSET

The Democratic Party is the little gem of South African politics. If politics were like a gymnastic contest where impartial judges hold up score cards for performance, the DP would get a round of nines and tens. It is the very model of a modern political party. It is scrupulously democratic, with a distinct leaning towards traditional democratic liberalism. It has changed with the times, starting off as the Progressive Party, becoming the Reform Party, then the Progressive Reform Party, then the Progressive Federal Party and, finally, phew, the Democratic Party it is today. Throughout this political safari, though, it has remained steadfastly true to its democratic ideals. In that time it has harboured outstanding individuals, notably Jan Steytler, Helen Suzman, Frederik Van Zyl Slabbert and Colin Eglin.

It has been unstintingly unselfish, invariably putting the national interest before its own: it has helped others, enlightened many, acted as honest broker, and its role as an intellectual resource and deadlock breaker in the tense years of Codesa was such that it is not far fetched to say that the new South Africa would not have happened without it. The DP's own processes have always been vigorous, open, honest and tolerant. There has never been even a whiff of scandal around the party or any of its members. Most of all, the DP is almost always right – its opponents, the NP and the ANC alike, have shamelessly appropriated its policies time and again. To see where the Democratic Party is in the present is to know where the other parties will be in the future. Naturally, all of the foregoing are reasons why the DP has been hopelessly ineffectual as an electoral force in the crude politics of racism and revolution in South Africa. They are also the reasons why the DP will remain as hopelessly ineffectual from here onwards. Even if it doubled its current national support, it still wouldn't have 5 per cent.

THE TUG OF HISTORY

It is likely that the course of politics in South Africa will affect the DP in the following way. As the split in the governing alliance looms, it will bring out something of the demagogue in Mbeki. The ANC and the Mbeki government will become increasingly authoritarian. Then a new breed of South African liberals will look around for a political home that will offer them the liberal ideals they will no longer experience in the ANC. These new liberals will be made up of two groups. One will be youthful, mainly professional, Afrikaners who would have learned from the new South Africa that a black government and the sky falling down are not the same thing. They will look for a vehicle in which they can broaden their concept of South Africanism. The National Party, despite its pretensions, will not do. They will be ashamed of it and the association of Afrikaner identity with it. The second group will be a newly emancipated, youthful, black elite. They will stake their position firmly in the high-tech, high-standards, high-mobility, high-individualism lifestyles of the new millennium. They will want their politics, like their cellphones and hi-fis, to be switched on and new age. The numbers of the new liberals will not be great, but they will be there. And the home they will look for will be round about where the DP is standing today.

However, something else will be happening around that time, remember? Anlap will be forming and by the time the election of 2004 comes round, voters who oppose its socialist drift will be faced with a dilemma. It will be a dilemma that sucked opposition voters into vortexes of indecision in the past in South Africa. In the Sixties and Seventies when the United Party was the biggest opposition party, many voters who would have preferred to vote for the more liberal Progressive Party or its successor, the Progressive Reform Party, didn't. They voted instead for the UP as a party that stood a better chance of winning against the National Party. Many white South Africans will recall the endless arguments about whether to vote conscientiously or strategically. Those arguments will return when the ANC becomes a strategically more promising alternative to Anlap for liberal voters.

Until the DP confronts that dilemma, however, it will continue to struggle with its single biggest drawback. The DP's political roots are in English liberalism and it remains almost exclusively associated with white English-speaking South Africans – who are a minority of a minority. To overcome the English-tag drawback, to provide a home for new liberals, and to be in there with a chance in the strategic voting dilemma, the DP, like the NP, has to metamorphose into something greater.

AIZIKA ZUMBA, ZUMBA

The question that the Inkatha Freedom Party has to ask itself is whether it will survive Mangosuthu Buthelezi. For, if ever there was a case of a political party being established to manifest the ambitions, the whims and the grudges of one man, the IFP was it. Buthelezi established Inkatha as a Zulu cultural organization (although it was nominally open to any black person) in 1975 when he was consolidating a power base in the KwaZulu homeland. In 1990, South African politics took a sudden turn with the ANC's entry to the arena, and rapidly became a two-man event, involving Mandela and de Klerk. Buthelezi determined to turn politics into a contest of 'the big three' by dealing himself into the process. He did it by opening Inkatha to white membership and converting it into a regular political party. The tactic he adopted, then perfected, and has since stuck to, was brinkmanship. It combined well with Inkatha's emergence in the violence that was part of the political vocabulary of both the ANC and the government. This made Buthelezi's participation vital to a political settlement. Having established that, he then played hard-to-get. In a variety of issues, meetings and agreements – from the 1991 Peace Accord, through Codesa and to the 1994 election itself – Buthelezi diverted attention to himself by keeping everyone guessing about his participation. Invariably, media coverage was as much about whether Buthelezi and the IFP would be there as it was about the issues involved. The Buthelezi brinkmanship enjoyed mixed success. It undoubtedly catapulted him to greater prominence than he would otherwise have had as a homeland leader – but it left him with an image of a petulant, contrary politician who often disagrees for the sake of disagreeing.

Although the IFP was open to all, and attracted a scattering of white and Asian political adventurers and wannabes, it remained a party of Zulu jingoism. Zulu territorial exclusivity topped its agenda and there have even been dark mutterings about succession. Closer inspection of its Zulu base, though, reveals an important distinction: repeated polls and voting patterns have shown that urban Zulus have little time for Buthelezi or the IFP. The support is almost entirely in rural KwaZulu, traditional home of South Africa's most numerous ethnic group. This has been sufficient to propel the IFP to a one-seat majority in the provincial government of KwaZulu/Natal, and to the 10 per cent it has nationally. Even that rural support, though, is split. It follows a fault line reflecting the long-standing animosity between Buthelezi and Goodwill Zwelithini, the ANC-leaning, but politically weak, Zulu king. The rivalry between the two Zulu royals – Buthelezi is a prince – has a curious dimension: while being the king's subject, Buthelezi is his uncle . . . making him the king's superior in both age and family hierarchy.

By the time of the 1999 election Buthelezi will be seventy-one years old, and the king merely fifty. Buthelezi is not a man in peak health. It is likely that if he doesn't retire or retreat to regional politics at the next election, his grip, at least, will be weakening. The intriguing questions are then raised – without the rivalry between Buthelezi and King Goodwill, will there be so vehement an ANC–IFP antagonism in KwaZulu? With Buthelezi fading or gone, will the IFP have the will or the support to hang on to the province? While some of the violence there is by now self-perpetuating, and some of it merely uses politics as a cover for timeless clan clashes in a tribe steeped in warrior traditions, the answer to the two questions is likely to be a simple no.

Without Buthelezi, the vehicle he created for his political ambitions will splutter to an end. But before it does, it will become caught up in a bid to form a new party to the right of the ANC.

FEW WRONGS MAKE A LITTLE RIGHT

Someone once said – actually, it was me – that if you proposed a radical change to three people, one would approve, another would wait and see how things turned out, and the other would be opposed. Following this rule of thumb, about a third of Afrikaners were deemed right-wing in the build up to the 1994 election. Since the election, change seen through the eyes of whites has amounted to little more than better sport on worse TV. Accordingly, the wait-and-see third has moved across to general acceptance of the new South Africa. For the same reason, many in the opposing third have decided that compliance with the new South Africa is a more sensible course than resistance. No matter how little they may like the idea of the new society, it hasn't affected their lives sufficiently for them to take the risks and make the sacrifices that would be involved in doing something about it. The result of this process has been to leave a much-diminished white right-wing.

DECLINE AND FALL OF THE VOLKSTAAT

The fact that the lurid imaginings of right-wingers about a black-dominated South Africa didn't materialize substantially lessened the impulse to a volkstaat, where the Afrikaner would be isolated and immune to the rest of South Africa. Nevertheless, the ideal of a volkstaat remains the rallying point of what remains of the right-wing. A volkstaat council was attached to parliament in a buy-off wherein the ANC secured the electoral participation of the Freedom Front, the leading right-wing party. True to the unchanging nature of right-wing Afrikaner politics, that council has been engaged in a ricocheting polemic with itself and the many right-wing groups, all of whom have different notions about the volkstaat. So confusing has the picture become, with proposals and counter-proposals, new demands, reverses and compromises, that it is worth reminding oneself of the only certain fact about the Afrikaner dream of an independent volkstaat: there will never be one.

The reasons there will never be a volkstaat are manifest and involve matters both of principle and practice. The principle of a volkstaat will never be countenanced by any South African government because no government will ever accede to Balkanizing its sovereign territory. Additionally, to give in to the Afrikaners' demands would open a Pandora's box of ethnic succession claims – if it's all right for the Afrikaners, why not for the Zulus, or the Ndebele, or the coloureds, or the Griquas? The practical considerations are equally self-defeating and explain why the volkstaat ideal has not advanced from the hazy notion it started off as. First among these considerations is that the term Afrikaner is roundly abused in this context – the right-wing has never been able to demonstrate, in an election or otherwise, that Afrikaners as a group want a volkstaat. What's more, the definition of an Afrikaner, for purposes of the volkstaat, has never been agreed on. Must an Afrikaner be white, excluding the millions of South Africans whose language and manners are Afrikaans but who are not white? If so, does that mean the volkstaat must be the world's only avowedly racist state? In any case, where does white end and coloured begin? What must happen to the people who live where the volkstaat would be created, given the fact that there is no region in South Africa where whites are in the majority? Must they be denied citizenship at their places of birth? That didn't work for apartheid and it certainly won't work for the volkstaat. Is it not preposterous to imagine that Afrikaners in significant numbers want to abandon their jobs and homes to move to a barren ethnic reserve? And don't all these questions highlight the underlying question, about which there is still no agreement after all these years: where could the volkstaat possibly be located?

What these simple questions reveal to any one who thinks about them even for a few minutes is that a volkstaat is a notion without the smallest chance of realization . . . so much so that they raise two disturbing conclusions: Nelson Mandela must have given an undertaking to negotiate about a volkstaat in the future, and agreed to the creation of the volkstaat council, in order to defuse the dangerous tensions before the 1994 election, knowing he could never accede to anything like a volkstaat when the promised negotiations happened. Not only that, the right-wing leaders must know it, too, and they are merely stringing along their followers while those of them that are in parliament hold on to their positions, waiting for an as yet unimagined solution to their predicament.

Worse, the two sides have only two options: one, given the pervasive loss of interest in the volkstaat idea, they can simply let it fizzle out by the time the 1999 election comes round and the Freedom Front can either fade or fudge it; or, two, they can let the matter come to a head and let volkstaat supporters see that the dream is in vain. Both cases would leave right-wingers with what has become common in the politics of white nationalism – an exercise in futility, liberally spiced with pinches of deception.

BOERE BOMBERS

The anger and dismay that will arise from the betrayal of the volkstaat ideal will provoke the one really meaningful question posed by the right-wing for future politics in South Africa: does it have the potential to be aroused to the point that a right-wing terror campaign can influence the course of events?

If the absence of real change affecting whites spiked the right-wing cause, then it follows that the social revolution that will begin in the Mbeki years, and will accelerate after the victory of Anlap, will spur a revival of right-wing feelings and activity. That, however, doesn't fully answer the question. A rise in sentiment and activities is one thing, but will it be enough to matter, to become a serious threat to the social order? The likelihood is no, it won't. The main reason is that the weight of future political action will be to the left of the ANC, not to the right.

That doesn't mean there will be no cause for right-wing activism. There will be. Working-class and middle-class whites will feel increasing pressure, finding it ever more difficult to make ends meet, and weathering increasing levels of crime. Unemployment, which, after a forty-year absence, has started eating into white society, will increase. Hardest hit will be the low socio-economic bracket of whites. This is traditionally where the bulk of right-wing support is to be found; the author of the saying 'Racism is the snobbery of the poor' could have had the thought at a right-wing gathering. From these people, unaccustomed to joblessness and extreme poverty, the right-wing will be able to recruit its militants. But these factors in this bracket of society will never reach the critical mass needed for widespread revolt. That's what has already happened, and will happen again, on the left of the spectrum.

There is another reason that right-wing militancy will not grow to proportions that could change the course of events in South Africa. It is that we have already seen its worst. The cause of right-wing revolt peaked in the months leading up to the '94 election. Then, the threat of the unquantified evil of black domination hung over the section of white society that saw it that way. An explosive mix of fear of the future, combined with fury at the betrayal of Afrikaner leaders, spurned an extremism that will not revive. At that time, too, the right-wing had a vital resource that has since been truncated, and will expire in time – the backing of substantial elements of the state's armed forces.

The right wing has done its worst. It has neither the will nor the resources to mount repetitions of the tragi-comic escapades of the past, such as the invasion of Bophuthatswana, when a phalanx of overweight Western Transvalers rode into the dusty homeland, shooting indiscriminately, only to beat an ignominious, scrambling retreat hours later. For the reasons discussed here, though, there will be a resurgence of white right-wing terrorism in the early years of the new century – but never enough to matter.

ADVENT OF A NEW PARTY

At the end of 1996, a popular political topic was a merger of the parties immediately to the right of the ANC – the National Party, the

Democratic Party and the Inkatha Freedom Party. It was a popular topic in the parties themselves and, before long, it will probably happen – for the biggest among them wants it the most. Because the NP once was in power, it clings to the belief that it could be once again. However, its strategists now know what anyone can see. The NP is not going to attract mass black support unless something significant changes.

In addition to reasons of morality and image discussed earlier, the NP has no political platform from which to fight the ANC. The ANC has moved to the right and deprived the NP of a distinctive economic policy. With its own unfortunate record, the NP cannot claim to be a viable alternative to corruption or inefficiency in the ANC. It cannot criticize the profligacy of public representatives – they are merely riding the gravy train set in motion by the NP itself.

The way ahead is clear. There must be a new party, but really a new party, not simply the familiar old nationalist dinosaurs with a new name.

CALCULATING POLITICAL PROFIT

The NP will put pressure on the DP to form a new party because the DP's participation will be the stamp of approval the NP would need. The participation of the unflinchingly-liberal DP would signify acceptance that the NP had made a true break with its past. That, of course, is exactly what the danger is for the DP. By going into a joint venture with the NP it will put at risk its most precious asset, indeed, its only asset, its good name. The prize, however, that is being offered to the DP for taking that risk is access to a support base nearly ten times greater than it has at present.

The participation of the IFP in the merger will give the partners immediate access to that which they seek most, a large black constituency. The IFP will probably be willing to contribute that stake because it would secure its presently precarious position in KwaZulu/Natal, and make it part of the ruling party in the Western Cape. This will put a brighter hue on the party's growing resignation to the fact that it is declining as a national factor and is devolving into a regional force.

All three parties will do their sums. At 1994 levels of support, a merger would give them the NP's 20 per cent, the IFP's 11, and the DP's 2: 33 per cent of the national vote. That's within striking distance of power, somewhere none of the three parties are right now, or could hope to be. Additionally, they will reason, a number of other elements can be factored in. Discontent with the ANC will funnel at least some black support to a high-profile, new, liberal party. Percentage polls in future elections will fall and that will eat into the ANC's majority, making 33 per cent an even better batting base then than it is now. When the ANC–Cosatu–SACP alliance dissolves, and a new party is formed to the left of the ANC, parliament could split three ways . . . and it's anybody's guess as to how the balance of power will tip then. A governing coalition between the ANC remainder and the new liberal party could be a distinct possibility.

So they'll go for it.

THE STARTER'S GUN MISFIRES

Between a decision to pursue a merger and it actually happening, the new party will blunder into a leadership crisis. F.W. de Klerk will feel that as the man who has walked the longest road to the new party, the man who willingly gave up power, who made all this happen, and who heads the largest unit in the merger, he is inarguably entitled to the leadership. Mangosuthu Buthelezi will not be anybody's deputy. No discussion. And the DP's current leader, Tony Leon, will figure if the new party is a place where he is going to get trampled in the leadership rush, then what is he doing in it? This will be the first consequence of the merger as a proposal. The clash will reverberate all the way down the party hierarchies as office bearers in the old demand undiminished status in the new. Big fish in little ponds never like their status being reversed.

The unavoidable reality of the new party will be that the NP will dominate it. For the NP it will be a method of getting back to power and NP members will want to be near the front of the queue. The NP's superior numbers will enable it to dictate widely in the new party. In an early battle over the name of the party, the rest will be lucky to defeat the NP's preference for the name Christian Democratic Party. In a compromise that the NP will finally buy into, the new party is likely to be called the National Democratic Party, the NDP.

Another unavoidable headache for the new party will be the Buthelezi factor. The idea of an alliance between the NP and the IFP is not a new one. Courting gestures passed between the two parties in the early 1990s. Before long, it became clear that there would be no marriage, and de Klerk spent much fruitless political energy in attempting at least a working arrangement with Buthelezi. But the Zulu leader's prickly nature and headstrong ways prevented it. The idea failed then and it could again, for the same reason, leaving the NP and the DP with a political booby prize – each other.

WAY TO GO

The idea of a three-way split in parliament in, say, 2004, between Anlap, the ANC and the NDP is not the primary scenario being put forward in this book. But it is a strong enough contender for second place to make the formation of the NDP worthwhile. The best way to form it, however, is the way it is least likely to happen. What the NP, the DP and the IFP need to seek is not an agreement to merge, but an agreement to disband simultaneously. Once this is done, a procedure can be followed for the creation of an interim management, setting up regional structures and holding a founding congress of a new party. Only in this way can the contaminated image baggage that the NP and the IFP, particularly, will bring to a new party be eradicated. At the founding congress all candidates for leadership and position will have to submit to the votes of regional representatives. Only then will the voting public be convinced that the new party is, indeed, a new party.

Failing this, the NDP will struggle fitfully into existence. It will simply be another missed opportunity. It will leave South Africa's former political masters in a *danse macabre* on the periphery of politics, and the wrong periphery at that, while the real fight for power takes place to the left of the ANC.

VIVA DEMOCRACY!

Anyone who has experienced both Western and African democracy knows that they are different. The root concept of Western democracy is accountability, and the root concept of African democracy is consultation. In the Western system voters select representatives from a particular party – that is, a particular philosophy of public administration, put them in government and expect them to get on with it. From that point, there are a number of interest groups, the media primary among them, who will keep an eye on how the selected representatives are doing. Any representative caught in any wrong-doing or betrayal of the public trust accepts that that is the end, and leaves, usually without question. At the end of a predetermined term of office, the government submits itself to the voters for reaffirmation or condemnation. The factors in the voters' decision are usually economic – growth in prosperity, availability of jobs and homes, and the general stability and efficiency of the society. That's why it has become a common wisdom to say, for example, that the election of a US president is in fact a referendum on the American economy.

In African democracy these things matter, naturally. But there is a tendency for voters to select a party that is familiar to them, and language and culture play a strong role in that decision. The emphasis of government is to engage the many organs of society in discussion and planning of public initiatives. Performance often takes a back seat to process. Africa is replete with examples of parties being chosen on grounds of their racial or ethnic make up, rather than their ability to perform as a government. South Africa itself is an outstanding instance where a particular tribe, the white one, repeatedly voted for a party despite the fact that it was demonstrably weakening the economy and endangering its citizens by driving the state ever closer to violent revolution.

The net effect of the African way is to make government big, to slow it down and to multiply the opportunities for abuse. It reduces its capacity to act as a concentrated, efficient catalyst in the economy, in facilitating foreign trade and brokering social harmony. Instead of being a catalyst, a facilitator and broker, government tends to penetrate the target activities and make itself responsible for them.

The Mbeki government will be particularly encumbered by this African malaise, especially when the new president introduces his ideas on social transformation – and the government goes into a new phase of policy development. Later, when the Mbeki administration gives way to an Anlap government, the severity of the impediment will increase. What this partial, and incremental, paralysis of government means for the way we live is that present trends towards self-sufficiency will continue. They will become even more a feature of life in the future than they are today. Already many areas traditionally regarded as the public preserve are being privatized. South Africans have realized that they have to take personal responsibility for their security; where the police were once guardians of public order, private security firms now proliferate. People in the upper echelons of society are realizing that they have to provide financially for their children's education. Health services and retirement benefits are ever more a matter of individual responsibility.

Concerning business, government will increasingly turn its ineffectiveness into a virtue: it will let the markets determine their own rules and operations. This process is already under way.

The tendency to self-sufficiency will be reflected in politics, and will accelerate as time goes by. At local government level many communities are in conflict with their local and second-level, metropolitan authorities. In the most visible of these, residents of Sandton, one of the country's wealthiest residential areas, rebelled against a manifold increase in their rates – ostensibly to fund development in more needy areas. Some of these conflicts will be resolved, of course, but the trend will be towards independence from former municipal services such as refuse removal, beautification of streets and pavements, and similar. At the next tier of government, provincial, a greater *de facto* autonomy will also develop. Already there is a great disparity in the levels of proficiency in provincial government. The Eastern Cape, for example, approached a state of near ruin. The Northern Province is in a parlous condition, while the Free State, Gauteng and the Western Cape are in good working order. As the social and political pressures on the central government increase and it becomes more inward looking, and itself enters a crisis of power, the provinces will be left to fend for themselves. The disparities between them will multiply, not diminish.

One might say this is not all a bad thing. The relationship between government and society is evolving towards the liberal ideal of small government, busying itself with essentials and leaving society and individuals to take responsibility for themselves. It's happening by default rather than design, but it's happening nevertheless. Yet it is an optical illusion of politics – because it is an effect that is perceived only when looked at from the perspective of society's privileged. In reality, government is not getting smaller. It is merely realigning its cumbersome armoury to direct its administrative battery at its real constituency, the workers and the un-people. The painful, final proof for the privileged will be that while they will bear the costs of small government, they will be denied its biggest compensation – small taxation. From this, then, we must turn the examination of our future lives to the nation's finances and the economy that determines them.

CHAPTER FIVE

FUMBLING THE FUTURE

The fate of the economy

It's the economy, stupid.

CLINTON CAMPAIGN SLOGAN, 1992

Forests have given themselves up to the newspapers, periodicals, academic papers and boardroom briefing documents that contain analyses and forecasts of the South African economy. The trouble is, though, they are usually 'if . . . then' arguments. If the gold price goes up, then the economy will be saved; if labour problems are solved then manufacturing will become more competitive; if corruption, crime and inefficiency are curtailed then there will be more foreign investment; if there is more foreign investment then the economy will grow; if tourism picks up then more jobs will be created; if unemployment goes down then there will be more social stability; if the government implements its economic policy successfully then the free market will be expanded. Well, that's just dandy.

What we really want to know is what likelihood there is of the if factors happening. Will the gold price, foreign investment, tourism, labour stability and productivity go up? Will corruption, crime, inefficiency and unemployment go down? And why? What are the consequences of present trends remaining what they are? If negative trends change for the better in the future, what are the currently absent factors that will enter the picture to bring about those changes? That's what we really want to know.

The answers are difficult to come by, and when we do get them they are often unpopular, or even dangerous, or just plain uncertain. So we normally avoid looking for them, or even asking the questions in the first place. Even when we do put aside our customary fears, we are curiously open to following false signs and being misled by experts who have developed a science that, in some instances, has slipped its moorings with reality. It is in economics, for example, that we have ungrumblingly embraced the banal expression 'negative growth' for an economy that is shrinking. It is touching that we express our determination to be optimistic in this way, but it isn't realistic. We content ourselves, too, with discussions of the growth rate of the economy as if the number of additional people who are living off that growth doesn't matter – so, for example, when an exceptional growth rate of 4.2 per cent in Gross Domestic Product (GDP) in 1988 was applauded, few felt like mentioning, and no-one felt like hearing, that measured as real GDP per capita it was actually a decline of 1.8 per cent.

Despite our anxieties about what might be revealed, we must ask ourselves questions that matter, and we must cast the answers in real terms. For the fundamental truth underpinning all considerations of economic growth, for example, is that it becomes meaningful only when it exceeds the growth of the population. Only then is there progress. Only then are there more people better off than there were before. Only then does a country prosper, get stronger and move up the ladder of nations. Until then there is no reason to celebrate an economy that is growing, but growing in such a way that it is creating an ever-greater deadweight of misery and want in the society.

An economy is merely a collective measure of the degree to which people have education, jobs, health services, housing, leisure and, in general, a quality of life that is desirable – and the means they have for achieving these things. Economic growth is always a developing country's number one priority, and particularly so if it has already straightened out its politics. An observation made earlier in this book is that in many of the economic success stories of the last three decades economic growth was put before political development. South Africa, of course, has done it the other way round and this has placed the country in an especially difficult position: political transition is most successful within the environment of a growing economy. In fact, political science is producing increasing evidence that vigorous economic growth is a necessary condition for lasting, successful political transition.

In 1991 two South African finance houses, Old Mutual and Nedcor, commissioned a scenario study of the country's prospects. The study was undertaken by local and international experts, and in the course of their analysis they examined forty other countries that had undergone a similar political metamorphosis. They found that there was not a single example of a country that had successfully moved from autocracy to democracy without a strongly growing economy. Drawing from these findings, the same study laid out a series of markers for successful transition in South Africa. In the four years following the study through to the beginning of 1996, South Africa dramatically underperformed against all but one of those markers. The study considered a conservative average of 5 per cent growth in GDP to be a vital condition for success; the figure attained was 0.8 per cent. Gross domestic fixed investment over the four-year transition, the study said, should grow by an average of 10.5 per cent annually; it grew by 2.75 per cent. The study said exports should grow by an annual average of 6.25 per cent; they grew by 3.9 per cent. Only in controlling inflation did the country exceed expectations: the study allowed an average of 14 per cent inflation a year; the actual rise was 10.4 per cent.

One might say: so what? The transition is more or less over and, sure, things haven't been as good as they could have been, or should have been – but they're chugging along and sooner or later we'll get to where we're supposed to be. That view, regrettably, would be an illusion. When one talks of voter discontent, the failure to deliver change and tidal political shifts – as was done in the preceding chapter – the origin of these happenings are to be found in the underachieving economy. The spread of poverty, in real terms, and the slow erosion of the well-being of the nation begin in the slack economy and gradually insinuate their way into the political arena. By the time things come to a head in some political manifestation, the cause-and-effect chain is so long that the head and the tail of events are often not perceived as parts of the same beast.

The South African economy today hovers in a limbo of critical uncertainty. Analysts, both the despairing and the optimistic, search for convincing signs of which way it is going. Until recently the South African economy was able to fall back on a ready-made excuse for its failure to perform – apartheid. From the fall of apartheid until now the country's special status as a modern political phenomenon has caused harsh judgements about its economic capabilities to be suspended. Those palliatives are no longer available. The period of transition from autocracy to democracy is over, and the country, and its economy along with it, is entering its democratic adulthood. Like someone leaving the supportive networks of youth for the self-responsibility and self-reliance of adulthood, the transformation is a little frightening. In the case of the national experience in South Africa, the country is undertaking this transformation without the assurance that its economy will be there to carry it through.

An exhaustive review of the political economy was undertaken for the South African Chamber of Business for the third quarter of 1996 by the South African political scientist Lawrence Schlemmer. Professor Schlemmer took into account macro-economic strategy, political stability and human resources. Along the way he assessed employment, management, housing, health, education, the government's Reconstruction and Development Programme (RDP), infrastructure, the impact of crime and corruption, affirmative action and productivity and training. He ranked each segment on a significance scale, and then gave each item a rating. To his evident surprise the professor's overall rating came out at exactly 50 per cent. It prompted him to the ringing conclusion that 'the cup is indeed both half-full and half-empty'.

That's the opinion of a learned analyst. Ordinary South Africans, aware of their environment and interested in its fate, can sense the same thing. Contradictory signals proliferate, the daily news is confusing, and the pattern is obscure. The question of which path events will follow into the future is as pressing now as it has ever been.

WIDE ANGLE – THE OUTLOOK FOR GROWTH

Boosted by hope after the arrival of democratic government in 1994, the South African economy showed signs of coming to life. Up to then, GDP had been falling steadily for more than a decade. In 1992 the economy contracted by 2.2 per cent. Then, in 1993, with tentative optimism about the future entering the picture, the economy grew by 1.3 per cent. By the time 1994 closed growth had risen to 2.7 per cent, and in 1995, emboldened by the political miracle of 1994, growth reached 3.3 per cent. The figures were paltry, admittedly, and they failed to amount to real progress, but they were heading in the right direction.

Then, in 1996, a new sobriety set in. Time tarnished the gleam of the miracle, and the growth shown up to that point first levelled off, then began to slip backwards. As 1996 drew on it was realized that early expectations for the year's growth had to be trimmed. A slowdown for 1997 had already been envisaged as early as the opening months of 1996. But when the 1996 slowdown itself proved to be more pronounced than expected, the forecasts for 1997 were revised, with most economists' predictions falling closer to 2 per cent.

As things stand, South Africa's growth pattern is locked in the 2 per cent to 3.5 per cent bracket. As self-evident as it might seem to say so, something fundamental will have to change if the country is to break out of that pattern after 1997. What is not so self-evident is what the positive element might be, lurking there in the future, waiting to reveal itself and create that change. In fact, there is very little evidence in the present to suggest that such an element exists at all.

WAIT AND SEE

It is generally accepted that the post-1994 economy has been plagued by a wait-and-see attitude among investors. The hallowed figure of Mandela loomed over the transition, but investor money wanted to be assured of a safe landing. The problem with Mandela was that he bore much promise but no delivery record. Money was simply not prepared to come in on anything less than a sure bet. Now, if that was the case with a leader of the stature of Mandela, wait until Mbeki comes along. Justly or unjustly, there is not a high quotient of confidence in South Africa's new democrats, who came to government in one mighty leap from an underground revolutionary struggle, when it comes to matters of the economy. The giddy drop in the Rand when Trevor Manuel, the first ANC minister of finance, took office illustrates the point.

The problem is compounded for the ANC because, with the notable exception of national reconciliation, it has not showered itself in glory in national administration – economic or otherwise. So, even the money that was prepared to back a Mandela administration will hold back until it sees whether the Mbeki government is a departure from, or a continuation of, what has become the norm. Because the wait-and-see factor will be even more pronounced in the case of Mbeki than it was in the case of Mandela, it will be more drawn out. The net effect will be to retard economic development that much further.

Economic growth traditionally relies on investments, productivity, constructive labour relations, exports, good government policies and free markets. The new world economy has grafted on to the traditional elements a second order of requirements that involve closing the knowledge gap, swimming with globalization and liberalization, and having a nation with the self-belief that it can be part of global prosperity. In both of these respects, the traditional and the contemporary, Mbeki is seen as a greater adept than the incumbent he will replace. Mbeki the technocrat is seen as more in tune with day-to-day realities than Mandela the icon. Mbeki's concerns with meaningful change hold more promise of grass-roots action than Mandela's lofty ideals of reconciliation. All of this is undoubtedly correct – the ANC's belated but well-received macro-economic policy was largely Mbeki's work. Yet none of it will be sufficient to cancel out the wait-and-see factor.

Within this context of suspended economic animation, Mbeki will launch his drive for transformation. Its sub-theme will be a hunt for money – money to make the envisaged transformation happen. The impact of this has been discussed in the previous chapter: a failure of the economy, hence the public purse, to deliver that money – or, at best, a sluggish delivery insufficient to head off the negative political ramifications; a resulting exertion of pressure on the business community and the media to become surrogate agents of change . . . to be met with roughly equal measures of unresponsiveness in each instance. In sum, Mbeki's dexterity in management, greater than exists in the presidency at the moment, will ameliorate some of the ills, blemishes and bumps in the economy – but will not be enough to overcome the pervasive inertia already contained within it.

Beyond Mbeki, when Anlap or a look-alike takes control of government, radical changes will begin to take place in the economic operating environment. Those changes will be unwelcome. They will, nevertheless, be depressingly familiar to those who, like former British prime minister Margaret Thatcher, are predicting a retrogression to socialism in some parts of the world. Anlap will not hesitate, as Mbeki will, over new taxes. Business will batten down for a long siege against avaricious government. A significant portion of its energies and the best of its brain power will, as in the later years of apartheid, be diverted into political avenues. Business is inherently obdurate and, besides, it is closer to the money than government is – so Anlap will not win its war with business. This, in turn, will lead Anlap to turn to areas that are wholly under its jurisdiction, like the civil service. Ambitious development schemes will be conceived within the public sector, which will begin to swell alarmingly. There are several examples in Africa – Zimbabwe is one – where the civil service grew by up to four times following independence. The burgeoning civil service will, in itself, be a drain on the economy, accompanied by further attempts by the government to raid the corporate sector and wealthy taxpayers. Along the way the government will try to tip the standing battle between capital and labour in the latter's favour. The wind-down cycle will be in spin.

Along the lines of the above, then, the operating environment of the economy will take shape in the future, with the following distinctive periods: the remainder of the Mandela era; the first phase of the Mbeki era with a protracted wait-and-see; the second phase of the Mbeki era, where there will be some return of confidence, but undermined by the onset of political disquiet at the formation of Anlap; followed by the Anlap period and the accelerated decline that will come with it. These economic periods, it will be noted, are defined in political terms. That's the way it's been in South Africa, and that's the way it will stay.

All of the foregoing reduced to percentages means that current forecasts for growth of around 2 per cent to 2.5 per cent for 1997 will doubtlessly hold true for the remainder of the Mandela years. The natural wave-like fluctuations of economic activity may push growth to 3–3.5 per cent in the first phase of the Mbeki era. The likelihood of economic growth breaking out of the 2–4 per cent range at any stage before the watershed onset of the Anlap era is unsupported by any evidence in the present.

HOW DOES YOUR ECONOMY GROW

Before this discussion moves on to specific sectors of the economy – the building blocks of growth – three qualities of economic growth need to be noted. The first is the central issue of how much economic growth South Africa needs to make progress in real terms. No-one knows for sure. The overall reason for this baffling uncertainty on such a fundamental issue is that South African social science is plagued by unreliable statistics. No-one, for example (at least up to the end of 1996), knew for certain how big the South African population was. That meant that no-one knew for sure the rate at which it was growing. That, in turn, meant that no-one could say with certainty how quickly the economy should grow to keep pace with the population.*

* This explains why figures vary according to different sources. I have made my own judgements about which sources I consider to be most reliable or, by comparing several sources, have worked with what I have been compelled to deem dependable aggregates.

To muddy this picture even further, some economists say that for real advances in national well-being to be made, the growth rate needs to be at least double the population growth rate. Nevertheless, without descending into an academic argument and an evaluation of sources, it can safely be said that nothing starts happening in South Africa in terms of real progress until economic growth gets to 4 per cent. To this must be added the often-overlooked requirement that economic growth of, say, 4 per cent would need to be sustained over a period of at least a decade before there is irreversible progress, of the like that can be compared to the success stories of the Pacific Rim nations. The corollary of this is that real-terms economic reverse, sustained over, say, a decade is cumulative and does damage that a nation needs more than a generation to recover from.

The second quality to be noted is that it matters where economic growth takes place – where in the economy, and where in the society. Recent economic growth in South Africa, for instance, has been propelled largely by expansion in the agricultural sector. According to some estimates, a subtraction of the agricultural sector would have reduced the recent growth of 3 per cent to about 1 per cent. Industry has recently shown little or no growth. Yet it is here that growth is desperately needed to overcome the problems of labour relations, employment and urbanization. If this ratio between industrial and agricultural growth doesn't change – and there is little to suggest that it will – it means that overall growth in South Africa will be the hostage of climatic conditions. One bad drought cycle and GDP is in trouble.

The matter of where in society growth takes place is equally important. In this regard some simplistic notions have been overturned in recent years. It used to be held that any growth at all was good, ultimately, for everyone. If the factories – and their owners – got bigger and richer, they would pay more salaries to more workers who would spend more, which would stimulate more production, and so on, ad infinitum. A rising tide lifts all boats was a popular defence of unbridled capitalism. Alas, this is not so: while it remains true that you cannot make the poor richer by making the rich poorer, it isn't necessarily so that the poor get richer when the rich do. Many Third World countries, who can afford this anomaly least, have seen elites prosper without any real benefit trickling down to the poor. In South Africa's case, particularly, this kind of growth will have dire political consequences.

The third observation deals with the ultra-long-term prospects for the economy. The argument has been forwarded up to now that the gathering forces in South African society will culminate in a radical political shift to the left in 2004. A feel for what will be experienced under an Anlap government has been sketched. But it does raise the question of what happens after that. In the opening chapter of this book the undertaking was given that a bid would be made to look up to twenty years into the future. The method that has been employed to look into the future is an examination of the continuum of events, from the past into the present – and, by extrapolation, from the present into the future. Of course, the further one looks into the future, the more tenuous that continuum becomes and the more science gives way to speculation. On this basis, though, the most likely course of events from the victory of Anlap onwards will follow what we might call the Mozambique syndrome.

Up to the 1970s Mozambique had a functioning economy. But it was so skewed to a privileged minority and so disregarding of the majority of Mozambicans that it engendered its own nemesis. That nemesis, popular discontent, needed only the trigger of events in far-off Portugal to set off a seismic political shift in Mozambique itself. In the uncaring way history works its ironies, independence under a communist government brought only greater misery to Mozambique until, officially, it was designated the poorest country in the world in the late 1980s. The experience has been a cruel cold shower for Mozambicans. Today they are abjectly welcoming to anyone who can bring development of any shape or kind to their benighted country. Workers are prepared to accept any work at any remuneration. There has been an attitudinal shift and Mozambique has embarked on a long, slow recovery. A similar cycle of events is likely to characterize South Africa's long-term prospects. Only at the nadir of the Anlap-induced wind-down of the economy will there be an abandonment of the culture of entitlement, of self-defeating labour strategies and of unjustified affirmative action. Only then will there be a realization that wealth must be created before it can be distributed. Thus South Africa's real recovery will not begin until some years into an Anlap administration – probably at least five, more likely ten. The beginning of real prosperity for South Africa is at least still one generation away, about fifteen to twenty years, in about 2015.

GOVERNMENT FINANCE – THE DEADLY DILEMMA

Delivering on promises of change is the central issue in South African politics, and will remain so for governments to come. It immediately calls up the question of the government's ability to deliver – 'capacity' is the buzzword. This question, in turn, taps into government finance – another way of saying: has the government got the money to put where its mouth is? To get to the answer, three things have to be weighed up. Together, the three govern the amount the government has at its disposal.

The first is that the amount of money there is in the public sector is directly governed by how wealthy the private sector is. Government is not, normally speaking, a wealth producer. It derives its revenue entirely by taking a cut off what's going on in the private sector. Hence, a government that wants money for its own ends must first ensure that the business world is making it. The simplicity of this observation is matched only by the frequency with which governments overlook it. The fact that the South African economy is not delivering, and is not likely to for a considerable time, has been discussed above. This is the primary restriction on the government's future spending plans.

The second factor is the efficiency with which the government can collect the money that is available to it, and this will be dealt with separately, below, under the discussion on taxation.

The third factor determining government finance is the effectiveness with which it manages what it's got. In this respect the new South African government is generally deemed to be moving in the right direction – tighter all-round fiscal controls. Its priorities are right – redirecting spending towards social investments such as health and education. It is also achieving a more sensible proportion between spending categories than its predecessor – apart from health and education, spending is up on police, welfare and housing . . . and down on agriculture, government services and defence. That leaves only the two big baddies of public finance: deficit and debt. And that's where things get ugly.

Every year the government budgets to spend more than it will collect in revenue. That doesn't make it different to most other governments, but it's the extent to which it is done, and the accumulative effect thereof, that is deeply troublesome. The deficit of income against expenditure, which is measured as a proportion of GDP, has crept up from 3.6 per cent in 1989, hitting an all-time high of 10.2 per cent in 1994, and easing to 5–6 per cent at present. This is more than double the level the seven richest countries in the world allow themselves, and more than three times the average for successful emerging economies. The problem with the deficit is that the government has to borrow to cover the shortfall; and the problem with borrowings is that they give short-term lift, and become long-term ballast. Government borrowing periods are lengthy – anything from five to twenty years, which is why succeeding generations pay for the profligacy of their predecessors. In international economics, lights generally start flashing when a country's borrowings reach 30 per cent of its GDP. In South Africa's case, they have reached a profoundly sobering 57 per cent. At this level of national debt, the following starts to happen: not only is there a mounting series of lump-sum payments looming over the economy, the interest on those debts becomes so high that the government has to borrow to meet those interest payments. That, classically, is the debt trap. In the words of one economist, Vella Pillay of the National Institute for Economic Policy: 'There is only a remote possibility of getting off this roundabout.'

The sum of all this is to present the next South African government, and those to follow, with an unhappy choice. It will be a choice that will also be drearily familiar to just about every South African family, which will be feeling the pinch just like the government: cut expenditure, or increase income, or both. As it happens, the ANC government has decided on the first: it plans to bring the deficit down to 3 per cent by 2000. To its credit, cuts are already evident. But if it does achieve its aim, it will do so in the face of serious political pressure to spend. If Mbeki's transformation plans are to have any substance, they will cost, and cost a lot. Add to that the fact that spending cuts mean, more than anything else, loss of jobs in state organizations. The political feasibility of this course is unpromising.

Sadly, even if 3 per cent is attained, it will alleviate the problem, not solve it. Therefore, it can only be a matter of time before the next government – certainly the one after it – moves to the second option: increase income. That means going to the taxpayers for a bigger cut of their wealth. That's another story. Don't go away.

TAXATION – THE GOVERNMENT TAKETH AWAY

If Karl Marx hadn't written *Das Kapital* in nineteenth-century Britain in the throes of the Industrial Revolution – a society that present-day South Africa strongly resembles – he might have done so now, in this country. This is a place where the many languish in want while the few flaunt the riches the economy is capable of producing. In such a place one's thoughts turn easily to big, benign government that equalizes obligations and rewards. Recent world history, of course, has taught us that it simply doesn't work like that. Communism's final egalitarianism is that it kills off the poor along with the rich, while capitalism at least spares the rich.

The ANC government knows all these things in its head, but does it know them in its heart? When capitalism and the free markets fail to uplift the poor, as they shall, a future government will feel compelled to intervene. Indeed, Mbeki's transformation vision implies nothing less than intervention. So, with the pressure mounting as the dissolution of the ANC–Cosatu–SACP alliance looms, the next government will toss on the horns of the public finance dilemma described above . . . and will emerge with the inevitable answer: get the money from those who have already got it. But it won't get it without a fight.

A recent history of abusive taxation has left South African taxpayers among the most burdened in the world. It wasn't always like that. In the 1960s and early 1970s, the economy boomed, apartheid had not yet fully started to take its toll, and fiscal life was good. Even in 1980, the tax picture resembled international norms. Government took its main tax bite from companies, followed by individuals, who provided about 20 per cent of the national tax cake, with sales tax in third place. By then, though, the government had discovered the sheep-like complacency of the South African voter, and began to take advantage. Today the payment ratio has inverted.

Individuals now get bitten hardest, and their contribution to the cake has risen to 40 per cent. The take from sales tax (guess who bears the brunt here) has more than doubled to about 27 per cent. And the contribution from companies, who have the clout, the accountants and the tax lawyers, has dropped vertiginously to around 13 per cent. And that includes the gold mines. A *Sunday Times* survey, in the last quarter of 1996, of the tax raid on salary earners showed that high earners (R20,000 a month) spent the first five months of the year working for the government. Earnings of R10,000 a month put the earner in hock to the tax man for the first four months of the year. The survey did not factor in sales tax and a host of indirect taxes such as those hidden in the petrol price, or local rates.

A wide-angle view of South African society reveals another important dimension of the problem: about 20 per cent of the economically active population is paying about 85 per cent of individual tax. The present government has launched an initiative to 'widen the tax net' – but the situation is getting worse, not better. The formal economy is shrinking in the sense that it is shedding jobs. Therefore the tax burden is falling on fewer and fewer payers. This, coupled with the unfairness of the burden, has provoked a mounting resentment among taxpayers. The inevitable has happened: alarming numbers of taxpayers have seized on the culture of dishonesty in the country to shrug off their tax responsibilities. Current estimates for undercollection by the Receiver run at about R21 billion, or about one-and-a-half times the amount that is levied on the entire corporate sector. Lawrence Schlemmer reported in his SACOB survey that prosecutions had been initiated against 60,000 people for non-payment in 1995. Answering a question in parliament in November 1996, the minister of finance disclosed that no more than 24 per cent of tax forms sent out for the 1995/96 tax year had been returned.

There are no realistic prospects for meaningful change. South Africa is likely to follow its northern neighbour, Zimbabwe. Seventeen years after independence, the country's tax profile remains largely the same as it was before independence. The South African tax bureaucracy is tackling its two main problems: structural deficiencies and a skills shortage. Some gains are being made with structural adjustments. However, these will be offset by the culture of avoidance (which will intensify as new bids for more taxes are made) and by the fact that the skills pool is getting smaller, not bigger.

The area that is likely to be chosen by future governments for new tax revenues is indirect taxes. The complacency of taxpayers who have dug ever deeper to pay up on their direct income tax has a termination point – which, in fact, has already been reached. So, already under discussion are taxes on pension funds, capital transfer taxes, death duties, and land taxes. The next government is likely to see that the only way to bring the growing informal sector of the economy into the tax net is to increase sales tax. It is only when traders in that sector buy that they come within the reach of the tax man. All in all, taxation is set to be a battlefield of the future, with gains and losses experienced by both the givers and the taker. Ultimately, the government, the taker, will have the upper hand. South Africa will remain a tax-unfriendly environment for the foreseeable future.

PRIVATIZATION – THE WINDFALL MYSTERY

It is a popular irony in South Africa that the apartheid government, while justifying itself by purporting to fight communism, adopted many of communism's ways. It transformed the bureaucracy into a central planning behemoth, and encroached on the economy to the point that, today, about half of all fixed assets are owned by the state. This sin of the past has turned out to be the biggest potential bonanza for the post-apartheid government: all it has to do is normalize the situation, that is, sell these assets back to the private sector where they belong. Estimates of the value of the assets vary. An upper estimate from a New York analyst puts the gross value at R248 billion, with R33 billion immediately saleable. Standard Bank in South Africa says R100 billion could be raised from the sale of state assets. With that money the government could get close to wiping out the national debt and providing a kick-start to some serious economic growth, or undertake some really imaginative political initiatives – like eradicating the housing backlog, or establishing nation-wide pre-school care, or an effective primary health care scheme, or whatever. So how come, having said it will do it, it doesn't?

The unions' opposition to privatization, with its concomitant loss of jobs as private-sector efficiencies are introduced, is well known.

But can the government be more anxious of antagonizing that opposition than is generally credited, even in this discussion? Especially when it can be bought off by some massive social recompense that can flow from the proceeds of privatization – think of the loss of jobs that could be made up in a new cycle of real growth, for example? Or in some government-backed public-works programme? It just doesn't seem plausible that the government cannot make a deal with the unions, especially when the benefits for all are so easily seen or sold. Dare one suggest that the answer is that Thabo Mbeki could be content to see the privatization programme start delivering results – that is, profits – only in his administration? Or could it be that there is a deep-seated psychological resistance to far-reaching change that would take its progenitors into unfamiliar territory? Neither of these is a question that any politician would, or could, answer honestly. So, personally, I prefer the latter explanation. Inertia is the strongest force in politics, and it is the only thing that explains why the privatization issue has been approached so gingerly.

For the purpose of privatization, the government divided its assets into three categories. The first contained those that it was deemed imperative the state should retain control over. They included electricity supply, telephones and telecommunications, railways, broadcasting and the Airports Company. The second category contained those of a lesser strategic importance, measured from a socio-political point of view – like Armscor and a subsidiary, Denel, both armaments manufacturers, South African Airways, Soekor oil exploration company and the controversial synthetic fuel project, Mossgas. The final category contained a number of companies among which the only common thread is amazement that the government should possess them in the first place. They include a holiday resort company, a parcel delivery service and two airlines left over from two former homelands. This latter category was divided into those that were profitable and those that were not, and it was decided that privatization would begin with the unprofitable companies. The exaggerated caution of this approach soon proved self-defeating: no takers were found. It was then decided to push Mossgas into the market place. The misbegotten project had already cost R40 billion, was running on a R400 million a year subsidy, and needed multimillion-Rand capital injections to keep it going. No-one was prepared to offer a price acceptable to the government and the sale flopped. The obstructions that lie in wait on the privatization road were highlighted, however, by the reasons given and conditions sought by the bidders. Several bidders wanted commitments from the government that it would get out of the rest of the fuel industry – like guaranteed deregulation of the retailing of fuel. Several would only bring their money in if it wasn't going to be trapped by exchange controls. One bidder reportedly wanted a free-trade area in the Eastern Cape, off which shore the Mossgas fields lie, partly as a strategic instrument to deal with the unions threatening to make any new owner's life miserable.

The point is that privatization has limited prospects in a highly regulated, unionized economy. This has particular relevance for the government's present plans to find minority shareholders in state corporations, such as Telkom and others. Prospective private-sector investors will have to be content with the fact that they are getting involved with a majority partner that is traditionally slow in taking decisions, has agendas beyond the business itself – political considerations like not being compromised in job-cutting exercises, and alliances with unions – and may change ideological garb at the next election. What successes there will be in privatizing in this hesitant manner will not be great.

It is most probable that there will be a burst of privatization activity in the twelve months leading up to the next election. President Mandela nailed his colours to the mast when he said, in the face of union opposition, that privatization was 'fundamental policy' for the ANC. For this reason the party could not approach the polls with nothing to record under this heading of its report card. It would be important for the ANC to demonstrate to its upper-bracket constituency that it is capable of manifesting the spirit of its macro-economic policy. And, speaking of which . . .

MACRO-ECONOMIC POLICY – PUTTING YOUR MOUTH WHERE YOUR MOUTH IS

The really worrying thing about the government's macro-economic policy is that it starts off by saying that if the economy continues on the tracks it is presently on there can be no progress in alleviating the fundamental ills of South African society, like poverty, unemployment and ignorance. It's really worrying because, first, the premise of this book is that South Africa is trapped on the track it is presently on, and has been on for some years now, by inertial forces that are bigger than any political initiative. Second, it's really worrying because it raises the question of whether this government has shown up to now that it has the insight, the boldness, the innovation and the resources to overcome that inertia.

The government's tardiness – more than two years after it took office – in producing the policy in itself counts against an encouraging answer to the foregoing question. What made things less auspicious for the government was that its two partners in the social compact, business and labour, each got tired of waiting and produced its own strategy for development. The corporate sector produced a document called *Growth for All* and labour produced *Social Equity and Job Creation.* This placed government in the unpromising position of having to satisfy both, or choose on which of the two demarcated terrains it would rest its weight. In the event, in mid 1996, it came to rest on the side of wealth creation, with a document called Growth, Employment and Redistribution, now known as the GEAR plan. Predictably, the plan was applauded by business and condemned by labour. The plan made South Africa a paid-up subscriber to post-modern economic orthodoxy, which hallows small government, free markets, low taxes, low national deficits and high growth.

GEAR applied the orthodoxy by making the following its resting pillars: fiscal reforms, removal of exchange controls, industrial policy reforms, for example, promoting competition, privatization, governmental focus on infrastructure, wage flexibility, and a social agreement for wage and price moderation. An integration of these, GEAR said, would bring a growth rate of 6.1 per cent and 409,000 jobs a year by 2000. While the spirit of the plan was well received, a forest of question marks rapidly formed over its prospects and practicalities. The governor of the Reserve Bank, Chris Stals, said immediately that the growth target was 'ambitious' and the prospects have been more fully dealt with above; exchange controls, by the government's own admission, will be with us for at least the duration of the GEAR term; the labour movement said the proposals on wage restraint were 'like declaring war'; the provision of infrastructure falls smack into the government revenue problem dealt with above; likewise privatization; industrial policy reforms have, since GEAR, been minimal and slow; and there has not even been an inclination in the direction of a social agreement. Only in the undertaking on fiscal reform has the government shown it has a sporting chance of success – it made early progress in trimming back the deficit.

GEAR's expectation of itself, it turned out, was too high. It was anticipated that the very presence of such a plan, so long called for by the investment community, coupled with its pleasantly surprising leaning towards the corporate world's view of life, would in itself lead to an investment surge. It didn't.

President Mandela sent a spurt of anxiety through financial society when he told a trade union audience that if the plan didn't deliver on its promises, it would be reconsidered. The absence of investment response to the plan, and the government's less-than-firm commitment to its implementation revealed by Mandela are linked – the one is both cause of the other, and its effect. If the plan doesn't work, there won't be any investment, and if there isn't any investment (hence no growth and no jobs) the plan won't work.

Several economists have pointed out that the plan's two fundamentals are privatization and the removal of exchange controls, and it is precisely with these two that the greatest problems exist. The advances made with pruning the deficit will not be enough in themselves to carry the plan through to its goals. These widely publicized goals will then become a yardstick by which the government will be measured unfavourably. The closer the next election comes, particularly, the more gleefully parties on the left and on the right will smack the government with that yardstick. The right will say the failure to meet targets is proof that the government doesn't have the capacity to run a modern economy successfully, and the left will say it is proof that the modern orthodoxy may work for developed economies but not for one with special development requirements such as South Africa's.

FOREIGN INVESTMENT – DON'T CALL US, WE'LL CALL YOU

The GEAR plan makes the definitive observation that all elements of economic status, the current status and the envisaged, are integrated. The uncomfortable result of that is it makes a discussion like this seem uncompromisingly – and, therefore, unrealistically – pessimistic. Regrettably, it is an unavoidable truth that the nature of one aspect of the economy will invariably mirror the nature of another. It is unlikely that government, business and labour will adopt a bold, innovative, co-operative and productive approach to one part of the economy, and not do so in other parts. Therefore, if one segment of economic life is in a poor and unpromising state . . . Mark Twain said it best: if you are on the wrong train, then every station you come to will be the wrong one. Accordingly, here we go again with that old cyclical effect: foreign investment will not pick up until that grossest of manifestations of a closed economy, exchange control, is eliminated – and exchange control won't go until foreign reserves build up and the economy has become a financial magnet . . . which are things that will follow substantial foreign investment.

Exchange controls are not the only culprit discouraging foreign investors. There are others and they are well known. Crime is a deterrent. The prevailing mood in Western, industrial democracies, where most investment comes from, is extremely sensitive to employees' exposure to danger while on assignment. Ethical aspects aside, companies fear the practical consequences of employees being robbed, injured or worse. Insurance, law suits and top executives' down time are all issues that swim into focus. Tax is a put-off. Where manufacturers could have a factory in Ireland, Chile or Singapore with a 5 per cent to 10 per cent tax exposure, that would rocket to 48 per cent in South Africa. The labour picture is uninviting. South Africa's labour is the most expensive of emerging markets, and among the least productive. The closed economy stifles interest. The country's many monopolies give newcomers the cold shoulder. Lastly, investors worry about the long-term political and social instability augured by an exceptionally high unemployment level – against scant prospects of a growth rate that will begin reversing the malaise.

Of all of the foregoing impediments to foreign investment, only one

– exchange controls, is subject to administrative fiat. Thus only this one factor could be eliminated merely by a decision to do so. All the others have their own volition and will be with us for some time to come. This is why the estimated R20 billion that has flowed into the country since the coming of democracy has not been in long-term, fixed investment that could lay a foundation for growth. And this is why GEAR's presuppositions of a doubling in real private investment by 2000 and a fourfold increase in additional foreign direct investment are simply and sadly beyond reach.

EXCHANGE CONTROLS – SOPHIE'S CHOICE

Exchange controls, which in effect mean that once you have money in South Africa you can't get it out, stand at the core of South Africa's economic problems; and an analysis that skips along the surface of the problems would suggest a simple solution: get rid of them. Many people urge just that. The difficulty with that is the authorities – who would love to be rid of this left-over of apartheid economics – are undoubtedly right in fearing that a sudden lifting of the barriers would lead to a fatal outflow of funds. Billions of rands left South Africa clandestinely when it was feared that apartheid would bring ultimate catastrophe to the economy. If financial channels to the global economy were now legitimized, investors wary of poor prospects at home would undoubtedly take advantage and send funds to safer havens. In addition to this, there would be a dam-burst effect: South African companies have been prevented by exchange controls from investing abroad and there is pressure from funds that have been turned inwards for too long.

Some alleviation of the exchange-control dilemma is provided by the fact that, to a limited extent, a piecemeal approach can be employed. The government has doubled the amount that a wholly foreign firm can borrow in South Africa, thereby reducing the amount of capital it would need to bring in to start or maintain operations. There have been other, largely technical, alleviations involving asset swaps and offsets of imports against exports. But the word limited is applicable throughout. Reserve Bank governor Chris Stals has categorically ruled out a precipitous lifting of controls, plumping instead for a four-to-five-year programme. That means that exchange controls will be part of the South African scene well into at least the middle of the Mbeki administration, protecting the money that's already in the country, but being an effective barrier to any new money coming in.

LABOUR – ON YOUR MARX

When the South African government accepted the recommendation of Professor Nic Wiehahn in 1979 that black trade unions should be legally recognized, it didn't see the big picture: it was sanctioning the only legitimate socio-political instrument available to the country's seething black proletariat. From that moment, organized labour became more than just organized labour. The unions became a substitute for political parties, the shop floor became a substitute for political platforms, and the hard bargain and the strike became the instruments for realizing political, social and economic aspirations. The black South African worker, politically and socially oppressed, looked to his shop steward in the same way that a worker elsewhere would look to his local councillor or member of parliament to represent his wishes. The unions formed themselves into a federation, Cosatu, and the ANC engineered an alliance with the federation. The rest was inevitable.

The question that the democratic victory of the alliance brought was: would there be a decline in harmful labour actions? The evidence so far is not conclusive. From the unbanning of the ANC until its ascendancy to power in 1994, strikes took a painfully high average of 3.9 million man days out of the economy each year. Then, in 1995, it fell to 1.6 million. At the time of writing, it seemed 1996 would show low strike activity, too. Some labour analysts say union membership has declined slightly. Does this mean the costly industrial war in South Africa is over? At the very least the evidence suggests that there is a truce. However, there are elements of the labour picture that give rise to long-term concerns. The decline in membership is merely consistent with the shrinking number of jobs in the market. Although strikes have been less protracted, a situation aided by the arrival of a new Labour Relations Act strongly favoured by the unions, union activity hasn't lessened – at least twelve new unions have been formed since the ANC came to power and more than 50 per cent of all South African workers are now unionized. In addition, it is axiomatic that the political quotient of union activity would be dependent on the political climate. As the above figures for strike days lost indicate, strike action is highest when expectations are highest. The unions are currently in a phase of disillusion with their alliance partner. When that disillusion mutates into a new cycle of expectation, along with political circumstances as described in the previous chapter, union activity will revive the mind-set the unions were conceived in, and become a potent political force once more.

There's one more important way to look at industrial relations in the future. On 15 June 1976 there was no objective social index to tell you that the following day Soweto would explode in riots that would change the course of South African history. But a few days spent in Soweto at that time would have told you sentiments were at boiling point. This is not to suggest labour relations are set to explode. However, some time spent in the workplace, listening to both management and unions, will tell you that, despite improved legislation and fewer strikes, attitudes and antagonisms between the two have deteriorated, not improved. One formal measurement that makes this visible is the phenomenon of jobless growth – industry is doing all it can to grow away from the unions, not with them. On another level, unions are flexing their influence in areas beyond the shop floor. A strike was organized when banks raised their interest rates, unions have pushed for the end of the reserve bank's independence from government, are pushing for new tax laws, and are working against government, not with it, on privatization. And in case there should be any doubt about organized labour's view of its role in society – there are ongoing discussions within the movement about forming a new political party.

And, oh yes, one last thing: can it really be very long before the unemployed organize themselves, paradoxically, into a union? With the unemployed making up 30 per cent of the workforce, they are a substantive part of society's make-up. There has already been one attempt to organize the unemployed. That bid, which has apparently come to nothing, was humorously called the loafers' movement. It can't be long, though, before a more serious organization comes into being. It might even start in some other country and catch on here. Think about an international agency providing funds and support for an organsation wherein the jobless try to help themselves; think of pickets at factories, riotous downtown marches and worse . . . the chaos power that futurists fear, at work in an entirely new guise – one that would form beyond the range of our social vision, until it burst onto our television screens. It would be a new force, and its natural ally would be the formal workers' unions. Ultimately, the buck will stop with government. But management will have to handle it along the way.

RECONSTRUCTION AND DEVELOPMENT PROGRAMME

Here's an outstanding example of how idealism is distilled by the realities of governing, funding and delivery. The RDP began as the thematic platform of South Africa's first democratic government, and promised 1 million houses, piped water for 1 million people and electricity for 2.5 million people. In addition, it undertook to 'change the approach to government'. The funding concept was based on a kick-off of R2.5 billion, to be increased by the same amount every year, so that the funding of the programme would reach R12.5 billion in its fifth year. The funding picture muddied a little when the RDP got R5 billion in its second year, all right, but that included just about all of the previous year's allocation, which had not been utilized. The picture got murkier still when the government turned to zero-base budgeting for its departments, disallowing roll-overs. Then the government surprised everyone by deciding the RDP fund would no longer exist independently, but would go directly to spending ministries.

Few of the RDP's initial goals seem within reach. But this does not mean the RDP has been a failure. Government officials say that in 1997 some 43,000 projects will be under way. However, this illustrates, more than anything else, that the RDP means what anyone wants it to mean. It raises the question of whether the RDP is an outstanding prestige of the first government of the masses, or is no more than could reasonably be expected of any, even moderately responsible, government in the circumstances. The founding allocation of R2.5 billion was only marginally more than a fund for similar purposes established by the previous government, and is now administered by the Independent Development Trust.

The supply of electricity is often pointed to as one of the RDP's goals that stands a chance of being realized, or coming close to it. That is so, but the electricity supply commission, Eskom, had reached a rate of 250,000 new connections a year (on its way to a target of 300,000 a year) when the ANC came to power. Additionally, Eskom raises its money independently of the government. If the electrification project is to fail – and there are some indications of problems on the horizon – it will be because its investors are not getting their money back. That is happening for two reasons: electricity is being stolen at a rate of up to 70 per cent of the supply in some depressed areas, and some of the new recipients are too poor to consume any more than one-quarter of the projected consumption.

What the foregoing illustrates is that the RDP was ultimately dependent on a growing economy. That is the point made by development guru Jeffrey Sachs, head of Harvard's Institute for International Development, on a recent visit to South Africa. An appropriate growth rate, he said, could do more for the country than an RDP; and growth, he added, lay on 'an outward-looking, manufacturing-oriented and low-wage' path. He backed up his views with his own study of ninety developing countries over the twenty-five years from 1970 to 1995. He defined fifteen of the ninety as having open economies. They all achieved growth rates of more than 2 per cent. Of the seventy-five closed economies – South Africa is one – average growth rates of sixty-eight were below 2 per cent. What it comes down to is that the RDP, whether by special undertaking or by what one would be entitled to expect, will alleviate some poverty, and will provide some stimulus to development. In this sense we are far better off with it than without it. But it can only really succeed if it is part of a wider success story.

What is really interesting about the RDP, however, is its political fate. The country's new government needed a point of focus, a symbol of regeneration, a flagship project. That focal point needed a name, a slogan, an office that the media could phone, and a person who would personify it. The RDP was all those things, and the minister installed in the corridor near the president's office, Jay Naidoo, was the person. Former head of the union federation, Cosatu, he stood to become the embodiment of the yearnings of South Africa's disadvantaged masses. Perhaps that was just the problem. The government decided, wisely, in April 1996 to integrate the fund with the budgets of the ministries ordinarily responsible for the respective functions and projects. But was it wise, or necessary, to close the office, assign the popular Mr Naidoo to the lowly ministry of telecommunications and broadcasting and transfer supervision of the RDP to, ahem, Mr Mbeki? It would be going too far to say that Mbeki had it done in order to clear a present or future presidential contender from his path, and I wouldn't. But it's funny how things work out, isn't it?

LAND REFORM

The ANC government's bid to right the wrongs of land distribution and ownership flies into the maw of South Africa's most scandalous contravention of natural justice. The Natives' Land Act of 1913 laid the foundation whereon was built an edifice of cruel legislation that culminated in reserving 13 per cent of South Africa as homelands for about 75 per cent of the population and saw some 3.5 million people being moved from the land they occupied. A bouquet of recent legislation has attempted to embrace the entire period from 1913 to the end of apartheid. It has done so in two broad categories – restitution of land where claimants can prove they were dispossessed by race-based legislation, and redistribution of land to achieve a more equitable sharing among the country's people.

At the start of this process white farmers, particularly, turned their eyes northwards to where Zimbabwe's president has continually threatened white farmers with expropriation and even confiscation of land he says they stole to begin with. In South Africa the process has been handled with a praiseworthy deftness and soundness of policy, which has obviated the Zimbabwean excesses . . . although it must be remembered that the process here has only just got under way.

The specially created Department of Land Affairs has estimated that 26 per cent of land in South Africa is owned by the state, although only 1 per cent is available for redistribution and development. The immensity of the task is revealed in complaints by the Land Claims Commission that it is receiving up to 300 claims a month, and that, although the deadline for claims is 1 May 1998, it may take up to twenty years to resolve all cases.

The restitution of rural land is relatively trouble free, as in cases where it is not feasible the law provides for compensation or the granting of alternative land. Clearly it is one of the latter two courses that will have to be taken in most cases. In urban restitutions, however, the policy is to pursue densification of urban areas in order to get the poorest people closest to their places of work. There is as yet no sign of projects of this kind, but they are inevitable and will lead to much controversy – and much change in the character of affected urban areas.

Redistribution, too, is on the face of it relatively problem free, as it is based on a willing-seller-willing-buyer policy. Here, though, as in urban areas, a change in the character of some land occupation must be anticipated. Rocky Drift Farm in KwaZulu/Natal was an early project that became an example in which both the protagonists and the antagonists of redistribution found evidence for their views. The farm was a large, conventional, commercial one, producing 100 tons of beef a year, when 230 families pooled their R15,000 government subsidies and bought it. Despite the government's inarguable assertion that the buyers are entitled to the purchase, others are undoubtedly correct when they say the farm will not remain as productive as it was in its new guise as a multi-owner settlement where many of the economically active adults work elsewhere.

What is at stake in land reform is a clash of cultural attitudes toward land ownership, the morally unavoidable restitution of wrongs, and competing interests. As things are positioned at present, however, its implementation will leave more people better off than before, and contribute meaningfully to a sense of national healing. Less comforting, however, are the long-range prospects, under a government less sympathetic to entrenched interests. In these circumstances the issue of land is likely to come to the fore as a primary political concern of the African peasantry, and government redistribution will be tackled far more aggressively.

AFFIRMATIVE ACTION – IT'S NOT WHO YOU KNOW, EITHER

Affirmative action and black empowerment are destined to obey one of the fundamental laws of public administration: a good idea will be badly implemented. The prospects, consequently, are mixed. Successes will be localized in particular areas of economic and social life – but with a pervasive lack of change in entrenched patterns that will leave these disruptive exercises with a lacklustre report card.

Counting in favour of these undertakings in social engineering is, chiefly, the sheer weight of the moral imperative behind them. It is beyond dispute that black persons suffered indefensible prejudice in the economic and administrative life of the society, and it is beyond dispute that special measures should be taken to redress the imbalance. Helping affirmative action along, too, are recent, high-profile black empowerment deals that have seen black business ending up in control of an estimated 10 per cent of the Johannesburg stock exchange. Although these have been criticized as benefiting a tiny elite, they will have a pull-up effect as black business will be more open to, and more adept at, bringing black candidates up the rungs behind them.

However, affirmative action means putting up with incongruous notions like the one that has just appeared – 'black business'. There is a strong sentiment in both black and white society that such artificialities should be allowed to die off. The result of this artificiality, albeit a benign form of racial discrimination, is that its beneficiaries end up with a hollow feeling that what they have achieved is not due to their inner qualities, and its victims focus on the sense of unfairness that can be extracted from the process. Making it even more difficult to implement the laudable aims of affirmative action, in South Africa now and in the future, is the critical shortage of skilled candidates who genuinely qualify on grounds other than their colour. In addition, the declining jobs market is making the competition for posts ever more intense.

The balance of forces has meant that affirmative action has been able to write up very little overall success. Several surveys found that by the end of 1996 not even 5 per cent of managers in corporate South

Africa were black. The great exception has been the civil service, where the majority of government departments now run under black directors-general, and the parastatal corporations – all environments where policy ambitions overcome economic restraints.

There are, and will be, exceptions in the commercial world too. Just as the taxi industry became a predominantly black business avenue, so there will be others. Retail, particularly in townships and eventually in downtown areas, will be one of these. The professional class will also show quick and noticeable change as the new black elite makes its presence felt and fills in the vacuums left by white emigration. The present trend of propelling black candidates into top management will continue, especially in non-production jobs such as human resources, marketing and public relations. There will be some further black penetration of skilled jobs, particularly in the building industry.

However, the broad middle stream of economic endeavour – middle management, technical and production jobs, and entrepreneurship at the level of the butcher and the baker – will remain largely unchanged for at least another generation, until general education levels and economic under-performance begin to improve. The evidence for this conclusion is to be found in the only noteworthy example in the modern world of an affirmative action programme applied to a majority (not, as is more usual, to a minority group) from which South Africa can extract lessons. Malaysia's twenty-year bid from 1970 to 1990 to elevate the indigenous Bumiputra people in relation to the dominant Chinese and Indians has been deemed a qualified success, although the programme failed to meet many of its targets. In 1996 an Anglo-American researcher, Ian Emsley, published a study of the Malaysian experiment, from a South African perspective. Emsley's disturbing finding was that the two primary factors that made Malaysian affirmative action work – and would be preconditions for even modest success in South Africa – were economic growth (the Malaysian economy grew by an average of 7 per cent over the period concerned) and a major upgrading of education. As neither of these conditions is within South Africa's reach, the prospects for broad-based success in affirmative action here are slight.

CIVIL SERVICE – STATISTICAL TRICKS

The observation is sometimes made that South Africa is now entering its second cycle of affirmative action. The first was a forty-year programme of affirmative action for Afrikaners, which made the public service its focal point. It was used to great effect: the public service ballooned under the National Party government so much that by 1970 about 20 per cent of the white workforce was in its employ. From a distinctly colonial service before the NP takeover in 1948, employment in the civil service became synonymous with being Afrikaans. The question evoked by this view is whether round two will cost the country as much as round one. It's a valid and worrying question. According to the RDP's Professor Ben Turok, the cost of South Africa's public service is the highest in the world, using up 45 per cent of government funds in salaries alone. At this level the public service has long since become a serious inhibitor of economic performance.

Sensitive to public anger at the country's inert and inept civil service, the Mandela government undertook to cut its jobs complement from 1.2 million to 900,000 in the last three years of its term, in annual targets of 100,000. As praiseworthy as the aim was, there appeared more than a little sleight of hand in it. The first 55,000 of the jobs were vacant posts, and the remaining 45,000 of the first year's target constituted less than 4 per cent of the full complement. This is worth registering in the light of the later revelation by the public service minister that the natural attrition rate in the service is 7 per cent a year. The magic of statistics was further revealed in questions in parliament that showed while numbers in the defence force had shrunk from 112,000 in 1989 to 101,000 in 1996, the permanent staff complement (as opposed to draftees) had more than doubled. It was also revealed that there are now 43,000 more employees in government and the public corporations than there were in 1994. Part of the reason for the confusing data is that there isn't agreement on what is meant by the public service. Should only central government count? Or should that include the public corporations and the provinces? And what about local government? The variations merely open possibilities for juggling with figures.

The benefits of the cut backs are additionally undermined by the fact that they have been matched by an undertaking to raise salaries, particularly of the lowly paid. Also, the mechanism of reduction – inviting voluntary retrenchments – lead to a damaging flood of applications by experienced personnel. Their reaction was not surprising. The employment benefits of the public service have been so grossly inflated in recent time that even a middle-ranking public servant can retire as a millionaire, and a senior one as a millionaire several times over. So, there are few cost benefits in the short term to the government's cutback plans.

In the longer term, political considerations are likely to dominate. It is unlikely that this government will make painful job cuts in the heart of its voting constituency in the eighteen months before the next elections. The Mbeki government is even less likely to do so when it faces the breakaway by Cosatu and the SACP, and when the Anlap government takes over, the public service will enter a new era of expansion. Between now and then, the process of de-skilling the civil service that accompanied the bid for Afrikaner hegemony will continue its lamentable course in the drive to African hegemony.

TRAINING – UNLEARNED LESSON

This subject is a vivid example of the silent dynamics that are shaping South Africa's future. In South Africa's circumstances one might expect to find special efforts being made to train people for work and progress. That is not so. South Africa lags behind the rest of the world. Experts in the field say the country spends 1 per cent of total employment costs on training whereas successful economies spend many times more – the USA spends 5 per cent and Japan 10 per cent. Not only that, training in South Africa is deteriorating. In recent years there has been a steady fall in the number of apprentices enrolled in artisan training programmes. A comparison between South Africa and its trading partners becomes even more distressing when it is understood that the training that is lacking is not only at the level of skills for a new-world, knowledge-driven economy, but for simple literacy and language skills in a land where several million employed people are functionally illiterate.

Training is not merely the social responsibility towards employees' development that employers often regard it as. Low training levels are one of the key elements in South Africa's dismal productivity performance; and low productivity means falling ever more behind in the rapidly globalizing economy. This culminates in the depressing cycle in which slack economic performance undermines the ability to launch and fund initiatives that would improve economic performance.

Utterances by government officials make it clear that employers are blamed for the dangerously low levels of training. Again, this is not so – or, at least, not entirely. The country's hostile unions are also to blame. If unions saw themselves as partners in a compact with management, subjects like training would come to new prominence in the politics of the work place.

At the time of writing there was talk in government circles about producing a white paper on training at some time in 1997 – and it may have appeared by the time you read this. It would be worth noting whether the intended policy takes into account recent international findings that training programmes don't work merely because they exist. Several studies in Europe have shown that training schemes failed to benefit those who participated in them. Attention has turned to the German model, whereby apprentices enter a firm's employ at wages below normal entry level in exchange for half-time training, both in the company and at schools for each discipline run by local governments. This system, however, demands an expensive, integrated approach between the public and private sectors and is not within South Africa's grasp.

The message here for black South Africans who want to be part of an economically emerging class is the same as it is in affirmative action: get into a business that has to train and advance black personnel to operate successfully. A recent survey showed, for example, that businesses with overwhelmingly black customer bases did the most in these fields. These businesses were all in the consumer sector, while engineering and mining were at the bottom of the scale.

JOBS – PROSPERITY DENIED

It is no revelation to say that, of all the ills besetting the South African economy, unemployment is the greatest. What matters now is the future of the problem – and how long the society can tolerate such an immense strain before something gives. After some years of argument about exactly how bad unemployment was, the Central Statistical Service pinned it down at the end of 1996: 30 per cent of people over the age of fifteen who wanted work didn't have any. And that was based on a most elastic definition of work: at least five hours over the five days preceding the survey. As with most statistics, however, that is only part of the story. The burden on those who are employed is very heavy – only something around 50 per cent of the adult population is economically active, or wants to be. For young people who enter the economy every year, about 350,000 of them, the picture is grim indeed – only six out of every hundred ever find a job. Does one really need a degree in political science to figure out what the social and political consequences of this are?

In the unemployment field, as elsewhere in the South African economy, figures vary widely. But one thing is clear – the jobs shortage is getting worse at an alarming rate. In 1995 the economy shrank by about 50,000 jobs. The mining sector alone has trimmed off about a quarter of its jobs in recent years. The private human resources consultancy, FSA Contact, found that no less than 4.8 per cent of the workforce had been retrenched in the second half of 1996. The really frightening thing about these job losses is that they occurred in a period in which there was modest growth in the economy – a case of jobless growth giving management the last laugh in its war with labour.

Where is all this going? The government's macro-economic plan sets a target of 400,000 new jobs a year by 2000, starting with a goal of 252,000 in 1997. But if the job market has been shrinking to the start of 1997, and economic growth is predicted to slump by about 30 per cent, there doesn't seem any hope of achieving the first target, even less so the 2000 target. And if the economy is in a cycle of jobless growth, and the government's plan envisages that 75 per cent of the new jobs must be grown in the private sector, then this target, too, seems beyond reach. That's bad enough, but it's important here to look at the prospects in terms of one of the primary themes of this book – casting the problem into real terms. In this case it means that even if the target of 400,000 new jobs were attained in 2000, it would be fewer than the number of new job seekers in that year. And that means that in the best possible scenario there will be more people with less work than ever before. To imagine that this is an issue that will continue to slumber beneath our plane of vision, remaining a set of statistics to tut-tut over, is foolishness of the blindest kind. A great reckoning is scheduled for the not-distant future. It will happen on the political terrain as discussed in earlier chapters.

HOUSING – FUTURE FOUNDATIONS

Housing is another of the silent dynamics – like training and unemployment, among others – that is writing our future in vivid letters. Nowhere else in the body politic is the rich–poor gap a more gaping wound. No-one feels the pain more deeply than those who cannot give their children a house to grow up in. Frequently they must bear the cut within sight of settled suburbs, often in the employ of households in which children have their own rooms and private gardens to play in. To put the numbers into perspective: there are more unhoused South Africans than there are white South Africans. More than half of urban South Africans do not have a proper home.

The ANC government came into office brandishing a promise to build a million houses in its five-year term. It was a rash promise. Unhappily for the ANC, the promise encapsulated the hopes of millions and it became the flying standard of the RDP. Now it haunts the ANC. At the end of 1996, the minister of housing told parliament that 70,335 houses – about 7 per cent of the target – had been completed in the first half of the government's tenure. Paradoxically, though, it is out of this, its greatest failure, that the country's first democratic government may be able to rescue its greatest self-vindication. For it is in housing that the government is poised to show it can improve its poor delivery record. One of the most informed independent commentators in the field, Dr Gavin Lewis, editor of the *RDP Monitor*, believes the delivery rate could go up to 165,000 units in 1997. In addition, about 400,000 subsidies (up to R15,000 each) had been approved by end of 1996, although the majority of these were blocked in bureaucratic channels and not yet applied. A further cause for optimism is that there is a conceptual change that will permit the building of high-density housing (blocks of apartments) – something that, curiously, was not contemplated before.

In the pale light of this hope in the gloom, it seems churlish to do what must be done – that is, look at the matter of housing in real terms. The number of houses desperately needed in South Africa is between 1.5 million and 2 million. Therefore, if the government had succeeded in its aim of 1 million houses it would have made a good dent in the problem, but it would not have come close to solving it. There's more to it than that, though. The rate at which the need for houses escalates is about 200,000 units a year. That means if the government did build a million houses in five years, it could only keep pace with the tempo at which the need was growing. Therefore, at the most optimistic projection of what will happen in reality – about 40 per cent of target – the net result will be to end up with many more people without houses than when the project began.

Housing, and its lack, represents a stream of frustrated yearnings of millions of people in South Africa. That stream will become a torrent and find a confluence with others, like joblessness, on the political plain. Together they will bring about the great reckoning.

PRODUCTIVITY – NO NEED TO RUSH

When Oscar Straus, a turn-of-the-century US secretary of commerce, said the cheapest labour is that which is most productive, he highlighted a key element in the cost of production that some economies, like ours, here at the end of the century, still haven't got right. South Africa consistently figures way down on global productivity rankings, coming forty-fourth out of forty-six countries in 1996's survey by the Swiss-based International Institute for Management Development, and forty-third out of forty-nine countries surveyed by the World Economic Forum. The current trend is downward – South Africa has been slipping on these scales in recent years. What trips up South Africa the most are its rock-bottom scores in the human development segments of these surveys – where training and skills promotion are measured. The surveys rate this division the most important because contemporary economies are knowledge driven, and will be more so in the future. The interlocking of costs and production is illustrated in international comparisons. According to *The Economist*, South African workers in the motor and clothing industries are slightly cheaper than Mexicans. But Mexican auto assemblers take one-third of the time their South African counterparts need to build a car, and Mexican clothing workers add four times as much value per garment than South Africans do.

Grey van der Hoff, principal consultant of South Africa's National Productivity Institute, says the problem is a direct result of the closed economy, where protected industries developed a false sense of doing well. The country's recent re-entry to the global economy has cast a harsh light on its deficiencies. Cultural considerations also complicate the issue. Productivity leaders like Germany and Japan have never been without a productive mind-set, whereas the attitude is foreign in the African way of life. South African workers, particularly, have been excluded from the effort-and-reward cycle that underpins a productive attitude.

The Productivity Institute is trying to promote improvement through training and development, instilling a culture of competitiveness, and relationship building between management and workers to erase distrust and build a sense of common interest . . . all things that will take time, even if they are successful. For the next decade, at least, low productivity will remain one of the main factors inhibiting economic performance.

TOURISM – SCUFFING THE WELCOME MAT

Tourism is an international boom industry, and the question is whether South Africa, which seems ready made for tourism, can become part of the fun and action. An estimated 11 per cent of global GDP is generated by tourism, and one in nine workers is in the tourism industry, making it the biggest employer in the world. On the face of it, South Africa should be an above-average destination, but it isn't. Tourism accounts for about 4 per cent of GDP and provides under half a million jobs – putting the country at less than half the international average on these scales, according to the government's white paper on tourism.

The prospects for improvement, to the ambitious levels stated in the white paper (10 per cent of GDP and 2 million jobs), are not auspicious. The problem is that the elements favouring tourism are all fixed – sunshine, wildlife, open spaces – and the variables are all negative inputs. The latter are crime, costs, poor service and lack of skills, and inadequate international promotion.

All of the impediments to growth in tourism are likely to be around for a while. Crime in South Africa is entrenched and the president of the Association of Travel Agents, Roger Mackie, made the astonishing disclosure in June 1996 that 1 per cent of tourists to South Africa were attacked. Greedy profit-taking has substantially eroded the cost appeal South Africa had for foreign travellers. A room in a good hotel in South Africa now costs about the dollar equivalent of similar accommodation in the USA or Europe, despite the devalued rand. Poor service and low skills are linked to training and an attitudinal shift in the economy as a whole, and a cash-strapped central government is making tough cutbacks in its funding of its tourism-promotion agency, Satour.

Recent statistics show the effect of these impediments. After the boost given by the political events of 1994, the high-season first five months of 1995 showed a 76 per cent growth in tourism. In the same period in 1996 the growth slumped to 6.5 per cent – and later figures given for May and June in 1996 showed a 49 per cent decline over the same months of the previous year. South Africa has distinctly palled as a destination for foreign travellers. If there is any growth in South African tourism it will happen because there are more tourists at large, rather than through South Africa's ability to enhance its own tourism resources.

MANUFACTURING AND EXPORT – WAITING FOR THE BOOM

Many of the elements of the economy discussed up to now have a point of intersection, and that intersection is the country's manufacturing industry. It's the economy's most vital sector – it's the biggest employer and the biggest contributor to GDP – and it's in big trouble. In the decade between 1983 and 1993 South Africa's global market share fell by 26 per cent from 0.46 per cent to 0.34

per cent. Sanctions played a strong role there, of course. Since then, however, political emancipation and the devaluation of the rand should have led to an export boom. Although there has been some improvement in exports, mainly to the rest of Africa, the boom didn't happen. South Africa's shock immersion into the global economy showed its factories sluggishly unable to compete in world markets.

Part of the malaise is that the only impressive export performance South African companies have shown is in exporting themselves. In a search for more stable and more promising environments, despite exchange controls, South African companies have, in the nineties, increased their foreign assets by 50 per cent to R135 billion, according to Reserve Bank figures quoted by *Newsweek*. Some of the country's biggest companies and best-known entrepreneurs have artfully left their industries seemingly intact in South Africa, but have in reality become foreign operations.

Myriad factors – low productivity, poor training, over-regulation, antagonistic labour relations, parochial management, to name just a few – make the manufacturing situation what it is. Yet one doesn't need to be an economist to know what's wrong. South African workers and factories have been outclassed. Others are better. It's as uncomfortable as that. As a result, business that should be done within the country is streaming abroad. You can't blame business people for going for the best deal.

The book you are holding now was written in South Africa but manufactured in England. The new South African flag that was enthusiastically waved at the country's recent sporting triumphs, if you please, was not manufactured in South Africa. In these cases, as in thousands of others like them, the business decisions have been motivated purely by costs and dependability.

The prospects for improvement are similar here to other aspects of the economy discussed thus far: each is an integral of the whole. It is unlikely that one aspect will shine brilliantly while others remain dull. For change to be effective, it must be pervasive. When it comes, it will announce itself on every economic platform and its presence will be unmistakable. A lot, however, has to happen before that time comes.

AGRICULTURE – THE ROOTS OF GROWTH

The parlous state of South Africa's biggest economic sector, manufacturing, is shown up by agriculture. Outstanding performance by the country's food suppliers, following good rains and bumper crops, has substantially beefed up the country's GDP. According to the Central Statistical Service, GDP growth in the second quarter of 1996 was 3.7 per cent, and 3.2 per cent in the third. Without agriculture the figures would have been 1.8 per cent and 0.5 per cent.

Agriculture, as an industry, is on a sound footing, and the government's land-reform programme is proceeding with no real disturbance to its short-term and medium-term productivity. Ultimately, however, the fate of agriculture is not in the hands of the farmers, or the government. A protracted cycle of drought, of the kind that South Africa is susceptible to, could knock the stuffing, albeit temporarily, out of both agriculture and the GDP.

Even the good news makes one worry.

HOUSING MARKET – LITTLE BOXES MADE OF . . . ?

It is a popular wisdom that the residential property market works in cycles, and that the present downturn will, consequently, soon be followed by an upswing. That is merely wishful thinking on the part of those of us who have an interest in the market. There are wave-like fluctuations in the graph, of course. Real prices in the housing market have been on a declining trend for more than a decade, and will remain in decline for many years to come.

In recent years, rising prices, inflation and higher taxation have changed the way middle-class South Africans distribute their income. The percentage of income available for housing has contracted. In the new South Africa, two additional demands on income have arisen – schooling and health costs. Families are having to trim their housing ambitions, either by not selling and buying upwards with the same ease as in years before, or doing so more modestly. The chief economist of Absa, one of the country's biggest home loans institutions, told *The Star* in October 1996 that, in real terms, housing prices had nearly halved since 1983. In the first three quarters of 1996, Absa said, they had dipped by 5.3 per cent and there was a likelihood of a decline of about 10 per cent running into 1997.

That's the change in the value of the market. There is also a change in the nature of the market. A fear of crime has driven South African families away from the traditional free-standing home with a large garden. Instead, there is a move to more secure cluster housing in walled and guarded complexes. Square metres of living and leisure space are no longer the factors determining price in middle-class suburbs. Metre for metre, in the residential suburbs of South African cities, the traditional home is now worth about half of its cluster counterpart. Almost all new development is along the cluster concept and many existing homeowners are living in rapidly dwindling investments.

There, then, is the South African economy. It is a patient suffering serious illness. It has been doing so for so long that complications have set in. If a medical bulletin were posted now, it would say 'critical but stable' with the prognosis for full recovery 'poor'. It is at a juncture like this that minds normally turn to thoughts of alternative healing and, as everyone by now knows, healing begins with an attitude.

CHAPTER SIX

WE ARE WHAT WE THINK

Attitude and behaviour in the new society

We speak incessantly of goodwill and co-operation and getting together as though the lack of these things were due to an oversight and could be remedied by words.

ARTHUR KEPPEL-JONES, 1947

Recent history contains a vivid example of the reciprocal effects a country's social order and the mind-set of its people have on each other. It's the story of the two Germanys. Until the Cold War divided Germany, it was a homogeneous nation. Then the East Germans gave up their individualism to authoritarianism, central planning and pervasive government. The West Germans, to put it plainly, simply got on with it, each pursuing a lifestyle commensurate with his or her ambitions and capabilities. Forty years later, when the wall came down, the difference between the two groups was astounding. By comparison with their Western cousins, the East Germans had become unsophisticated, insecure, suspicious and resentful, and economically backward.

The interplay between politics, attitude and the mood of a nation had wrought a sad and fascinating change in the German character. It was a telling illustration of how powerful this combination of factors could be in determining the life of a nation. Even more intriguing, though, is the realization that just as an individual can have a certain attitude, or a certain mood, so can a group of people – even an entire nation.

Right now the mood of South Africa is a little confused, a little anxious, and a little depressed. And so are the circumstances, the acts and the character of this nation in transition.

VIVA THE PARADOX

It's a pity, a big pity, about the mood of South Africa. Just when things were supposed to be getting better, we find that the big questions haven't gone away. Are things getting better? Or are they getting worse? And what should we do about it? Are the people who are leaving wiser than I am? Or should I stay and have the last laugh?

On the rational level, it's quite clear that things have got markedly better. The whole world celebrated the coming of democracy to South Africa, and the miraculous way in which we achieved it. Besides, we are rid of all those things that every decent person abhorred – apartheid, the police state, censors, sanctions . . . it's a long and unlamented list. We should feel good about it. So, why don't we?

The fact that we don't feel good about it makes us feel guilty – and that makes us feel even worse. The problem, of course, is that we haven't resolved the paradox about things getting better and worse at the same time. The paradox confuses us, and because we are confused, the future seems uncertain. An uncertain future makes us anxious, and that anxiety makes the present an unsettling experience. You don't need to go back to your first-year psycho books to know that prolonged confusion, uncertainty and anxiety result in depression.

WHO YOU ARE IS WHAT YOU THINK

South Africa has long been notorious for offering varying, often contradictory, experiences to different people. That hasn't changed, although the roles may have reversed. If you are a middle-class white parent today, faced with declining living standards, rising costs of education and health, diminished job prospects, and threats to your personal safety, you would understandably be unenthusiastic about your own experience of the new South Africa.

If, however, you were a young black person whose parents had fought the odds and provided you with an education, and you were entering a job market hungry for someone like you, and you were faced with a range of choices about where to live, work and play such as you hadn't dreamed of until not so long ago, then you would – equally understandably – be aggressively supportive of the change in society.

These are simplistic divisions, of course. Reality is more complex than that. Many white people have wholeheartedly embraced the new society. Most have done so partly with enthusiasm, partly with qualifications. Many black persons have recoiled from bewildering changes, and new threats such as crime and an estranged youth. Chief Buthelezi has said on more than one occasion that things are worse now than they were before, and the black left says they are no better. Nevertheless, there is a level at which generalizations are valid, and do reveal trends and collective attitudes. It's that level that this discussion will explore.

WHITE ATTITUDES

1 Glum together

Cape Town psychiatrist Anthony Teggin has studied what he believes to be collective depressions that descended on that city in 1985 and again in 1990. He backed up his findings with anecdotal evidence of the rise in the number of people seeking treatment for the illness during those periods – as well as reference to a manifestation of the phenomenon elsewhere in the world. Teggin identifies stress resulting from people's erosion of earnings, political uncertainty and the progressive breakdown of social support networks as the causes of the collective depressions. My own observation is that 1984–86 was the apogee of political protest and turmoil, particularly in Cape Town, and 1990 was the year that de Klerk turned history about with the release of Mandela and the unbanning of the ANC. The depressions coincided with the times of greatest change and upheaval – and the escalation of uncertainty that comes with such times.

If one extends Teggin's findings, there is a sombre outlook for the collective mood of white South Africans in the future. All the elements in the periods under Teggin's observation remain in place. That includes the political uncertainty created by Mandela's imminent departure, and the break-up of the governing alliance and its consequences that will follow.

2 New stresses

There are three new sources of stress that have entered white society since the periods observed by Teggin. The first and greatest of them is the effect of the crime avalanche. The threat to personal safety of the ordinary citizen is many times greater now than it was then. A fear psychosis has gripped suburbia.

There has also been an escalation in alienation. It flows from radical changes to the familiar, however welcome or indicative of improvement those may be. From an ultra-conservative, taboo-beset society, South Africa became a place where pornography was legalized, abortion is performed on demand, and gay rights are propounded. The figures of authority in society look, act and speak differently. The type of journalism broadcast on radio and television has changed, and the news is often in a language you don't understand. 'I don't feel as if I'm living in my own country, any more,' is one overheard reaction that illustrates a feeling shared by many.

Lastly, white South Africans are being affected more than ever before by something we might call the departing monk syndrome. Teggin quotes accounts of acedia, recognized in earlier times by the Church as one of the seven deadly sins. Acedia is also known as sloth or apathy. Today, more generously, we label it depression. A monk stricken by acedia in a monastery will begin to feel scorn and contempt for his brothers, he will become lazy and uncaring, he will come to feel that his teaching is benefiting no-one, and he will begin to see far-off monasteries as places more conducive to accomplishment and well-being.

It's when the monk leaves, though, that the interesting phenomenon sets in. Those he leaves behind fall into a collective melancholia. Each brother asks himself: was the departing monk right? Did those who remained deserve his scorn? Were other places better and was it wise to enhance the soul by going there?

All of the remaining monks' questions, and their mood, are a perfect paradigm for the effects of emigration – which, with the exception of a peak in 1994, is now at an unprecedented level. Emigration is similar in its nature to resignations from a political party, described earlier. For every person who does it, there are many more wondering whether they should, or wishing they could. It represents a substantial loss of morale and spiritual energy in the society.

3 Guess who's getting together?

Curiously, the above malaise is more true for whites who are English speaking, who are inheritors of the tradition of liberal thought associated with the English-speaking world. As much as they huff and puff about their African roots, their cultural framework is European. They read *Time*, not *Bona.* Few have a vocabularly of more than ten African words. The situation with their Afrikaans-speaking compatriots is different. The Afrikaner's cultural point of reference is African. It might not be the same as a black African, but it is African nevertheless. The upshot of this has been that there is a pre-existing cultural platform on which Afrikaners and black Africans can meet and start the long, tentative and fraught process of forging, if not a common identity, then at least a shared identity.

The rural areas of South Africa abound with examples of white farmers who have accepted the new circumstances, internalized the ramifications, and got down to making things work. Like rural communities the world over, they are headstrong, they are difficult to deal with and they tend to do things their own way. The point is they are doing them. It is no accident that the land-reform programme is one of the most successful undertakings of the new government.

In the country's new parliament, too, the new ANC members found, surprisingly, that the white members they had the greatest affinity with, and could work most productively with, were those of the white conservative parties. The feeling was reciprocated. I asked a prominent conservative MP to explain. He replied gruffly: 'Mandela is an honourable man. He talks straight. I can work with him, and his people.'

Afrikaans has its own word for rapprochement. It is *toenadering.* I know this is a view shot through with contradictions, and it isn't the whole story, by any means. But this is the way it is. Just take my word for it.

BLACK ATTITUDES

1 Entitlement

Liberation was a yearning and a promise long held by black South Africans. Over time it became a Holy Grail which, when attained, would be the font of goodness and plenty. This was the mythology of liberation.

Meanwhile, officialdom kept black South Africa in limbo. According to apartheid, black South Africans were here, but not here. They were here, in the cities, towns and farmlands as working sojourners. Their real home, said apartheid, was in the homelands. That meant that what they needed while on sojourn would be provided – in bare minimum, of course. The last thing the masters of apartheid wanted was black people deciding for themselves what they wanted, where and how. A predisposition towards receiving, rather than making, was thus engendered among black South Africans.

These two great impingements on the minds of the country's black citizens have resulted in a post-apartheid society that expects to be taken care of – what is called today, with some exasperation, even by the country's new rulers, the culture of entitlement. It is an ethos that is responsible for a lack of self-help get-up-and-go, that permeates industrial relations, underpins poor productivity, and has helped make the phrase 'our demands' one of the most common in South African political discourse. It is an attitude that has caused self-improvement schemes to run into trouble when their participants demand higher wages.

A large part of the problem is that the leaders of the revolution, the authors of the promises that kept the fervour alive, are still in power. It will take a new – and very brave – generation of leaders to inculcate the idea that liberation meant no more than acquiring the opportunity to pursue the good things in life.

The United Nations Interaction Council, a gathering of former presidents and prime ministers, decided in 1995 that on the fiftieth anniversary of the Declaration of Human Rights, in 1998, the UN should convene a conference to consider a Declaration of Human Obligations. Presumably, there will be a South African delegation at the conference – but this, like all attitudes, will turn around slowly.

2 Complacency

Africa's unhappy masses are distressingly tolerant of abusive rulers. Dictators arise who then gather the wealth of the nation within the precincts of the palace, and the populace unquestioningly accepts that that's the way things are. Potentates like Houphouet-Boigny, Bokassa and Mobutu reign, or have reigned, in what are among the world's poorest countries in a lavish personal splendour that no Western leader would dare assume, even if it were possible. The right and power that the Western person-in-the-street assumes to appoint and dismiss governments is an attitude that is foreign to Africa's people.

In South Africa things are both similar and different. The complacent African character is to be found, all right, but the country's people have the enervating, recent experience of toppling an abusive government. The question arises, of course, which of the two facets of the character will have the upper hand when it comes to holding the ANC accountable for its acts and omissions. Whichever way it works out, the complacency factor, combined with the loyalty retained by the ANC as the true liberation movement, is the strongest force militating against a change of government in 2004. The argument put forward in this book is, however, that by then the silent dynamics, such as population pressure, joblessness, urbanization and the like, will have built up to a force that will manifestly overcome the inertia of complacency.

Complacency, it must be pointed out, is not a character trait exclusive to black South Africans. The stolid acceptance by white voters of decades of economic mismanagement, blundering and corruption by the National Party government is testimony to that. In the South Africa of today it is compounded by a reluctance to criticize the new government – for fear of being branded racist, or becoming victim to an insidious tendency to see critics as reactionary spoilsports who secretly yearn for the way things used to be.

3 The new tribalism

Tribalism is the dirtiest word in the vocabulary of an emancipated African. It carries connotations of backwardness and it echoes the argument that was used as apartheid's rationale. Or, at least, it did. Tentatively, very tentatively, tribalism is coming out of the closet. Elsewhere in Africa it is being looked at again to see if it can produce an antidote to the terrible strife that racks the continent. The creation of tribal states or some form of tribal geographic autonomy is the subject of an avant-garde discussion in pan-African politics. The reason is not hard to divine. Africa's colonial powers, themselves ethnically homogeneous states, carved up the continent with no regard for how the African people organized themselves. The colonial overlords, for example, didn't pause in their assumption that rivers formed natural borders, as they did in Europe. In Africa tribes regarded rivers as precious assets, from which they derived their living. Consequently a tribe would live on both banks, and regard the river itself as common property. The colonials, in their race for African possessions, split people who belonged together, and lumped together those who didn't. The discussion in neo-African politics is a speculative bid to see if the egg can be unscrambled.

In South Africa it is not likely that tribalism will ever become part of the national political debate. But it will remain the subtext to political alliances and strains, within parties and organizations, that it is today. When the chips come down at the time of the break-up of the governing alliance, the tribal subtext will be yet another stone on which the knives will be honed.

Outside of politics, though, it will be different. The crush of urbanization will multiply the stresses and tensions that currently exist in the overtaxed cities. The squatter settlements that form part of the metropolises are already dangerously unstable communities. Tribal and clan affiliations are natural faultlines where conflict and abrasion will occur when the social earthquakes come. It has happened already. Squatter settlements around Cape Town – Crossroads and KTC – erupted in violence over a brew of social and political issues in 1986. Clan allegiances weren't the cause of the eruptions, but they figured in the way events unfolded. Scores were killed and more than 100,000 made homeless. Inter-tribe and inter-clan animosities underlie sporadic but continual violence on mines. It is only a matter of time before the social tensions caused by urbanization and poverty intersect with ethnic animosities in another Crossroads . . . and others after that.

LEGACY OF THE PAST

1 Erosion of belief

Living with apartheid meant living with lies. We were told that apartheid, and the many names it was given, was the best way. But we knew the people to whom it was applied had never been asked if they thought so, too. In fact, it was quite clear they didn't think so. And if we couldn't see that, the simple act of reasoning that we wouldn't like it ourselves would have revealed it. We knew it was a fallacy that the movement of black people to the cities would halt, then reverse. And we knew that even if it did, 75 per cent of the population could not live on the 13 per cent of the land that the homelands comprised. But we pretended not to know these things. Or we pretended that those who told us these things had to know what they were talking about.

In maintaining the edifice of apartheid, based on these big lies, society necessarily became infused with lesser lies. The government and its ministers were caught lying to the country and to parliament in the notorious info scandal of the late 1970s. Before that, in 1975, everyone knew that South Africa's invasion of Angola was being reported around the world and that the government was lying when it denied it. There was dismay but little surprise when it turned out that government-backed newspaper publishers were burning portions of their daily print run to keep an appearance of buoyant circulations. The false denial became a daily instrument of public life.

The lies had a devastating impact on a society steeped in patriarchy and authoritarianism. The deep shock was that the symbols of authority did not value the truth, and thereby sent a message into the society: it's OK to say what you need to say to get what you want.

Black South Africans, of course, had these and other, more dramatic, reasons to become disaffected from authority. The instruments of authority were patently contrary to their interests. Into this attitudinal arena came the campaign for ungovernability, making the imposition of authority difficult or impossible. It was accompanied by a latter-day revival of the medieval children's crusade, where the young, scornful of the passivity of their elders, took the lead in bringing about change.

The combination of all of the foregoing factors resulted in a society with little inherent belief in authority, or respect for it – despite the prima facie loyalty to the ANC by the majority.

The erosion of credibility is not being reversed, for the simple reason that the inheritors of the legacy are now in power. The present government practises the false denial as a matter of course. You can find it in tonight's paper. The pattern of disclosure in the public arena, followed by confirmation by an unpremeditated official, followed by contemptuous denial by a higher official has been visible in the *Sarafina 2* debacle, allegations of racial favouritism in the Truth and Reconciliation Commission, the financial state of local authorities, arms deals, and many more.

No-one wants a return to patriarchy. It would be out of step with the liberal ethos of the new government and with the rest of the world. But a society needs something to believe in. It needs a symbol of credibility. This is the single greatest reason that Mandela became the icon that he did. Those that are to follow him give no reason to believe that they understand the burden of credibility that rests on them. South Africans remain condemned to be a society with a crisis of self-belief.

2 Culture of dishonesty

If an extrapolation may be made from measured crime, fraud and corruption, then South Africa must be one of the most dishonest societies in the world. Above I have sketched what I believe are the origins of falsehood in the country's national life. Regrettably, it goes further. Once it was established that the public would tolerate even the most blatant deception, officialdom threw off all restraint. People in police custody would slip on the (wink) soap and die in the shower. As people died daily in pre-election train violence and drive-by shootings, the government had no idea (nudge) who was responsible.

This awful betrayal of public credibility and trust set the tone – predictably – for citizens in their private lives. Business was particularly affected. Today, entire economic sectors, particularly those based on importation, are distorted by wide-scale dishonesty in the granting of permits and other customs and excise abuses.

In the dying years of white hegemony, the novelist J.M. Coetzee captured the spirit of the time in his highly praised novel *Waiting for the Barbarians.* It captured the moral dissolution at the end of an epoch. A 'last-days' psychosis gripped whole segments of society and the axiom became: get it while you can. It has carried over into the present day and many forms of dishonesty have been institutionalized into recognized social practices. For example, stealing product from one's place of work is a practice that has a name. It's *mokabelo* in Sotho, *uMshanqani* in Zulu, and just plain *brood* (bread) in the patois of Soweto.

What will end it? The answer, sadly, is elusive. But example in public life would be a good place to start.

3 Non-payment

The breakdown of respect for authority and institutions and the culture of dishonesty intersect in the social plague of non-payment of dues to local government. These cover water and electricity, rates and taxes – and even housing rentals. At the end of 1996 the shortfall in payments on rates and services stood at R5.6 billion – more than double the first annual funding of the RDP. In addition, local authorities owed R1 billion to the electricity supply commission, Eskom.

Figures given in parliament said that forty-eight of the country's local councils couldn't pay, and ninety-five could not cover one month's wage bill. The figures also revealed that the situation was getting worse, not better. The government's Masakhane campaign, launched – and re-launched more than once – had had no measurable effect.

The above figures reveal only part of the seriousness of the problem. They, for example, do not include non-payment of rents. In the private sector, lending institutions struggled in the first half of this decade to overcome bond boycotts and ignited much controversy with a practice of red-lining – demarcating certain areas, mainly in townships and inner-city districts, where they would not grant loans.

If there is a lingering suspicion that I might be exaggerating the claim that the culture of dishonesty and breakdown in institutional respect runs through the society from top to bottom, one might like to register that by the end of 1996 the non-payment of local government dues by businesses in Johannesburg's CBD had reached R100 million. The truly hard-to-convince will be interested in the director general of public works who, in January 1997, praised members of parliament who had started paying their rentals for government-supplied accommodation. It's the sort of news that leaves one not knowing whether one should be glad there's improvement, or be outraged that the situation existed in the first place.

NATIONAL CHARACTER

1 Cultural splits

One of the underlying themes of this book is that South Africa is two worlds in one – a First and a Third World. Accordingly, it contains a Western tradition and an African tradition, each representing a different philosophy of society. The essential difference is an emphasis on individualism in the Western case, and a contrasting emphasis on collectivism in the African case. This is not merely ephemera. It's the sand in the cogs that often prevents the smooth turning of daily life.

The subject is tackled in Mike Boon's *The African Way*, reported in the *Financial Mail.* Boon says African belief is in 'an external locus of control' while Western belief rests more on individual responsibility. In business, the dichotomy makes the Western mind see commerce as an activity that is essentially individual and private. Joe Citizen runs his business the way he wants, selling to those willing to pay his price, and employing those willing to work for his wages. The government administers taxes, with which it provides roads and other infrastructure that help Joe run a better business, so that he can pay more taxes. Joe Citizen can be anybody, and anybody can be Joe Citizen. The system works by creating a prosperity cycle and that's the end of it. The African mind sees business not as private and individual, but as part of the body politic. It's an integral part of civic society, to employ the favoured expression. This leads comfortably and easily to notions of collective responsibility to the people, and to participatory ownership of enterprises.

The function of competition in commerce is similarly affected. The Western mind sees the Joe Citizens pitted against one another so that individuals can decide between them. In the African view there are strong group and territorial impulses. The taxi industry is a prime example. Associations are formed on the bases of geographic and other common interests, and then literally go to war with one another over territory. Competition in the Western sense is foreign and simply not tolerated.

Boon says that where Western attitudes reward individual performance, the African preference is to be seen as part of a winning team. This explains manifestations that invariably perplex the Western mind – wage negotiators find that performance-linked rewards are not popular; students conduct 'pass one, pass all' campaigns.

A country's newspapers, radio and television are usually mirrors in which a nation can see its own reflection. In the Western view, unsurprisingly, information is regarded as just another commodity, independent of all else, and consumers choose the level of quality they want. In the African view, journalism is part of the nation-building undertaking. It is a view clearly revealed in Mandela's and Mbeki's admonitions of, particularly, black journalists. My aphoristic conclusion from my own experience is that Western journalism is determined by what is of interest to the public, and African journalism by what is in the public interest. It's a subtle distinction, I grant you, but it makes a significant difference to what you eventually see, hear and read.

Cultural traditions change slowly, if at all. If nation-building is to succeed, white and black South Africans will have to define an overarching level of identity, one that values diversity and sees in it the spring of the nation's psychic energy. We humans being what we are, it's a tough call.

2 Fair shake?

It is worth asking whether the criticism of the ANC government, including the criticism in this book, is fair. It's worth asking because it makes a big difference to public attitudes to the government, and to how the government responds to public perceptions of the administration.

Criticism of the government revolves around the central issue of its perceived failure to deliver meaningful change successfully. But is that fair? Doesn't it take some time to turn a tanker round? Especially in this case, where the crew was catapulted onto the bridge without any previous experience of steering a complicated vessel – through no fault of their own, mind you. And wasn't it wise first to become acquainted with the levers of power before starting to yank them round? Wasn't it precisely the criticism of the previous government that it bulldozed over the wishes and interests of the people? And so what if the process of consultation took a little long, but eventually ensured a government that was manifesting the will of the people? Isn't it the African way to take a little longer over things, and isn't it better, after all, than the frantic Western rush?

Any person of only moderate generosity of spirit would concede the truth implied in these questions. Unfortunately, history will not be as indulgent. The great forces driving South Africa's destiny – the failure to make progress in real terms, the growing impatience of swelling multitudes of the un-people, and an unforgiving emergent global economy – demand a government of great boldness and innovation. No questions asked. No explanations entertained.

3 Government attitudes

Governments have feelings, too, you know. This one came into power buoyed by the exhilaration of victory over a life-long foe, eager to please and demonstrate that it did, indeed, have the answers to the country's wrongs. The barrage of criticism being levelled at the government – now coming even from allies in the struggle and other sympathetic quarters – is in danger of producing a counter-productive reaction. The more the government is criticized, the more resentful it is likely to become. The more resentful it becomes, the greater the breakdown of positive morale at the helm of society, the greater will be the tendency to rationalize its shortcomings, the more arrogant and impervious to advice it will become. The outcome of this is a state of collective paranoia. Fitful early signs of it can be detected in assertions like those by senior government members that top policemen are purposefully limp in fighting crime because they believe it is the one thing that will bring the ANC down. Worse, this mind-set is pre-eminently the psychic breeding ground for the get-it-while-you-can mentality, which will become much more pronounced among the government's morally weaker members. In other words, more government corruption, not less.

It will be a profound pity if this happens, for this government's great service to South Africa has been to bring the country into broad alignment with world norms. In terms of openness and the pursuit of laudable goals, it has brought a refreshing new tone to public life. The obstinacy and bellicosity of its predecessor have vanished. Curses be, that these afflictions should ever return.

BAD HABITS

1 Informal privatization

South Africa's citizens have long been the victims of a sullen and inept civil bureaucracy. Now an alternative is opening up – but at the cost of turning the country into one of those places where 'unconventional methods' become the only way to get anything done. Already, if you need anything from a telephone line installed, moved or repaired, to an import permit, the most effective way is to strike a private arrangement with an official.

My partner, two days before departure on an overseas trip, finds that her passport has expired. 'No problem,' says the travel agent. A call to an ex-employee of the passport office, who escorts the applicant into the inner recesses of the office and through the procedure. R200 and fifteen minutes. The ex-employee and her former colleagues gleefully explain how they grow their market by excessive delays of applications that come through the conventional route.

A brutish simpleton is being interviewed in a television documentary about men who batter women. The simpleton brags about his violent ways with women. 'Won't it be a problem for you if one of them goes to the police and lays a charge against you,' asks the interviewer.

'No,' he says, laughing dismissively.

'Why not?'

'I'll just go to the police station and buy the docket,' says the simpleton.

I get stopped for speeding on a country road. The traffic officer asks me to accompany him to view the read-out on his meter. He tells me the fine for the speed I was doing is normally R250. The 'spot fine', however, is R100.

In many countries where these sorts of incidents have become prevalent, they have become more than random corruption. Sometimes, in fact, to see such practices as corruption is merely to employ a Euro-centric prejudice. Not every society has the same concept of organization and uniformity. Often these practices are necessitated, either by a breakdown of organizational structures left in place by departed colonial administrations, or by the absence of such organizational structures to begin with. For example, in Zaire, the organizational infrastructure to pay a policeman in a small station frequently does not exist. Or, the state's ability to pay him adequately and punctually may be limited. So the policeman does an honest job. Only, he gets paid directly by the people to whom he provides the service. And so the principle is extended to other public-service jobs.

But South Africa isn't one of those countries.

2 The culture of inefficiency

In years gone by, when South Africa contemplated a post-apartheid society, it also had to contemplate a paradox: in order to become a better society, South Africa had to become a less efficient one, for a while at least. A temporary loss of efficiency is unavoidable in any major act of transformation, such as that which South Africa is experiencing. The transformation did not begin from a high base of efficiency, and there is a looming danger that the systemic inefficiency of the change-over phase will become the norm.

Transition in South Africa involves a paradigm shift, from a strictly Euro-centric view of society to a more indigenous, African one. It is unpopular, but it is true, to observe that African culture, at large, places less emphasis on efficiency than European or Oriental cultures do in the main.

South Africans, consequently, are going to have to make a choice they haven't yet made – whether to embark on the European–Oriental path or the African path in respect of effectiveness and efficiency. The outcome will be determined by an intricate interlocking of the productivity question, the effort-and-reward cycle and self-belief. The outcome will be measured in the global market place, which is an unforgiving arena.

SOCIAL TRENDS

1 Living with stress

The discussion opened in this chapter with the assertion that nations, just like individuals, can have moods. Stress was pointed to as one of the major influences on the current South African mood. The society's stress is the combined effect of the silent dynamics at work in the community and the transformation that accompanies them. In August 1996 the Psychological Society of South Africa called for the urgent implementation of a national strategy to deal with the levels of stress South Africans were living under. The society said South Africans were among the most stressed people in the world and the causes were urbanization, unemployment and the constant need to adapt emotionally to change. The results were violence, aggression, family breakdowns, child abuse, drug usage and depression.

The statistical picture provides the evidence. South Africa, it is well known, has one of the highest divorce rates in the world. In 1995 more than 40,000 children were involved in the divorces of their parents. The problem has been escalating in recent years, and seems to be taking on run-away proportions in the black community, where the stress factors hit hardest. Divorce statistics for the black community have been available only since 1993, which doesn't provide a base for definite conclusions. But the measure of black divorces leapt from 4,754 in 1994 to 8,174 in 1995. These figures are only scant indications of what the real picture is. In family and kinship matters South African society conforms to several different cultural norms, and the official statistics measure only one of these.

Family disintegration is one of classical ways of measuring disintegration in stressed societies as a whole. There are many other, informal, signs that point to a disintegration of the social fabric. About 3,500 corpses a year turn up in police mortuaries, the identities of which are never discovered and which are given anonymous burials. More than a thousand items of registered post a month go missing and are never delivered, according to figures given in parliament. Armed criminals march on parliament to demand their 'rights', as happened in response to vigilante attacks in Cape Town in 1996. Gangs of schoolboys, in school uniforms, roam the streets of small towns and rob stores, as reported also in 1996. The really bad news about all of this is that the underlying causes are set to get worse, not better – as discussed in the case of the national mood above.

2 Critical mass

It is a fundamental tenet of the ideas set out in this book that social dynamics have a critical mass. Just like there is a platform at which fissile nuclear material will enter a chain reaction so it is in society. There is a point at which the stresses induced by population growth, unemployment, urbanization, poverty, homelessness, crime, the erosion of authority and community disintegration will overcome inertia, complacency and the remnants of authority to produce a chain reaction that will be unguidable and unstoppable. The chain reaction will course through society, wreaking deep-running changes on our living patterns, and emerging, ultimately, in the political arena where convulsions seemingly unconnected with their root causes will bring about a new order.

It's no use preparing for the onset of the chain reaction. We're already in it. Look around you. The pattern is in place. It's merely the

Carletonville Sinkholes Syndrome of Change that makes us think today is normal.

3 Atomization

The erosion of authority, the de-skilling of the bureaucracy and administration, and the roll-on of the culture of inefficiency will increasingly produce an effect of contraction of authority and responsibility in social and economic activity to ever-smaller and more intimate spheres.

Ultimately, if it doesn't prove impossible for plush Sandton and deprived Alexandra, idealistically lumped together as they are now, to find common aims and methods, it will prove, at least, impractical. The responsibilities of each will contract to each. This is already happening – try calling the Sandton municipality and asking a question regarding Alexandra. In the long term the influence of central government will not be equal over, say, Gauteng and Northern Province. Nor, for the foreseeable future, will the capacities of the two provinces for governing themselves be equal. That means each will take on greater responsibility for itself, and each will develop a character distinct from the other. Whole towns will stop waiting for central and regional authorities to provide education and health services. The responsibility for these services will consequently contract not only to specific areas or towns, but to the individuals concerned. In the long term even some municipal services like refuse removal and beautification will contract into privatized undertakings. Residential security has long since begun contracting from the public into the self-initiative sphere.

New rules and practices of commerce will arise from within commerce itself. The manner in which the informal sector is creating itself, along with its places and methods of operating, is an example of this. Rules and practices that emanate from an external source will be imposed by the realities of the global economy, by-passing central government. The informal privatization described above, with all its attendant opportunities for corruption, is likely to continue apace. Formal business will have to learn to live with it.

The government's efforts to extend public services to those who have never had them will, of course, have a degree of success. There will never be nearly enough to meet the needs of the un-people – but there will be more than before. It's the upper-echelon communities, however, that will have to learn, more and more, to take care of themselves. The great safety-net that has protected the privileged in society from harsh falls and social and economic injury will be removed. The lifestyle of the individual will be more the responsibility of the individual than it has ever been before.

4 Disenchantment

The alienation of First World populations from politics and politicians is by now so substantial a phenomenon, making so great an impact on elections and the nature of government, that in Germany, for instance, it goes by a well-known expression – *politische Verdrossenheit.* Elections in Western countries have, over the last two decades, been showing a marked downward trend in the number of citizens who bother to turn out for the polls. In the United States the Clinton–Dole contest was decided by only 49 per cent of the nation's voters. Many European countries now have joke candidates in elections. Often hilarious, the pranksters nevertheless have a serious function and intent. They set out to focus voters' scorn for the politics and the politicians, and they succeed. The cause of the *Verdrossenheit* is a loss of belief in the ability and the sincerity of politicians in responding properly to the rapidly changing world that sophisticated populations perceive and experience.

In South Africa this negative political force will flow down three streams. The sophisticated segment of the voting population will respond in the same way as sophisticated voters in the West, and for the same reasons. Another segment of voters will be ANC supporters who become disenchanted at the lack of change in their lives, abandon hope of its possibility, and withdraw interest from politics. These two groups of voters, combined with those who stay away in active protest, will become one of the ANC's, and other moderate political parties', biggest electoral problems.

The most powerful of the three streams, however, will flow among the un-people. In this – as in so many other ways, for instance, their agitation for socialism – they will go against world trends. The un-people will see in politics their salvation. The fact that they will be the most committed and most motivated political constituency in South Africa in future will be just one more element that will bring them to political dominance.

5 The future of racism

In the years leading up to Namibia's independence there was an exclusively white party in the territory, and a white-dominated party. The first, the National Party, advocated white supremacy, and the second, the Republican Party, proposed accommodation with black Namibians and their parties. White political support fluctuated between the two parties according to the way the big political picture was drawn at any given time. When the prospect of independence under international auspices, with a Swapo victory, was in abeyance, the Nationalists held the sway among whites. When the stop-start negotiating process brought a Swapo victory more prominently into the picture, white support would veer markedly to the Republicans. Back it would go to the Nationalists when white Namibians thought they wouldn't, after all, have to contend with a Swapo government.

The lesson to be extracted from the Namibian political Paul Jones is that when people are faced with what they perceive as a big threat, they put aside small differences between themselves. The same process is happening in South Africa. As the threat posed by the un-people wells up from the underbelly of society, the privileged are abandoning – and will continue to abandon – petty concerns about what colour members of their own class are.

It is a maxim of politics that when competition for resources in a society increases, group dynamics come to the fore. In this respect it might be argued that racism will entrench in South Africa, not dissolve. A maxim is a maxim, of course, but in South Africa's case it must not be applied in a simplistic way. Faced with the menace of an increasingly impatient underclass, society's elite will stay intact. It's in that underclass, however, where cracks and fissures will run along ethnic lines as the pressures pile on. (This is yet another reason why there will be an impulse among the un-people to seek a common political identity that will transcend their differences. It's a social survival mechanism.)

For the privileged to unite across racial and ethnic lines will be no more than a natural evolution of a process that is already under way. One of the silent changes since 1994 has been the manner in which a black elite has quietly taken its place in the leafy suburbs of the cities. As one of its consequences, school benches across the country are being shared by children of all hues. A new, largely colour-indifferent, generation of the elite is preparing to emerge with common ambitions and common qualities for realizing those ambitions.

South Africa will always be a profoundly divided society. It's simply that it is evolving from a race-divided society into a class-divided one.

6 The day of the Jacobins

There's always someone who takes things too far. The Jacobins, for example. They were the ones who, after the French Revolution, deposed the moderates, guillotined the king and began the Reign of Terror.

One of the great fears of whites in South Africa before the 1994 election was that it would be followed by an outbreak of black anger, directed at whites for the generations of oppression endured by blacks. One of the great surprises after the election, shared by the world, was that nothing of the kind emerged. The decisive factor, of course, was Mandela – and the priority he placed on reconciliation. Implied in saying this, though, is the question: what happens when Mandela goes?

The prospects for an outburst of black anger have by no means been laid to rest for good. In June 1996 the president of Zimbabwe, Robert Mugabe, launched an amazing attack on whites, fully sixteen years after independence. According to South African newspaper reports, he said his government was tiring of its policy of reconciliation because whites showed no remorse for their actions of the past. He called them 'the enemy' and said they deserved to be shot and have their carcasses thrown to dogs and vultures.

Nothing that graphic has been heard in South Africa. There is, nevertheless, an unmistakable undertone of resentment, and it would be incredible if there weren't. No less evolved a spirit than Archbishop Desmond Tutu revealed it at a gathering of commonwealth newspaper editors in October 1996. He spoke with scornful bitterness of some white-owned newspapers as 'these new converts to freedom'. *The Citizen* reported him saying: 'It is all a matter of credibility . . . it is a bit thick for someone suddenly to be a paragon of virtue criticizing alleged government incompetence and corruption when they were so conspicuous by their deafening silence in the face of the ghastly awfulness and excesses of the past.' Similar flashes – in their general nature, as readily understandable – have been glimpsed in Mandela himself. Curiously, they have also concerned white proprietors of the media. As discussed in earlier chapters, these are sentiments shared by Mandela's certain successor, Thabo Mbeki.

So, is it possible, without the restraining presence of the great conciliator, that black anger at whites could flare? Isn't that anger there already as a subtext, for example, to the wave of violent crime? Isn't it there already in sentiments in some businesses to 'get the whites out'? How unthinkable is it that the post-Mandela rulers, dogged by the same inability to deliver change, will look for a scapegoat – and find a white one? Just as Mugabe has?

It is most likely that something along these lines will happen. It will never become a dominant trend, and it will never come from someone as sophisticated as Mbeki. But Mbeki will be significantly less inclined than his predecessor to remonstrate with those who do divert frustration down this lightning route. The scapegoat thing, anyway, is overtly present in his admonitions of business and the press for what he says is their failure to bring about change . . . a point which, to a degree, is valid.

In the end, though, black anger will be like white terrorism – an expression of extremism. Neither will ever be more than a side show to the great battle being fought between the privileged and the unpeople in the centre of the public arena.

7 Value shifts

A change in values in the new South African elite is taking place. Blacks can afford the things whites used to have. But whites can't afford the things they used to have. Affirmative action and fast-track empowerment have created a new, high-earnings black elite. In addition, the established black elite has emerged from the shadows of the townships, where conspicuous consumption was something to be indulged in with circumspection. Jointly, this newly emancipated class is, like many in Eastern Europe, intensely materialistic and discreetly eager to be accepted in the club of the privileged.

The white privileged, however, are undergoing a somewhat different experience. New expenditures in security, education and health are resulting in the big house being exchanged or sacrificed for a medium-sized one, the BMW for a Toyota. Increased competition for jobs is making advancement in the workplace not quite the automatic thing it used to be for whites. Whether they like it or not – naturally, they don't – whites are going to have to adopt new values to accommodate more modest lifestyles.

8 Africanization

Back in the bad old days, a colleague, a foreign correspondent based in South Africa, was asked how he found being here. 'Like living in California and working in East Germany,' he said. Well, now the East Germany part has changed, and the California part is going to. South African society, in the main, will become more recognizably African than the Western-coloured element of it has been up to now.

There is a specific debate around Africanization. At present, however, it revolves mainly around the country's universities. That's not surprising because, apart from obvious matters such as increasing African staff and student numbers, the abstract notion of an African identity, and the search for it, is something suited to academic discussion. Nevertheless, in the practical world, the presence and influence of Africans will multiply in schools, in business, in the media and in entertainment. Along with it will come more of a mood of Africa. It is a mood that is more leisurely, more philosophical, more voluble and more given to discussion. It is a mood that is not only more carefree, but, alas, more careless. More than anything, though, it is a mood more concerned with people than with things.

Both South Africa's white Africans and its black Africans face many adaptations of character if they are to ride the storms ahead as successfully as practicable.

CHAPTER SEVEN

THE REIGN OF THE HAVE-NOTS

Numbers and the impotence of policy

I was compelled to participate in worldly affairs, which excited the envy of fools, but which made the wise pity me.

AL-BIRUNI, CIRCA 1025

Population size and growth are the key elements in a developing nation's efforts to break out of the poverty cycle. The uncomplicated fact is that the number of people determines the number of slices that have to be cut from the economic cake, and the rate at which the number of people increases is the minimum rate at which the cake has to replicate itself, just so that things stay in balance. For a country to enhance its prosperity, of course, the cake must get bigger faster than the population. The point has been made earlier that this has not been happening in South Africa for a long time, now – and that the country is presently hovering, and is likely to continue hovering, at the break-even point.

Just recently, a seductive economic theory was put about that population growth was, after all, of not very great concern because more people would create more economic activity, and the balance would thus be maintained. The persistence of poverty in the face of explosive population growth, especially in Africa, quickly banished the proponents of that school of thought to muttering obscurity. Instead, the simple truths of the relationship between economic growth and population growth continue to spotlight the obvious conclusion that governments of developing nations should pursue economic growth policies in conjunction with population growth-control policies. The argument tempts one to take a step further, and brave the Orwellian overtones: if a government cannot ignite economic growth, it could achieve the desired effect by limiting population growth. That's what China did with its one-child family policy. Now, of course, it's achieving both accelerated economic growth and declining population growth . . . and is emerging as an economic giant of the new millennium.

The other side of the Chinese coin is the terrible havoc that can be wreaked in a nation's social and political life by growing masses of the un-people. It is no coincidence, for example, that the great social earthquakes and population dislocations that struck Rwanda, Burundi and Zaire in 1996 occurred in an overcrowded continent's most densely populated and (hence) poorest region. The mercifully lesser consequences of the same social forces for South Africa were discussed in preceding chapters. In this chapter we will take a closer look at the origin of these forces – the population dynamics.

WHAT GOES UP

The straightforward see-saw connection between economic growth and population growth is complicated by the fact that economic growth has proven to be the only effective, long-term way of curbing population growth. It means that there is a chicken-and-egg dimension to the problem. But it also means that if an economy can be prodded into meaningful performance, a cycle of self-generating benefits starts up.

A basket of factors is involved in the effect of economic growth on population growth. Families experiencing better living conditions want to protect and maximize these by not diluting them among overlarge families. There is a shift of values from the number of children to the quality of life of those already present. Job opportunities open up for women. Their emancipation from menial roles evokes a desire to lessen their child-rearing burdens. Along with greater prosperity comes better health; infant mortality drops and parents can count on greater survival of fewer children. Material prosperity enables the elderly to care for themselves, or to be provided for, thus decreasing the need for large numbers of children as 'old age insurance'.

The prosperity that brings about these social changes is ordinarily found in the cities. Therefore, it is the scourge of the Third World, urbanization, which brings massive problems of its own, that is also the most effective weapon in the struggle against population growth. This built-in mechanism does not, however, excuse governments – like South Africa's – that do nothing, or nearly nothing, proactive to cut down the birth rate.

THE FARMYARD FACTOR

An additional refinement needs to be taken into account when considering the ratio between economic growth and population growth in South Africa. The economy has shown that overall economic growth and growth in employment are not the same thing. In fact, the South African economy has demonstrated that it can grow at 3 per cent while the job market, by contrast, shrinks. This has led to a conventional economic wisdom that South Africa's economic growth rate needs to be at least twice the population growth rate before there will be progress in the greatest social, economic and political problem – unemployment. That means at a conservatively estimated population growth of 2 per cent, the economy would have to grow at 4 per cent.

We know, however, that the most critical dimension of the unemployment problem is in the cities, the centres of industry and manufacture. We also know that those sectors are responsible for only about one-third of the country's economic growth, at best. Therefore, under present conditions, the economy would have to grow at an unthinkable 12 per cent in order to begin reversing unemployment, itself a creation of population growth, where it matters.

HOW MANY IS TOO MANY?

Any remarks about the size of the South African population must be prefaced with the observation that it is already too big and growing too fast. Even the most ambitious goals of the government – which, at any rate, it does not have the capacity for realizing – are inadequate for the national need and the rate at which it is escalating. This was demonstrated through the example of housing in an earlier chapter.

A population census was conducted in October 1996. It promised to be the most reliable census up to now, and its results are expected, at the time of writing, towards the end of 1997. So untrustworthy were censuses of the past that most social agencies, including the government itself, have worked with estimates in recent years. There will thus be a lot of red faces around if the result doesn't produce a South African population of about 43 million – give or take a million or two either way. It will mean, by the way, that South Africa will exit this century with a population ten times bigger than it entered with.

The census was not free of controversy, with something of a cloud already cast over its findings. The Johannesburg daily *The Star*, sent reporters into the city's streets after claims by many people that they had fallen outside the census net. The reporters found that more than 25 per cent of the first 300 persons they interviewed had either not received census forms or didn't return the ones they did receive. The Central Statistical Service, however, has remained adamant that the undercount would not exceed 5 per cent, which is tolerable in the circumstances.

WHO GROWS WHERE

Recent estimates of the South African population's rate of growth have ranged up to an annual 2.75 per cent. There is now a trend towards a lower estimate, and the University of Stellenbosch's Institute for Futures Research says it is 2.02 per cent. Whatever, it looks good against sub-Saharan Africa's 3.4 per cent, not so good against the industrial nations' 0.6 per cent, but not too bad against the world average of 1.7 per cent. There's further comfort to derive from the fact that the growth rate is slowing down. In one generation from now, about twenty years, it should be down to 1.4 per cent. Mind you, the world average will dip commensurately. It's only in sub-Saharan Africa that the trend continues its frightening climb.

What matters for South Africa, though, is that different segments of the population are growing at dramatically different rates. The country's political time bomb, the un-people, are to be found overwhelmingly among the black population. That sector is currently growing at 2.4 per cent, while whites are increasing at 0.6 per cent. In a generation's time, when the overall population would have grown by 50 per cent to 60 million, blacks will be increasing at 1.6 per cent – while whites will have slowed to zero and coloureds and Asians will both be well below 1 per cent. This means that whereas whites now form 12 per cent of South Africa's population, against blacks' 76 per cent, in a generation's time whites will have declined to 9 per cent of the population while blacks will make up 81 per cent. The remaining 10 per cent will be coloureds and Asians. These figures do not take immigration or emigration into account.

The socio-economic picture of South African society is that of an inverted pyramid, balancing precariously on its apex – while the sky-borne base gets heavier and broader, and the apex gets narrower and sharper as the weight and pressure on it increases. The country's new, multi-ethnic elite is already beginning to stagger under its burden.

NATURE'S WAY

Nature's remedy for population growth, death, is also changing. It's coming later for the old, and not as frequently for the young. Life expectancy has grown from forty-seven years in 1960 to sixty-six at present. Infant mortality has been reduced from 89 deaths per 1000 live births in 1960 to 50. (This is not as encouraging a performance as may appear at first sight, when measured against the world average's drop from 128 to 60.) Future trends in these areas are hard to predict as the government is now realigning its health policy towards primary care. Undoubtedly there will be at least some measure of benefit to those among whom life-shortening diseases and infant mortalities strike hardest.

Macabre speculation about the effects of Aids usually enters the argument about here. The truth is it will slow population growth a little, but not make any meaningful difference. If the current growth rate of the Aids epidemic is superimposed on the population growth rate, then the figure of 60 million people in South Africa in about twenty years' time will adjust to about 59 million.

Another new entrant to the population discussion is the recent legalization of abortion in South Africa. It has not seriously been suggested in any quarter, however, that abortion could become so widespread as to affect population growth in any noticeable way.

GET UP AND GO

The population is not only big, large parts of it are on the move. Like rural populations everywhere, South African peasants are bundling up their belongings and heading for the bright lights of the big cities. They are more desperate than rural dwellers in the industrial nations of the West, so the rate of urbanization here, as in other developing countries, is several times greater. No-one knows for sure just how great the pace of urbanization is, but most social agencies agree that South Africa, like the globe as a whole, is on the fulcrum of a great historical turn where, for the first time, the majority of people have abandoned rural life, and now live in urban areas. The Centre for Development and Enterprise estimates that 60 per cent of the population will be in cities and towns at the end of the first decade of the new millennium. Although, says the Centre, the tempo is easing up. Professor Schlemmer, on the other hand, points to the household surveys conducted by the Central Statistical Service in 1993 and 1994. They showed that people living in the predominantly urban Western Cape and Gauteng – who were not born in these areas – increased by 27 per cent and 17 per cent respectively. He raises the valid conjecture that the shift would have increased since then. So, as before, national averages are deceptive. It depends who you are and where you are.

Once again, the haves and the have-nots are subject to different forces; their population movements are happening in different ways, for different reasons. South Africa's privileged classes have reflected the global trend of the last three decades to move from the cities to the suburbs. Communications technology and changing work patterns are now provoking a nascent move from the suburbs to the 'exurbs'. There is also a trend, in the USA for example, for people emancipated by technology to move to 'sunbelt' states for a better quality of life.

In South Africa the move from Johannesburg's central business district has been pronounced, resulting in a 30 per cent drop in the rental value of office space there, according to some estimates. The moves beyond the suburbs are less common in South Africa than in some other countries, but are detectable nevertheless.

For South Africa's privileged, though, there is a stronger motivation than the liberating technology of fax modems and e-mail: crime and the deterioration of cities like Johannesburg. The principal move is to the Cape peninsula in the Western Cape. The province is perceived to be more stable (its economy grew 4.5 per cent in 1996) and to have lower levels of crime. In 1996, according to a *Sunday Times* report, the value of residential property sold in the Western Cape increased by 60 per cent. Hout Bay, which offers village life close to Cape Town, saw prices rocket by 200 per cent.

The country's industrial heartland, Gauteng, will remain the commercial magnet it is, retaining an increasingly reluctant professional and managerial class. Smaller inland cities like Kimberley, Bloemfontein, Paarl and Oudtshoorn, however, may experience minor growth in about a decade as some relocation of business takes place. Companies will, in time, have to respond to employee pressure for safer environments. Losers in the rankings of the provinces will be KwaZulu-Natal, Eastern Cape and Northern Province, where the greatest confluence of population pressures, slack economic growth and social flashpoints exists.

WORMS IN THE BIG APPLE

South Africans' future is in their cities. On the face of it, it's a curious destination in a country rich in the natural resources of soil, climate and space. The great economic awakening of India, under way at present, is based largely on a successful stimulation of its rural economy. Nothing like that is in sight in South Africa,

South Africa's cities are in a parlous state, and in no condition to welcome their millions of new inhabitants over the next two decades. By the time that period has run its course, South Africa's urban areas would have added to themselves the equivalent of another Johannesburg and another Cape Town. The cities are paying the price of having been political cauldrons, and are ailing in the after-wash of boycotts, unpaid services and rents, and campaigns for ungovernability. There is now an irrecoverable history of failure to provide the infrastructure and amenities that make city life productive or, at least, tolerable – electricity, clean water, drainage, sanitation and cleansing, transport and recreation. As recounted in the previous chapter, many cities and towns are now in technical bankruptcy. At the time of writing there was an argument whether the country's biggest metropolitan government, Johannesburg's, was or was not facing bankruptcy. The confidence of taxpayers in the management of their money has been irreversibly eroded. Anti-discrimination court actions have been brought against local authorities by upper-bracket ratepayers demanding equal treatment and obligations. A rates boycott by top-segment ratepayers in Sandton has been the first of its kind, but it would be surprising if it were the last.

Still the pressure piles on. In *Preparing for the Twenty-first Century* Kennedy discusses at length the potential for social unrest contained in the unstemmed migration to shanty perimeter-cities – in the face of diminishing resources and employment opportunities. South Africa's urban dwellers will not escape a fate predestined for other Third World cities, if Kennedy and others like him are right. There are many signs that they are – 1997 opened with gun battles between residents and police in Johannesburg's coloured suburbs, and the privileged everywhere are under siege by a criminal subculture.

The government is unfairly criticized for its inadequate response to the challenge of the cities. The kind of action that would work lies beyond its powers. It is likely, instead, to pursue political kudos by implementation of its policy of densification of suburbs. The poor, unquestionably, should not be where they are today – consigned by apartheid to far-off dormitory townships. Facilitating their migration closer to their places of work will be good for the poor . . . but the rich are going to hurt even more, and they aren't going to like it.

PAPERS, PLEASE

By a conservative estimate, based on police and other official statistics, at least 10 per cent of South Africa's population doesn't belong here. There are about 5 million people who have fled the economic wastelands of sub-Saharan Africa for the honey pot in the south. Their numbers swell by an estimated 1 million every year, and they are not reckoned into the population size and growth statistics given up to now in this discussion. They come by foot, some risking being eaten alive as they cross the Kruger game park. Those that have met this fate do not deter those that follow. They come by road in coaches that bring shoppers from Zambia and Zimbabwe. Many 'shoppers' never go home. They come through legitimate points of entry by paying off customs and immigration officials. Several corrupt officers have been arrested, but no-one knows how big the problem is.

Once here, illegal immigrants become another burr in the social friction of the cities. Locals refer to them by the collective term 'Zimbabweans', and resent them because they are notorious for their contribution to the crime wave. When they go straight they cause more resentment by working for lower wages, or being more motivated and entrepreneurial. A small percentage of them is caught and repatriated. In 1996 157,000 of them were deported. But at an approximate cost of R2,600 a person, deportations are not likely to grow markedly. In addition, the governments of the two countries receiving most of the deportees, Zimbabwe and Mozambique, can't cope and have urged the South African government to ease up.

The origin of the problem lies within South Africa's sub-Saharan neighbours, where population growth rates are, at a rough average, 50 per cent higher than South Africa's, and where incomes per capita are sluggish, stagnant or declining. There is no cause to think the tide may soon be reversed.

Emigration is a profoundly emotive topic, and the statistics are manipulated by all to back up cases for and against, and conclusions about what the figures say about the image of the country.

Overall, only a handful of incontestable truths can be extracted from the official records. Have-nots don't and haves do. Emigrate, that is. It is an expensive undertaking and only educated and economically successful people emigrate. That there is a drain of home-bred brains is not in dispute.

Foreigners, loosely speaking, have more confidence in South Africa than many South Africans. In the two decades from 1975 to 1994 South Africa showed a net gain of 230,534 immigrants. That confidence, however, is waning. In the second decade, immigration fell to only 24 per cent of what it had been in the first.

The political situation in South Africa is decisive in determining the movement of people to and from the country. In the twenty-two years since 1975 there have been only seven in which emigration has exceeded immigration. Those years are 1977 and 1978, 1986 and 1987, and 1994, 1995 and 1996. The overlap with the peaks of political turmoil in the mid-seventies and mid-eighties, and the arrival of democracy in 1994, is unmistakable.

There is only one significant variable to introduce: the emigration figures are almost certainly under-reported. The reason is that departing citizens are not compelled to state that they are emigrating, and many do not want to burn the bridge behind them by doing so. The *Financial Mail* gave an example. In the year ending 30 June 1995, 1,330 South Africans emigrated to Australia, according to the South African authorities. Yet Australian records showed 2,792 immigrants from South Africa entering that country in that period. The equivalent figures for the year ending 30 June 1996 were 1,855 and 3,190. It means that real emigration figures could be as much as 50 per cent higher than known.

The impact on society of emigration has been dealt with under other headings – in the similarity with resignations from a political party: for every person who does it, there are a several more contemplating it; and in the departing monk syndrome: those who leave plunge those who remain into sombre reflection about what the most advisable course is. The sum is a net loss of energy, enthusiasm and belief in the society.

The prospects for emigration, and the further loss of skilled South Africans, are cause for dismay. The trend is rising, and the examples of other countries in Africa that have been through similar processes do not encourage. Since independence in Zimbabwe in 1980 no less than two-thirds of whites have emigrated. Since independence in Kenya in 1963 the white population has declined from 60,000 to 40,000 – but only 10 per cent of those living there today are citizens.

Just as the haves in South African society are surrounded by a growing sea of want, so the country as a whole is surrounded by an underachieving community of nations in the subcontinent. The governments, including ours, are either lax or impotent in the face of the overpowering challenges. For now, and well into the new millennium, it will be up to the individual to throw up the ramparts.

CHAPTER EIGHT

COLOURED GREEN

The environment and longevity of resources

Land is not something you inherit from your parents. It is something you borrow from your children.

CANADIAN MP, 1978

Environmental issues do not normally make it on to the main public agenda in developing countries. It's a curious omission because the environment is often their primary asset, or contains their primary asset. This is the case in South Africa. Until recently, the issues in South Africa have been black and white, not green. The future was fought out in the cities and their ghettos. Clean air, clean rivers and the fate of the whales were far from most people's minds.

The country's new ruling elite, however, is made up of many exiles who have returned from capitals where they have been sensitized to environmental concerns, and are receptive to South Africa's small, but increasingly vociferous, environmental lobby. Consequently, the country is on its way, at last, to a comprehensive environmental policy and, it may be hoped, to a body of legislation to back it up. In years to come, though, laws will only be able to protect what is there to protect. Some important resources are throwing up disturbing signals that they are not inexhaustible.

GREEN RULES

South Africa lacks the legislative muscle needed to enforce environmental standards and controls. In fact, it lacks the standards to begin with, and the lame legislation that exists relies mainly on the voluntary co-operation of actual and potential polluters.

Environmentalism is a terrain patrolled by ragged squads of politically correct Stalinists, and so a tediously protracted process of consultation has been under way, called connepp (consultative national environmental policy process). By mid-1996 the process had produced a set of principles. Some were unremarkable, such as those holding polluters responsible for the costs of damage they cause, placing the onus on developers to show that projects will not harm the environment, and recognizing that South Africa shares a global responsibility in protecting the environment. Some, though, seemed destined for deep controversy. One allows 'decision-makers' to act against projects with potential for damage – even in the absence of convincing scientific evidence. Another proposes that communities whose consumption is low – and, therefore, whose environmental impact is low – should be compensated for their environment-friendly status. When 1997 opened, this process was still in the long chain of multi-level discussion, leading to a government green paper for setting the basis for policy, then a white paper for the policy, and legislation to follow.

When the legislation is finally produced, it will probably reflect the government's desire to be seen as a progressive administration by current world standards. Industry should brace itself for a new environment regime. Yet society as a whole lags behind other countries where public awareness has advanced, where domestic garbage sortment and recycling are routine, there is public pressure for clean products, cycling paths are ubiquitous, unleaded petrol is common and there are rules for vehicle emissions.

South Africans can expect, nevertheless, that the national and provincial governments will become more active in these areas. It is a common occurrence that when governments are failing on over-powering central issues like poverty, unemployment, urbanization and economic growth, they turn their attention to manageable, peripheral matters in order to answer their critics with an image of successful, proactive governing.

GREEN TURNS TO BROWN

South Africa evokes images of clear, blue skies and unspoiled open spaces. This is misleading. The country has the mixed blessing of abundant coal reserves and its current and projected burning of this fuel source is several times the world average. About 85 per cent of South Africa's electricity is generated from coal, and about 80 per cent of that is produced on the highveld. In his book *Back to Earth: South Africa's Environmental Challenges*, James Clarke, a leading environmental journalist, quotes a 1989 study of pollution in the main coal-burning region, then known as the eastern Transvaal highveld, undertaken by the Council for Scientific and Industrial Research (CSIR): 'The emission densities are between five and just under ten times greater than those found in West Germany and the United States, and approximate the worst conditions found anywhere.'

As a consequence, South Africa is a significant producer of carbon dioxide, culprit number one in global warming, and a by-product over which South Africa exercises no statutory control. As one rectifying measure, however, an initiative was launched to plant 5 million trees in South Africa in the 1990s decade to increase the natural absorption of carbon dioxide. However, Clarke says that, at current rates of carbon dioxide emission, 5 million trees will neutralize only the carbon dioxide produced by South African industry every six hours, and that the South African plan compares unfavourably with a similar one in Australia to plant 1 billion trees.

In the next two decades South Africa will experience the disturbed weather patterns that have troubled the world in the decade gone by. The absence of adequate legislative action on factors that are within government's control will intensify the discomfort of that experience. The impact for South Africa of the upward creep of world temperatures involves more prolonged droughts, declining food production leading to greater importation strains on the economy, and an acceleration in the advance of the Karoo which already constitutes a third of South Africa.

GREEN GLOW THE LILACS

South Africa's only practical alternative to coal, nuclear energy, is not likely to be pursued further than it is at present. A plant such as Koeberg, the nuclear generating facility in the Western Cape, has sufficient capacity for greater Johannesburg. Such a plant would replace several of its coal-burning cousins, and would be cheaper to run than any one of them. The reason, though, that there is not likely to be another one is not the public disquiet over the dangers of nuclear power, but that the start-up capital cost is so enormous. A government facing the broad developmental demands that this one does, as will those after it, will simply not be able to justify such expenditure.

The danger is that the South African government will deal through the back door of the nuclear market, as it has done in the past. With its remote areas and stable geology, South Africa is an ideal place to bury nuclear waste – and is, reportedly, the only country that does so. Koeberg's low-level waste is buried at Vaalputs in the Northern Cape, and its high-level waste is stored at the plant. Countries that cannot bury and have limits to their storage abilities will pay handsomely for someone to take their waste. South Africa has been tempted more than once, and, as fiscal constraints tighten, will be tempted even more in the future. The fact that toxic wastes can often be received clandestinely will increase that temptation.

The prospect of underground waste dumps in Namaqualand and the Richtersveld with toxic life-spans of tens of thousands of years is not only unnerving, but would lead to incendiary clashes between the government and lobby groups, and an international scandal.

IN THEM THAR HILLS

Before South Africa became synonymous with apartheid, it was synonymous with gold and mining. The discovery of gold and diamonds, and the flurry of immigration from all over the world it provoked in the nineteenth century, created the rise of modern South Africa. Today, eight of the country's top ten export categories are filled by products of its mines.

This is not a good thing. In a report published in 1996 Wharton Econometrix Forecasting Associates said countries, like South Africa, with abundant natural resources evolved a dependence on them, and called it the 'resource curse hypothesis'. While South Africa's dependence on its natural resources was growing, the world was moving in the opposite direction, heading for a market dominated by value-added, manufactured goods. The result has been a steady decline in the price of raw minerals and base commodities. On a world price index, they fell from 130 points in 1981 to 71 in 1992.

This was double trouble for South Africa because, while mineral prices were falling, manufactured goods went up in price from 109 to 164 on the same scale in the same period. It meant that the price of South Africa's exports was falling while the cost of its imports was rising. Little surprise, then, that the country went from one of the cheapest places in the world to live to one of the most expensive.

It is, therefore, not the size and quantity of South Africa's reserves of raw materials that is the concern. In 1996, Anglo-American announced preliminary plans for a R10 billion development of two possible new gold mines, the discovery of new platinum deposits was announced, and plans were revealed to bring the country's first oil field into production during 1997 – with oil pumping at a modest, but ground-breaking, 20,000 barrels a day. The concern is rather the pattern of dependence on assets of declining value, which has played a big role in creating the country's economic predicament. It is a pattern, furthermore, that shows no signs of reversing.

ALL THAT IS GOLD DOESN'T GLITTER

Gold is the biggest headache in South Africa's minerals-dependency habit because of the way in which it dominates South Africa's exports. Gold accounts for more than 70 per cent of total exports – about three times its nearest rival, diamonds, and about twelve times the value of fruit shipments. Worse: as much as gold-mining executives may deny it, South Africa's gold-mining industry is heading for a crisis.

One fact about Anglo-American's proposed new mines illustrates the problem: to get the envisaged gold the company will have to go between three-and-a-half and five kilometres below the surface of the earth, deeper than anyone else before. The difficulties, the technologies, and the costs of doing so are staggering. So, while 30 per cent of South Africa's total deposits still remain in the earth, the science and the economics of getting to them are becoming intensely problematic.

Since 1985, North America has doubled its output of gold, and Australia has tripled its output. South Africa's production, in contrast, has declined steadily since 1980, and was overtaken in 1986 by the rest of the world's total (which excluded the production of the Soviet Union, and which South Africa had exceeded until then). Local mines have to go deeper, and haul up more rock, to extract ever-diminishing quantities of ore. The quantities of ore recovered fell from eight grams a ton in 1979 to five in 1988. The result has been (there have been other factors, of course) that South Africa's gold production costs have nearly doubled since 1985, turning the country from the world's cheapest producer at that time to the most costly today.

Average world production costs for gold are about $285 an ounce, and some shallow, short-life mines in Australia and elsewhere are producing at costs as low as $150 an ounce. South Africa's production cost is about $305 an ounce. The graph of operating costs is rising, and that of values of recoveries is falling. Even a 10 per cent decline in the price of gold, from its early-1997 level of about $340 an ounce, in the next decade could dump the country's biggest export earner in a catastrophic predicament – with nigh-unimaginable consequences for the economy.

THE FLOW OF THE REVOLUTION

Water is the most basic and life-sustaining of all resources. The right of access to it is enshrined in South Africa's new constitution, and it is likely that very few politicians among the ANC's opposition saw the ramifications of doing so when they agreed to this provision.

There is a consensus of opinion that South Africa's water supplies are sufficient for the next twenty-five years. But that is of little comfort to an estimated 18 million South Africans who do not have proper access to water, and at least 12 million who do not have clean water within five kilometres of where they live. One in five deaths of children are from intestinal infections that could be avoided by clean water supplies. Apartheid grossly distorted the supply of fresh water to the country's peoples.

This is the situation the new government set out to rectify. Under one of its most capable ministers, Professor Kader Asmal, the extension of water supplies became perhaps the only unqualified success of the RDP. Efforts by the water affairs ministry will ensure that as many as 6 million people will have improved water supplies by the end of the ANC's first term of government. Once again, though, against the enormity of the need, the achievements will have been insufficient, however praiseworthy.

The doughty Asmal realized that a radical approach was needed – and he came up with one. On his recommendation, the cabinet approved a new principle late in 1996 – that would lead to legislation some time in 1997 – which decreed that water could be used . . . but not owned. It meant the end of private ownership of water and water sources. It meant that all water rights reverted to the state and that the government could levy a charge on any and all water.

The impact of this decision will be felt for many years to come. For a start, the availability of water has traditionally been one of the decisive factors in determining land prices. Along with the private ownership rights went what are known as riparian rights – the right to the use of rivers by those who own land along its banks. Boreholes on private properties become public property, or, at least, their water does. The scene for many clashes has been set. Organized agriculture has already complained, and demanded that landowners should be compensated for their loss of rights. Contemplate a regional authority coming to an obstreperous farmer with his own water source . . . and telling him that he would henceforth pay for what he used, and that supplies would be led from his source to an underdeveloped settlement near by.

Apart from this kind of conflict, the new water laws will open the way for far-reaching adventurism by a future government more imbued with revolutionary zeal – and not averse to seeing white landowners hurting a little. And that speculation would be leaving aside the intriguing breach of principle: if a basic resource like water is deemed unsuitable for private ownership, then why not another, like land, for instance?

None of this, however, gets past the fundamental truth: that there should be citizens in a land of relative plenty who do not have something as elementary as clean water to drink, or that children should die for want of it, is offensive to any decent person. The privileged, defined here by the most rudimentary of distinctions, will simply have to put up with the difficulties of a transition to a more equitable distribution of nature's most basic resource.

CHAPTER NINE

YOUR MONEY AND YOUR LIFE

Crime, corruption and the defeat of prosperity

My friends, you would not tell with such high zest
To children ardent for some desperate glory
The old Lie: Dulce et decorum est
Pro patria mori.

WILFRED OWEN, 1917

How sad an irony it is that the most prominent characteristic of the new South Africa, and the most talked about, should be a run-away crime scourge. The great election of 1994 made South Africa a normal country, and it joined the well-subscribed club of nations of modest achievement who are lagging behind in the race to catch up to the industrialized West. It distinguished itself, though, by showing itself to be among the most violent, dangerous, aggressive, dishonest and undisciplined of all.

Many South Africans, of all hues, understood that achieving a new society would entail sacrifices. But they baulk at those sacrifices becoming their hi-fis, their TVs and video recorders, their motor cars, their personal safety, their daughters and their elderly parents – and even their own lives. Ordinary South Africans are bewildered at becoming one of the most life-threatening peace-time societies in the world. They are groping for answers to questions which they are humiliated even to ask. Why is it so? How did it get like this? Will it get better or worse? If, in every newspaper, every news bulletin, one reads and hears stories of corruption in high places and murder and rape in the quiet streets and homes of the suburbs, does it mean we are on a slide to anarchy? Does the government understand the depth of the problem? And, even if it does, can it do anything? What do all the stories about corrupt and criminal police amount to? Is there anything dependable standing between us and the rampant criminals?

The government's flaccid and fitful response has, distressingly, left these questions without answers.

THE UNWANTED DISTINCTION

Measures of crime, within South Africa and relative to other countries, vary. But the picture of South Africa's leading violent status doesn't. In 1993 the Centre for the Study of Violence and Reconciliation at the University of the Witwatersrand said, at 47 murders per 100,000 of population, South Africa was more than twice as violent as its nearest rival, the Caribbean island of St Lucia, with 23 murders per 100,000. In 1995 the World Health Organization agreed with the most-murders status, but not with the figure, saying it was 54 per 100,000. In 1996 a South African banking group sponsored a private study of crime in the country. The Nedcor Project on Crime, Violence and Investment said the murder rate was 45 per 100,000 – but that it was higher in the Bahamas, Swaziland and Lesotho. Whatever. The international average is 5.5. In the USA it is 14, and in Britain and Japan it is under 1.

On the crime of rape there is no dispute. With more than 3,300 being reported every month, South Africa has far and away the highest rate. The Nedcor study said the overall crime rate in South Africa, at 5,651 reported crimes per 100,000 people, was similar to that in Norway, France and the United States . . . and about a third of the rate in Sweden and New Zealand, half of the rate in Canada, and about 60 per cent of that in Britain. This seems to defy common sense and is probably due to different rates and methods of reporting, and the fact that in those countries, minor incidents that would be overlooked in South Africa are considered reportable crimes. A South African police study in 1996 said about 80 per cent of all South African households experienced crime one way or another, and one can hardly imagine this being the case in Sweden or Canada.

On average, in every hour that passes in South Africa, two people are murdered, four women are raped, a vehicle is hi-jacked, ten are stolen, twenty are broken into, ten robberies take place and thirty houses are burgled.

There is an important variable influencing the measuring of crime in South Africa – the fact, which has emerged in several studies, that at least 50 per cent of crimes go unreported. Complex reasons lie behind this phenomenon, many of them not known or fully understood. Some, though, like lack of faith in the judicial chain and an absence of confidence that anything will come of reporting, are self-evident and stand out. Non-reportage affects different categories of crime differently. A credible estimate is that only one in thirty-five rapes is reported. Experiences of corruption by officialdom are reported in only 3 per cent of cases, according to one study. Reportage of vehicle and other thefts is high, but it is apparent that the reasons here are not belief in the ability of the police to recover the goods, but to comply with the formalities of insurance claims.

Beyond the academic quibbles over statistics, the distinguishing features of crime in South Africa loom malevolently and undiminished. They are its excessive violence and the fact that the graphs of all crime categories, despite temporary bumps and dips, and with the exception of public violence, are rising steeply.

CRIME'S HIDDEN FACE

The worst aspect of South African crime, its violence, is one that statistics cannot measure successfully. If they could, what would be wanted is a quotient that would establish the minimum degree of violence necessary to commit a particular crime, and then the degree of violence actually employed. Many criminologists have remarked that the degree of 'unnecessary' violence would be found to be very high, and, in particular, it would be very much higher than in other countries with similar crime problems. No such quotient exists, of course, and one has to be guided by the anecdotal evidence of how housebreakings are frequently accompanied by vicious assaults on homeowners, and how shootings of robbery victims often appear as afterthoughts by the robbers.

The obvious question of why this should be so will be addressed shortly. First, though, it is necessary to note that the predilection towards violence is accompanied by a dramatic rise in crimes to the person – murder, rape and assault – and an increasing tendency to target the vulnerable in society. Attacks on the elderly occur at about 100 a month, and are rising. The isolated are in increasing danger – in an eighteen-month period from January 1995 to June 1996, 167 farmers were murdered on their farms.

The most shameful blot on any society's character, however, is the abuse of its children. It is a pestilent trend that has long been hidden in this society, and is now being increasingly uncovered. The true reach of it will undoubtedly never be known – the incidence of non-reportage among children, for obvious reasons, must be very great. The known dimensions are staggering enough: more than 200 cases of child rape are reported to the police every week.

GETTING AWAY WITH IT

Committing a crime involves surprisingly little risk for South African offenders. According to the Nedcor report, of every 1,000 crimes that are committed, 450 are reported; 230 are solved and 100 go to court; 77 convictions ensue, resulting in 36 imprisonments, 8 of which see offenders serving for longer than two years. The seventy-seven convictions mean that, statistically, a criminal stands an 8 per cent chance of being punished for a crime – alternatively, a 92 per cent chance of getting away with it.

Although the emphasis in crime in South Africa is on its crudity, the country has become a fertile field for organized crime. No doubt the relative impunity that the country offers, described above, and the ready availability of cheap and expendable criminal foot soldiers and hit men have been significant lures. According to police intelligence, there are 481 known criminal syndicates operating in South Africa. Some are home-grown, having germinated in the shadows of the corrupt previous regime, and some are branches of international networks that have taken advantage of the new democracy. Between them they have varying degrees of infrastructure, manpower, international reach, ability to import and export their contraband, connections and even members in the police and government, and ability to buy themselves into and out of the judicial process. Of the syndicates, 136 are known to be in drugs manufacture, import and sales, 112 in vehicle hi-jacking, theft and export, 85 in various forms of commercial fraud, and 71 specializing in illicit buying and exporting of gold and diamonds. Against this awful array of criminal power, the South African Police Service (yes, the acronym is SAPS) has an organized crime investigation unit of 28 officers who, in mid-1996, had 32 of the 481 syndicates under investigation.

A dominant feature of organized crime is that, sooner or later, it penetrates organs of society – local and national government, the police, the courts and banking. Innocuous areas of business are affected, too. For example, the profitable and active Western Cape property market is a popular mechanism for laundering criminal funds – once a property that has been bought with such funds has been sold, the proceeds are legitimate.

The degree to which organized crime has penetrated society in South Africa is not known. It is not as extensive as it is in Russia, for instance, where the syndicates are established at all levels and in all corners of civil life. There are, nevertheless, disturbing early signs of similar penetration in South Africa. A high number of the 176 policemen murdered in 1996 is thought to be 'eliminations' by crime syndicates. In at least four recent instances, SAPS vehicle-theft units have been discovered running or implicated in vehicle-theft operations. Police complicity in crime is well established, and leads to mirth-producing events like the theft of the commissioner's fax machine in August 1996, and the disappearance overnight from police headquarters of an automatic teller machine . . . and the R22,000 in it. In 1995 a bugging scandal erupted in police headquarters. A National Intelligence Agency investigation (the agency itself being the initial suspect) led to a report that was submitted to the Parliamentary Committee on Intelligence and the National Intelligence Co-ordinating Committee. The report never emerged from the two committees but insiders later said the blame for the bugging had shifted to organized crime.

The penetration of civil organs is organized crime's main growth point – and, while the police counter-force remains merely a puny obstacle to the syndicates, that is where they will make their greatest gains.

BUSINESS AS CRIME

Police say the known crimes of the syndicates amounted to about R518 million in fraud and counterfeiting operations in 1995. However, the crimes investigated in that year by the SAPS' commercial division, that is, crimes committed by persons who have regular careers and are not in the ordinary sense criminals, involved a missing R7.3 billion . . . roughly the 1997 value of the RDP.

Dishonesty and inefficiency flourish in one another's company. The erosion of the moral fabric of society caused by these two attitudes and practices were discussed in Chapter Six. Here they are seen at work. The accountants KPMG Aiken & Peat run a fraud barometer, which shows that the majority of fraud crimes are committed by the victim companies' own managers, not outsiders.

A KPMG survey, reported by the *Mail & Guardian* at the end of 1996, said two-thirds of respondents had experienced fraud in the preceding year – and almost all believed it was on the increase. Three-quarters said the biggest reason for the fraud plague was the weakening of social values. It's worth noting, however, that out of the 1,000 companies targeted by the survey, only 129 bothered to reply. There has to be a connection.

The capabilities of the front-line defenders, the police and the courts, are once again cause for mounting concern. The police units are understaffed and underskilled, and the courts are swamped. The result is that the rate of convictions against reported frauds is only 11 per cent.

THE IMPACT OF CRIME

The Nedcor project calculated the cost of crime to the economy in 1995 at R31.1 billion. Fraud and vehicle theft alone run at about 2.5 per cent of GDP. Foreign investment is taking a tumble: the South African–German Chamber of Commerce and Industry said in 1996 after the financial manager of AEG was shot dead by hi-jackers that sixteen of the thirty chief executives of German subsidiaries in South Africa had been victims of violent crime. Tourism is taking a knock. Commercial trucks get hi-jacked at a rate of five a day in Gauteng alone – and police say the drivers collude in 90 per cent of cases. Losses incurred by thefts of copper telephone wires touched R130 million in the first six months of 1996. A member of the *Financial Mail*'s board of economists says: 'We seem to be moving, at least perceptually, into a war situation.'

However, it is the impact of crime on general development and on society as a whole that is equally, if not more, damaging in the long run. A housing development for Phola Park squatter camp was shelved after most of the members of the elected committee piloting the project were shot and killed by a gang of residents who used the shanty township as a depot for stolen vehicles and other contraband. The gang's refuge would have been compromised by orderly development.

Social patterns are being disturbed, with incalculable results. Half of the adult population, women, has had its freedom of movement meaningfully curtailed by being particularly at risk, especially when alone and more so at night. Urban lifestyles are far more insular than they would otherwise have been. Protection from criminals is a major reason for the rise in popularity of shopping malls, an architectural paradox in a subtropical climate. At night, many people select restaurants, cinemas and other entertainment located in malls so that their vehicles are under guard in their absence . . . and can be reached with reduced risk afterwards. The rise of the malls represents an economic trend away from smaller, self-standing and more casual businesses – a move that not only chokes an important artery in a developing economy, but imposes uniformity and robs social life of colour and vibrancy.

The crime wave has substantially reversed advances that have been made in defusing racial antagonisms in South Africa, and will continue to undermine positive trends. Crime knows no racial barriers, of course. But the perception of the ordinary person – not entirely inaccurate – is that car hi-jackers, store robbers and house breakers are almost always black. The tragic consequence, in the highly charged atmosphere of fear in the suburbs, is that the mere sight of a black man or men at a drive-way entrance (a favourite hi-jacking location) is enough to provoke a mixture of fear and anger in the homeowner.

THE NEW CLASS WAR

Crime in South Africa is no longer an aberration on the fringe of society. It is too pervasive to be regarded as an anomaly that will resolve itself in time and through normal means. It is part of the make-up of the new society. In the introductory chapters of this book, the assertion was made that crime in South Africa had evolved into a low-intensity class war. Here, in addition to the description given there, are the reasons.

Criminals are simply numerous enough, and their activities by now have enough of an impact on the culture and economy of the nation, and the life of its communities, for them to be considered, legitimately, a distinct class of persons . . . a class unwanted and abhorred by the majority, but a class nevertheless.

Criminality has brought into being a sub-economy in South Africa. That portion of it that arises from the illegitimate activities of the un-people who, by their status, are denied access to the main economy, exists in tandem with the formal economy. Examples of this are the theft of communications cabling, which is traded as scrap metal, and organized stock theft that supports a sub-wholesale meat supply channel to squatter communities where the commodity is then sold at the sub-retail prices the people there can support.

Another segment of the sub-economy is created by the organized syndicates that employ the otherwise unemployable. The drones of this sub-industry hi-jack vehicles for their employers at a reputed going rate of R1,000 for a luxury vehicle – which may then be converted or hybridized by other workers in chop shops, or may be exported to neighbouring states, or even shipped to buyers on other continents. At work here are mirror images of conventional business. The criminal organizations have profit-sharing bosses and salaried employees. They trade, bank and exchange currencies as would occur in the legitimate economy.

Yet another segment of the sub-economy is more intimately interwoven with the formal economy. It is that shadow economy that is fostered by the white-collared middle manager next door who is running a scam at work with one of his company's suppliers, the proceeds of which he is using to pay off his bond in half the time that you can, or he otherwise would.

Crime has the dimensions of a class war because it has become an outlet for social aspirations. A seventy-five-year-old woman lying trussed up on her bed asks one of the three black men robbing her of her television, radio and microwave oven why they are doing it to her. 'You (whites) have always had everything. Now it's our turn,' he tells her. Echoes of the sentiments expressed in this incident can be heard in any number of victims' accounts.

Crime is an outlet for social anger. Not every black South African subscribes to Mandela's reconciliation. Many oppressed, brutalized and illiterate persons, rejected by society, are incapable of articulating such elevated sentiments. A recurring pattern in South African murders is one in which homeowners are killed by casual labourers, who have often been employed as gardeners – and who make off after the killing with some household item or a car. In how many of these murders, it is worth asking, was the initial spark provided by some insult or ill-treatment, with the robbery as a postscript to the murder, not a motive for it. As with the hashshashin, who practised murder as a social instrument and gave their name to the word assassin, killing as a form of retribution has long since become an established practice in some areas of South African society.

Crime has become democratized. The black townships have always experienced rampant lawlessness. It was one of the many distortions of apartheid that kept it, preponderantly, penned to those districts. Now suburban whites are feeling it – at least, much more so than they ever did before. Leaving aside the fact that the social dynamics would have created an overspill of crime from black to white districts even if there weren't a new South Africa, whites now sense a gulf of perceptions between them and their new black rulers. When Mandela says, as he did in August 1996, while launching a new anti-crime initiative: 'At the same time, one must understand the frustrations that have been bottled up over the decades,' and Gauteng premier Tokyo Sexwale says people in Johannesburg's plush northern suburbs must stop whining about crime and do something about it themselves, then middle-class whites feel their torment is not empathized, that in the background of government attitudes there lurks a rationalization of crime and a reluctance in the new ruling class to deal with it harshly, and that, consequently, a solution to their number one problem is not yet in sight.

FIGHTING CRIME

1 Policy and police

The police service has become ensnared to its detriment in praiseworthy broad policies of the government. In the overall drive to cut back government spending and reduce the deficit, the police budget has been frozen. In the plan to cut back on the civil service, a moratorium was placed on police recruitment, and retrenchment packages were offered to members of the force – as in other government departments. In the course of 1997, 1,300 policemen will take their payouts and leave the 140,000-strong force. More than fifty generals retired in 1995 and 1996. The frozen budget has reverberated down the ranks, culminating in a freeze on promotions.

In the face of the crime onslaught, it seems outrageously irresponsible of the government to follow this policy course. The argument offered in defence is that the challenge of South African policing does not lie in numbers – either of personnel or money. The country already has an exceptionally high police-to-population ratio: 328 people per police officer, compared with an international average of

1,014. What the force needs most is to be restructured and remanaged. For example, the Democratic Party disclosed early in 1997 that one of the country's most active police stations, Hillbrow, had a staff of 314 – but an amazing 274 of those were in administrative and back-up functions; only forty were active police officers, many of whom were illiterate and inadequately trained. It is this sort of misallocation of resources, the argument runs, that accounts for revelations such as that by a divisional commissioner that detectives – only a quarter of whom had been on detective courses – handled up to 164 serious crime cases a year, leaving around 80 per cent unsolved.

The morale and integrity of the police force hasn't waited for the outcome of this argument. In 1996 an average of fifty policemen a month were fined in Soweto alone for wrongdoing. At the time of writing, the Gauteng attorney general was investigating more than 8,300 cases of criminal offences by, or involving, police officers. The number of police suicides has grown alarmingly. In the eighteen months up to mid-1996, civil claims against the police amounted to R278 million. An internal police probe found that avoidable potential losses of more than R300 million arose from 'indiscipline, negligence, bad training and corruption'.

Against this background of depleted – and still dwindling – resources, the police ministry and the force launched a number of crime-combating initiatives. They began with an overall National Crime Prevention Strategy (NCPS) that targeted a number of right-sounding objectives – improved intelligence gathering, anti-corruption drives, better training and management development. The NCPS was followed by a series of on-the-ground operations – sword and shield, eagle, rooikat, iron fist, anvil and urban strike. Despite their upbeat names, they failed to elevate public confidence – probably because there were no lasting changes in crime patterns. After the biggest of the operations, sword and shield, which aimed to arrest the country's 10,000 most-wanted criminals in one month, the police announced they had captured 7,099. A public dispute then broke out between the commissioner of police and the minister of justice, who said there was no discernible rise in the number of court appearances. The question of whether the arrests were really those of most-wanted criminals, or simply arrests, was never satisfactorily resolved. In addition, the operation left in its wake the disturbing implication that the police only try hard in special circumstances (why weren't the 10,000, or, at least, the 7,000, arrested in the many months preceding the operation if the police had the capability of rounding them up in a mere 30 days?).

Weaving in and out of the policing debate is the issue of using the defence force to help crack the crime scourge. The government is coy about it, subscribing to the abstract notion that a defence force should not be extensively deployed in a civic role within the country's borders. Not quite though. The defence force disclosed that in 1996 it had deployed nearly 8,000 troops and flown 1,700 hours in support of the police. While there would appear to be a clear case for further such deployments, the argument that the policing problem is not one of numbers alone does carry considerable weight.

2 The courts

A make-over of the judicial system applied by the courts smacks of tackling the crime problem from the wrong end – punishment instead of prevention. Yet it is inarguable that the parlous state of the country's courts has been a significant contributor to the erosion of people's confidence in public justice and, therefore, to increased lawlessness. Overburdened and underpaid public prosecutors have been warning in recent years of the imminent collapse of the courts system.

Their warning has been heard. Early in 1997 the government announced a R1.4 billion upgrade of the justice system, to be spread over four years. The biggest single designated project was a R300 million computerization of the records of the police, courts, prisons and juvenile care system. R60 million of this money was to go towards a computerized fingerprint identification system, eliminating the present system that takes up to eight weeks to provide a result – another of those pronouncements that leaves one not knowing whether to feel joy at the solution or anger at learning that the condition existed in the first place.

Accompanying the upgrade will be a tightening of the screws in bail and sentencing legislation. Laws scheduled for promulgation in 1997 included the right of courts to refuse bail in certain cases of rape and a compulsory minimum sentence of fifteen years for crimes of violence. The minister of justice took the edge off this undertaking, though, with the postscript disclosure that the stiffer measures would be only temporary. The minister, it appears, anticipates a rapid normalization of crime in South Africa.

3 The prisons

At a total of about 125,000 inmates, putting prisons at 130 per cent of capacity, South Africa's incarcerated population was at an all-time high early in 1997. At a shortage of 7,000, the prison staff complement was at an all-time low.

Although the government has planned a new maximum security prison that should be completed early in 1999, it doesn't have any option on what to do in the mean time: it has to release prisoners. It will not be the first time it has happened. Several releases of prisoners (the penal term is 'bursting') took place in the lead-up to the 1994 election. They doubled neatly as acts of clemency on the part of F. W. de Klerk, president at the time. In 1995, according to one estimate, about 100,000 prisoners were released before the full termination of their sentences. The early release of about 30,000 prisoners is envisaged for 1997.

Naturally, releases focus on minor offenders. But the bursting principle clashes with New York's successful 'broken window' crime and punishment policy, wherein even the most minor offences are treated seriously. Escalation of criminal activity by individuals is thereby cut off at base. Opposition parties have already loudly complained that the releases send the wrong signals into the community. One is tempted to wonder if it matters – since 1993 an average of 100 prisoners a month have been escaping from the porous prison system and its chaotic jails. Up to 1,000 accused persons a month, released on bail, do not turn up for their trials.

ORIGINS OF CRIME

The direct causes of crime are not known. If they were, we'd be living in a very different world. What can be said with certainty is that conditions of poverty, crowding, unemployment, the dislocation of communities and the disintegration of families are circumstances in which crime flourishes. In the atmosphere of despair and alienation found with such urban conditions, crime can present countless numbers of young people with their most attractive career choice. In an environment where an average of only six out of every hundred job seekers find employment, crime can frequently be the only career choice. In any event, in most cases it offers disaffected youth greater excitement, bigger rewards, and not significantly higher risks than the kind of work that would be available to them, or in starting some undertaking for an independent income.

These conditions, therefore, can explain crimes of need. But there are many aspects of crime they cannot explain. Poverty and unemployment alone do not explain why many other societies that suffer from these afflictions do not have the same incidence of crime. The combination of conditions does not explain crimes of greed. It does not explain fraud, corruption, endemic dishonesty and other white-collar criminality. It does not explain the excessive violence of South African crime, and it does not explain the escalating crime against persons – child abuse, rape, assault and murder.

To understand these phenomena one must look to circumstances peculiar to South Africa. The most prominent of these, of course, is apartheid. It spawned a battery of factors that culminates in a severely dysfunctional society. The racial creed's unadorned message was that some lives were worth more than others. Some persons were entitled to decide on the fate of others. The absolute sanctity of the individual, and of life itself, became relative. Once it had become relative, it could be cheapened and abused. Apartheid society was, above all, an engineered society. The social engineers shifted neighbourhoods like flags on a map. They interfered with the natural, organic growth of communities. Like engineered communities everywhere – the housing estates of Britain, for example – South Africa's manufactured communities became places where normal social patterns and networks unravelled, where families disintegrated, and criminal behaviour bloomed. In 1995, 15,000 urban children were arrested for crimes ranging from pilfering to murder.

South Africans, especially white South Africans, learned to live the big lie, as described in Chapter Six. Dishonesty became a cultural norm. Also discussed in Chapter Six was the erosion of belief in authority. Apartheid was a brutal concept and the state soon found it could enforce the policy only through the instrument of brutality. The nation's experience of brutality – whether it fell into the category of those who suffered it, or the category of those who sanctioned it – combined with a corroded belief in the sanctity of life . . . and produced one of the modern world's most criminal, murder-prone societies.

CATALYSTS OF CRIME

Three further elements, associated with apartheid, and beyond it, influence crime in South Africa.

The deterioration of the justice system, as described above, and the fading deterrent that it poses, has played its role in the spread of crime in contemporary South Africa. With faith in the system lost, people – especially those in depressed communities – have increasingly taken the law into their own hands. Kangaroo courts were not only features of the liberation struggle, they mete out rough justice in many neighbourhoods today. A cycle of lawlessness and alienation from the system is in place.

Also, the fact that the police were, in recent decades, primarily a political instrument for the enforcement of apartheid has deprived the post-apartheid police force of a running start in the fight against common crime.

Finally, underdevelopment in South Africa's neighbouring states fuels crime. Growing tides of illegal immigrants flood into South Africa – only to find, once they arrive, that they have no legitimate means of supporting themselves.

THE FUTURE OF CRIME 1

South Africa's current crime statistics conceal a dangerous development. In a land where guns are probably already more prevalent than driver's licences, thousands more are entering the country – and then disappearing. In a recent publication, *Small Arms*

Proliferation and Control in Southern Africa, author Glenn Oosthuysen says about 40,000 AK-47 assault rifles have been smuggled into the country in the last few years. The police estimate that the 1,400 they intercept each year are about 10 per cent of the total that make it into the country. That's bad enough, but the really worrying part is that only a few hundred turn up in crimes each year. What's happening to the rest? Are they part of an illegal arms trade to other African countries? Or are they being stockpiled? If so, by whom and for what purpose? By the same measure, are any of the many bank robberies the work of underground groups funding political causes?

There is a strong probability of a connection with right-wing activism – the question is simply how great. The National Intelligence Agency says it has evidence that a 'third force' is dormant, but still in existence in South Africa. The opinion was expressed in an earlier chapter that right-wing insurgence will never be great enough to influence the course of events in South Africa. But that doesn't mean a lot of hurt and damage couldn't be done.

One place where illegal weapons are certain to emerge is in a future rise of vigilantism. The emergence of the Western Cape vigilante movement, Pagad (People Against Gangsterism and Drugs), was accompanied by such an upsurge of public sympathy that Pagad is most unlikely to be the last of its kind. Vigilantism is not, incidentally, a feature only of chaotic developing environments. London and New York both experienced a vigilante movement in the 1980s in the form of the Guardian Angels who patrolled the subways. In the USA there have been a number of high-profile trials of individual vigilantes, and vigilantism is a popular theme in American cinema. All that is needed is the right mixture of rampant crime, official apathy and public impatience.

THE FUTURE OF CRIME 2

Laudable efforts are being made in South Africa to improve the efficiency of the primary crime-fighting tool, the police. Doubtless, some of these efforts will succeed to some degree, and things will not always be as bad as they are now. But the idea that the SAPS will turn from a largely demoralized, substantially corrupt and inept force into a slick and powerful civic instrument inside of anything like a decade is simply naive. The inertia of decay is too great. The depressing likelihood is that organized crime, which is more motivated, will improve its reach and efficiency more quickly than organized crime-fighting will.

THE FUTURE OF CRIME 3

Under Mandela South Africa had its best shot at going straight. Mandela was a luminous and influential symbol of honesty, integrity and the virtues of a principled life. It's not to say that Mandela's successor will not have these qualities, but the active agent of the symbolism will not be there. When Mandela goes, the outlook for corruption and the epidemic of dishonesty is bleak. If they didn't reverse under his reign, they are unlikely to under any other.

THE FUTURE OF CRIME 4

The circumstances in which South African crime has thrived fall into two broad categories: the classical explanation of deprived social conditions, and the factors that are unique to South Africa. In respect of the second category, the view was expressed above that apartheid has been the major progenitor of the abnormally high level of crime in South Africa. This means, then, that the further the new South Africa moves away from its apartheid past, the fainter its effects will be – and the greater hope there is for a decrease in crime. Unfortunately, this is only partly true. Many of the effects of apartheid, such as the propensities towards dishonesty, violence and disregard for authority, have become entrenched and will remain part of the society for a generation, at least. The wave of factors in the first category – unmanageable urbanization, the cultural dislocations that come with it, the disintegration of families and the social fabric of communities, unemployment and poverty – will roll on and swell as it gathers momentum.

The unhappy conclusion is that only a future generation, with new values, can bring about a reversal in the crime patterns of South Africa. Until then, they must continue on the path they have taken . . . and get worse before they get better.

CHAPTER TEN

PULSE OF THE NATION

Health services in the waiting room

It ought to be remembered that there is nothing more difficult to take in hand, more perilous to conduct, or more uncertain in its success, than to take the lead in the introduction of a new order of things.

NICCOLÒ MACHIAVELLI, 1513

In the past, South Africa had a First World health service. It made medical advances, and provided a level of care comparable with the best in the world. This was both a good thing and a bad thing about the old South Africa. It was fine for the country's First World population. Some pains were undertaken to make the point that that didn't mean whites only. Baragwanath Hospital in Soweto was pointed to, and a mantra was recited about it being the biggest hospital in the southern hemisphere and that services were provided at a nominal fee.

That was all very well, but it disguised the millions of South

Africans, mainly black inhabitants of the rural areas and around the small towns, with almost no access at all to health facilities. Where clinics and health centres existed, they often lacked the most basic amenities. Sometimes that meant water, electricity, medicines and telephones. This explained why South Africa could pioneer heart transplants on the one hand, yet had a shameful infant mortality rate on the other. It was a gross imbalance that could not be allowed to endure. The National Party government made a failed attempt to put it right. When the ANC came into power, newly converted to free-enterprise philosophies, it clung to one socialist policy – a national health service.

What has happened since to the provision of health services in South Africa is quite straightforward: there has been a massive reassignment of priorities and money from the First World component of health care to the Third World component, where the need is greatest. This has had the effect of creating some praiseworthy successes in the one case, and leading to pitiable declines in the other.

THE GRAND PLAN

In 1995 an influential report was published jointly by the Health Systems Trust and the World Bank. In graphic terms, it outlined what was wrong with health care in South Africa. Although the public and private sectors together spend 8.5 per cent of GDP on health services, South Africa's people were less healthy than those in comparable countries at a similar level of economic development. The report said South Africa's health services focused on curative, hospital-based medicine. More than 80 per cent of the money the government spent on health went to hospitals – and more than half of that amount went to academic hospitals and those with intensive care and other specialized units. Non-hospital primary health care accounted for only 11 per cent of government expenditure.

The ANC government needed little further prodding. Already imbued with ambitions for a national health service, it responded quickly with a plan that set a March 1996 target of 152 new clinics, upgrades to 3,170 and the purchase of 144 mobile units. By June 1996, 60 of the new clinics had been built, upgrades had been undertaken at 120 and the mobile units were being awaited. As an aside, this failure to convert plans into practice points to one of the important red herrings in the health debate – the government proposals are so controversial that its ability to implement them is often obscured in the dust of the argument.

Nevertheless, there were more significant developments than plans for clinics. The ANC had come to power with a promise of providing free health care to pregnant women and children under the age of six. Mid-way through the ANC's first term of office, this was one of the only meaningful election promises it had fully delivered on.

In addition to the free pre- and post-natal health care, the government devised a primary health care (PHC) system that embraced aspects such as basic eye care, rehabilitation, communicable and chronic diseases, immunization, family planning, health education, screening for diseases, and trauma services. An elementary drugs list was also drawn up. In April 1996 the PHC service became free at designated health care centres.

The above initiatives were to be supplemented by a national health insurance scheme, the policy outlines of which the minister of health said would be available by the end of 1997. An early indication was that the scheme would involve a compulsory insurance levy on the wages of all employed persons who were not members of private medical aid schemes.

In the period that these radical innovations in health care in South Africa were taking shape, government expenditure on health – the second biggest item on its budget after education – remained steady at around 11 per cent. That, furthermore, is where it will stay. The government's commitment to bring down its deficit is a macro-policy imperative that overrides its health plans. That means the money for the PHC must be found from within an unchanged health allocation, that is, is must be diverted from the secondary and tertiary health care sectors. The principle was illustrated when, in the period in which all these developments were in gestation, the government stopped heart transplants – a hi-tech, high-cost procedure that benefits only the few – in all hospitals except the Western Cape in order to reallocate resources downwards to where the needs of the many existed.

The effects of the reassignment of health resources on the country's most important hospitals has been near catastrophic. The government began pruning their budgets mercilessly. Expectedly, the hospitals tried first to save in non-essential areas such as maintenance and cleaning operations. These have, though, begun to affect the main function of the hospitals – in at least one case unhygienic conditions in a major hospital have led to deaths of patients. Equipment has become obsolete, but not replaced. The minister of health herself acknowledged it would now take about R10 billion to rescue the country's main hospitals.

In the circumstances, medical personnel have turned elsewhere for their career paths. Emigration by doctors has increased by nearly 500 per cent since 1993. Those that haven't left the country have left the public sector for private practice. Their exodus has been helped by the government's overall policy of cutting back on the civil service payroll by offering retrenchment packages. At the end of 1996 in the Gauteng health department alone 3,000 medical staff members had applied for the packages.

Professor Dave Morrell, a prominent medical academic and expert on public-sector practice, gave *The Star*'s medical correspondent this dismal picture: 'There are 10,500 posts in state medicine, but 5,500 of these are in academic medicine at the large teaching hospitals. This leaves 5,000 posts in primary and secondary hospitals, of which only 4,000 are filled. Of these 4,000 state doctors, 2,000 are foreign doctors with limited registration from India, Pakistan, Eastern Europe and several other countries. A further 500 doctors are foreign doctors with full registration. This leaves a mere 1,500 South African doctors in the service, the vast majority of them junior doctors seeking experience before moving into private practice or specialization.'

Johannesburg's busy central hospital had, by mid-1996, only three of its original fourteen specialized nurses in its cardio-thoracic unit's intensive-care section. Over 1995 and 1996 Groote Schuur Hospital in Cape Town experienced a 25 per cent increase in its number of patients, and a 31 per cent drop in its staff.

Apart from the ravages the hospitals are having to endure as a result of a changing health service, they are falling prey to the more ubiquitous South African diseases of dishonesty, theft and non-payment. The superintendent of Baragwanath Hospital says about R500,000 worth of medical and other goods is stolen from the hospital every month by patients and staff. Gauteng hospitals were owed R162 million at the end of 1996, nearly half of what they had charged patients in the course of the year. An investigation by *The Citizen* revealed that ambulance despatchers were delaying sending ambulances to scenes of serious accidents until they had haggled and settled commissions for tipping off tow-truck operators. Even then, despatch was not automatic – Gauteng's health department said of the initial 450 ambulances it had to service the province, 150 had been scrapped and of the remaining 300, only 160 were operational at any one time. The entitlement culture has wreaked its havoc, too – in 1995 strikes occurred at ninety-four hospitals around the country. In Johannesburg's ambulance depot a strike left critically ill patients stranded while management and staff bargained over pay and working conditions.

The net effect of the foregoing has been to leave middle-class South Africans with deep anxieties about what would await them if they had the misfortune to end up in a state hospital. The head of surgery at Groote Schuur Hospital, Professor John Terblanche, told the *Financial Mail*: 'My advice is: don't get sick, injured or run over because you are likely to end up at one of our academic institutions. Despite the best will in the world, we will treat you badly. You could sit slobbering for five days with a broken jaw because we don't have the staff to see to it.'

It appears he wasn't exaggerating. Johannesburg hospital said in 1996 there was a two to three-year waiting list for cataract, hip, knee and heart surgery – and that approximately 2,000 patients were waiting for such operations.

ONLY AS SICK AS YOU CAN AFFORD

The upshot of the changes in health practice in South Africa is that, while the wealthy have never contemplated anything else, the middle class is more or less compelled to rely on private medicine. This has its own problems. Two things are happening in private medicine, which is dominated by the medical aid schemes: membership costs are soaring, and young people are increasingly opting for alternative methods of health insurance. The two trends are interrelated; the more the one happens, the more it fans on the other.

First, the matter of costs. Medical costs are rising, but medical aid costs are rising even faster. In fact, the upsurge in costs is nothing short of amazing. In the decade up to 1993, medical aid members' contributions had rocketed by more than 1,000 per cent – from an annual average of R442 to R5,220, according to a credit-ratings agency. Apart from the rise in doctors' fees, hospital costs and the price of medicines, the industry pins the blame for the rise on increased inefficiency and widespread abuse of the schemes by medical practitioners and patients alike. Equally significant, too, has been the decline of youthful membership.

This, the second trend, is caused by a combination of the first – declining affordability – and the availability of alternatives in the form of medical 'catastrophe insurance'. The latter covers only serious illnesses, accidents and hospitalization, leaving the individual to carry routine medical costs, and doubles as a form of investment saving by being cashable after an agreed term.

The turning away from medical aids is not merely resulting in a loss of customers, however – it is a trend that is dismantling the basic mechanism by which medical aid schemes work. The contributions of younger members of a scheme, who are not frequent users of medical services, subsidize more frequent use of the schemes' reserves made by older members. The more that a scheme loses its young members, the more it has to increase its membership dues in order to cover its costs. In addition, medical aids are having to pay ever-decreasing percentages of the medical expenses incurred by a member. In 1980, for example, doctors' charges and medical aid reimbursements were equal; today medical aids pay an average of only 45 per cent of such charges.

At present only 17 per cent of the South African population participates in medical aids. For the foreseeable future, that is likely to be a peak. The only real source of membership growth for medical aids would be from the corporate sector, fuelled by climbing employment levels. But the economy will not deliver that increased employment.

In the meanwhile, the trend to alternative forms of medical insurance will continue. Before long employers will be under pressure from employees either to increase the company's contributions to medical aid memberships or to allow employees to opt out of group schemes. The compulsory national medical insurance envisaged by the government, and which could be in place in 1998 or 1999, will also severely limit the private medical aids' market, particularly among wage earners, as opposed to salary earners.

All of these factors mean a future of sharply climbing medical costs for middle- and upper-bracket South Africans, and a pronounced shift to individuals of the burden for ensuring that they have planned medical cover for the course of their lives.

THE PLAGUE OF AQUARIUS

Of all the perils facing South Africa, Aids will probably be the most expensive in direct costs – apart, that is, from the misery that comes with it. The pandemic spread of the disease is, in addition, a wild card, a variable that is destined to have a measurable effect on economic growth, the implementation of the RDP and the provision of overall health care.

There are an estimated 22 million people in the world infected with HIV. Twenty million of those are in the southern hemisphere, and 14 million of them are in sub-Saharan Africa – South Africa's neighbours and source of its illegal immigrants. In 1997 there were about 2 million people in South Africa infected with HIV, although estimates vary and at least one major life insurer believes the real figure could be as much as five times the official estimate.

In South Africa, as in the rest of the countries of the subcontinent, Aids is predominantly a heterosexual disease and 90 per cent of cases occur among black Africans. Whites constitute 6 per cent of those infected, and in their cases 80 per cent of infections stemmed from homosexual or bisexual contacts. The department of health estimates that by 2010 the level of infection will have climbed from the present approximate of 4 per cent of the population to about 12 per cent – and will be the biggest single cause of death. The areas of South Africa most affected will be KwaZulu/Natal and Mpumulanga.

The point about Aids is that it is a time bomb: the number of infected people grows exponentially, and deaths from Aids illnesses happen five to ten years after infection by the HIV virus. Aids deaths tallied so far in South Africa account for about 2 per cent of those currently thought to be infected with HIV. By 2000, according to the government's estimates, that will have climbed to 16 per cent – nearly half a million people.

The observation was made earlier that the greatest effect of Aids will not be on the overall size of the population. It will slow the pace at which the population is growing to a degree . . . but only a degree. The biggest impact of Aids will be in its socio-economic effects. Aids strikes down its victims in the prime of their economically active lives, in the thirty to forty-five age group. This severely erodes the stability of families and the balanced presence of breadwinners. Ultimately, say experts in the field, its effects will be measurable on per capita incomes. This effect throws the economic burden on those least able to carry it – the old and the young. The disease is in the process of creating millions of Aids orphans that the country will have to deal with in ensuing years. The minister of health estimates that 15 per cent of pregnant women in South Africa are infected with HIV, that the figure rises to 30 per cent in KwaZulu/Natal, and that those mothers will probably die before their children finish school. The incidence of transmission of the virus from mother to child is about 30 per cent. In Soweto alone, the head of the maternity unit at Baragwanath Hospital estimates, 50,000 mothers will die by 2001.

When education became a sacrifice of the liberation struggle in the 1980s, there was considerable anxiety about the future of the 'lost generation'. Present-day South Africa is dealing with the effects of that great social dislocation in its current crime wave and general instability in communities. A new lost generation is being created by Aids, with equally dire consequences.

The costs of dealing with the pandemic – campaigns to contain it, and treatment of its victims – are appalling. The Washington-based International Food Policy Research Institute estimates that Aids could retard the per capita growth rate of sub-Saharan Africa by as much as 1.4 per cent. If that happened, it would plunge the region into an irrecoverable tailspin. The Aids unit of another South African life insurer says that the disease could reduce GDP by 1.5 per cent a year (this is not the same method of measure as in the figure for sub-Saharan Africa, above). The unit estimates that the direct costs of Aids in 2000, which goes beyond the ambit of the health department, will be R20 billion. That is more than the total current government allocation for health. The indirect costs, according to the insurer, will be about R80 billion. In future, more than 30 per cent of the national health budget will have to be spent on Aids.

Aids measurement and prediction, and its impact on social and economic life, is an imperfect science. Whatever the variations and exact figures and projections might finally prove to be, however, the direction the problem is taking, and its scale, is quite apparent. It will be the single biggest challenge the department of health will face, and its other, flamboyant, plans might remain largely the dreams of bureaucrats. At the levels of cost that are currently being predicted, broader government initiatives, like its RDP, will also be affected because of the imperative for diverting funds to efforts to fight Aids.

The prospects would, on the face of it, be enough to fill South Africans with dread. Their confidence, however, has been more profoundly shaken by the way in which the health ministry has dealt with Aids issues up to now. In 1995 the Aids programme of the National Progressive Primary Health Care Network collapsed, reportedly because of a lack of funding. Following that, extensive graft and shady dealing was revealed in the government's funding of *Sarafina 2*, a musical with a purported safe-sex message. As the government approached the end of its first term, nothing had been done to inspire a revival of confidence that public funds for the Aids threat were under judicious management.

CHAPTER ELEVEN

EDUCATION AND THE THREE Rs

Restructuring, rewriting and retrenchment

If you think education's expensive, try ignorance.
ADVERTISING SLOGAN, USA, 1988

The subject of education contains a simple and profound truth: the quality of a nation is a direct function of the quality of the education it provides. Education has been the key, not only to the success of the industrial nations of the West, but to the tiger economies of the Pacific Rim. All of the emerging countries who have enjoyed high achievement threw massive resources into education. And just as it is a recognized mark of quality to refer to someone as 'well educated', so the same is true for a nation.

In South Africa education takes the biggest slice out of the national budget, and quite rightly so. Yet this country has massive structural, organizational and attitudinal problems to overcome in education before its schools, colleges and universities can become the driving force of the nation's success.

EDUCATION PROFILE

From a global perspective, South Africa has a lot of catching up to do with the world. From a domestic perspective, South Africa has a lot of catching up to do with itself. For not only does South Africa significantly lag behind world norms in education, the gross disparities within South African education are the origin of the biggest division of its people.

A 1996 survey of half a million school pupils in forty-one countries, the third International Mathematics and Science Study, saw South Africa placed bottom in every category of the study. It said South African teenagers were dramatically under-equipped for the knowledge-based global economy. *The World Competitiveness Yearbook* in 1996 said of the forty-six countries it surveyed South Africa had the least number of students in science and technology-related courses. The South African Foundation for Research Development places the country eighteenth in a twenty-nation survey of levels of knowledge in natural and environmental sciences. The seventeen countries placed ahead of South Africa were all trade competitors. The brain drain has depleted South Africa's scientific and technological community, and the country's share of academic papers published in these fields in the world has been falling steadily since the 1980s.

In education, South Africans differ from one another as much as they differ from the rest of the world. Only 1 per cent of South Africans have a degree, and 3 per cent have a diploma of some kind. As many as 23 per cent have been educated only to standard five, and 25 per cent have had no education at all. But, after decades of discrimination, the greatest divide is predictably between black and white: 80 per cent of white children reach the final year of school, matric, while only 20 per cent of black children do. In 1994, for every R2.40 spent on educating a white child, only R1 was spent on a black child. This was after the gap had been closed from its 1983 ratio of R12 to R1. Predictably, again, while the matric pass rate for white pupils between 1990 and 1995 was 97 per cent, it was 42 per cent for black pupils. At university, after matriculation, the picture does not brighten: liberal arts courses are the most popular choices for both black and white students, although 43 per cent of black students make that choice, as opposed to only 23 per cent of whites. The next greatest number of black students, 18 per cent, choose to become teachers, while commerce is the second choice for whites, attracting 20 per cent of students. A remarkable 0.6 per cent of black students are interested in becoming engineers, as opposed to 8 per cent of white students. At graduation, although blacks make up 81 per cent of the school-children in the country, they eventually receive only half the number of degrees and diplomas awarded to whites entering the economy.

The cause of this appalling racial disparity is not a mystery. What Verwoerd, apartheid's architect, said when explaining his philosophy for Bantu education is well known. 'If the native in South Africa today in any kind of school in existence is being taught to expect that he will live his adult life under a policy of equal rights, he is making a big mistake . . . there is no place for him in the European community above the level of certain forms of labour . . .' From these words flowed a system of education tailored for suppression, endured by two generations of South Africans, a system that would tear the country apart in the student-led riots of the 1970s and 1980s, and a system that will damn the futures of millions of South Africans for at least a generation to come.

In 1996 that system ended, officially. Integrated schooling and equal curricula were instituted, and a campaign to transform the universities began. The questions that the coming years must answer are: how successfully will the methods that are being employed break the grip of the apartheid past? Will South Africans bring anything meaningful to the table in the knowledge-driven economy of today and tomorrow? Or will they be left fiddling glumly with the cutlery while the world talks business?

THE SCHOOLS

1 Re-writing dogma

Some time after Zambia became independent, its school history books were rewritten. Where, for example, they had said the Victoria

Falls were discovered by Livingstone, they were changed to read: Livingstone was the first European traveller to see the falls.

A similar broadening of perception, aligning it more closely with the way things really happened, will happen in South African schools. A new generation of pupils is to be spared the burden of learning the heroic minutiae of the lives of Afrikaner icons like Paul Kruger. The conventions that South African history began with the landing of Jan van Riebeeck, and that black South Africans made appearances in it only as warring tribes or distant influences on policy-making by the white government, are to be dispelled.

In a review by the *Sunday Times* of three new history textbooks attention is drawn to a crisp, four-line reference to van Riebeeck's landing in 1652, his founding of a ships' refreshment station, and a later reference to him as head of a household to which a Khoi woman is sent to learn Dutch.

The new textbooks, and a new, African-centric way of looking at African history, are to be introduced in 1998 as part of an ambitious new curriculum which will encompass many contemporary innovations in the learning process. What is less encouraging than news of new perspectives and new learning methods is that the new practices will depend on teachers' ability to teach them. This will entail a massive re-education of teachers, involving three of education's weakest areas – administration, teacher training and teacher quality. More about that shortly.

2 Neo-Bantu education

The integration of South African schools has been a very unequal thing. In cities and towns formerly all-white and mainly white schools opened to a mixture of children of the established white families of the district, the children of new black families in the district and the children of parents in domestic employment in the still predominantly white suburbs. This created a curious anomaly. Elsewhere in the world, it is common for a school to reflect the ethnic, social and economic status of the neighbourhood it is located in. Not so in the new South Africa – the child of a professional family could be sharing a school desk with the child of the possibly illiterate domestic worker employed by his or her parents. The outcome of this will either be a classless society or a social reshuffle over time in which schools will become more homogeneous reflections of their communities. Probably, a bit of both will happen, with more of the second than the first.

It is, however, in the majority of the country's schools, the black schools of the townships, where the greatest inequality is being perpetrated. This is because nothing has changed at these schools, nor is anything likely to for a very long time. Crippled by a history of underfunding, unrest, and underqualified and frequently incompetent staff, these schools can't simply stand up and walk. What's worse, the way they are now is the way they are going to stay for the foreseeable future. It's not a question only of money, even if the government had it, which it doesn't. A survey of matric results by the South African Institute of Race Relations' *Fast Facts* early in 1997 showed that in the twenty-five years in which the funding gap between white and black schools had closed from a ratio of eighteen to one, to three to one, the matric performance gap between white and black pupils had widened. (Incidentally, the group that has consistently out-performed all others, and by a wide margin, has been the matriculants of Indian schools – a minority group whose pupils make up only 2.4 per cent of the total. So, while the data show up racial disparities, they do not support racist conclusions.)

In the tenth issue of *Frontiers of Freedom*, another publication of the Institute of Race Relations, an unnamed lecturer who spent many years training black teachers in schools of the North West province recounts his experiences – dilapidated schools devoid of books and teaching equipment, pupils who travel long distances to school, arriving when they do and leaving when they please, the teachers who complain about 'the children of these nowadays', the chronic absenteeism among pupils, teachers and even principals, teachers who spend a school day basking in the sun, teachers who ignore timetables . . . The dismayed lecturer ends his report: 'There is a crisis of gargantuan proportions in the schools. Schoolchildren (one lost generation after another) are getting a raw deal. Who knows about it? What is being done about it? Is there any research to support anecdotes like mine? Am I unnecessarily pessimistic or critical? I really hope that these questions will reach someone, somewhere and that, somehow, something will be done about it.' One trusts the lecturer is not, as they say, holding his breath.

There will always be good schools and bad schools. That is true anywhere. But the differences are so pronounced here as to perpetuate the chasm between the haves and the have-nots, between those with a chance in life and those with none, and to increase the rate at which they are growing apart.

3 Private pedagogy

One of the most successful privatization exercises in the new South Africa is taking place without any involvement by the government. The number of private schools, according to Gavin Lewis, editor of the *RDP Monitor*, has grown from about 200 in 1990 to more than 500 at present. Listed companies in private education became one of the hottest stock items on the shares market in 1996.

When schools integration took place in that year, it included a ban on state schools setting means tests or aptitude tests, or any other method that could be used to deny a child entry to the school. Even inability on the part of parents to pay school fees could not be a bar to a child's acceptance. Against the background of racism in South African education, and the need to thwart resistance to integration on the part of individual schools, such provisions were necessary. The result, however, has been that children of greatly differing grounding in language and other basic skills equipping them for the learning experience have been melded together in the classrooms. A decline in the pace and quality of teaching and learning has been inevitable.

In turn this has created a demand for providers of excellence in education, hence the rise of private schools. There are many heart-warming success stories in the integration of state schools, and many thousands of children now have prospects that they didn't have before, but the overall decline in state schools is not over and, therefore, the rise in private schooling isn't either.

One of the country's leading private schools, Michaelhouse, advertised in the Sunday press early in 1997 its entrance examinations 'for boys wanting to enter Michaelhouse from state schools' – a tone resonant with an elitism that will soon lead to South Africa having a three-tier school system: private, state and township schools. Private schools will proliferate and represent 'the best'. As such, parents will make, and will increasingly be compelled to make, sacrifices to make the best available to their children. State schools will continue their great levelling. Their contribution will be inclusivity and the extension of opportunities to the previously deprived. When ideologues talk of the 'massification' of education, this will be what they mean. Township schools will remain the backwaters of education and will contaminate those who are immersed in them.

THE GREAT TEACHER EXODUS

Seen from an administrative point of view, there were two decisive imbalances in South African education after the 1994 election. They concerned the supply of teachers and the funding of provincial education departments by central government.

In general, it was held that there was an oversupply of teachers. In particular, there was an oversupply of teachers in urban areas, and an undersupply in rural areas. This over–under imbalance was reflected also between provinces with an urban preponderance, like Gauteng and the Western Cape, and those with a rural preponderance, like Northern or North West. Even more particularly, there was an oversupply of white, Afrikaans teachers, and a shortage of teachers in the disciplines vital for development – English, maths and science. Quite how the education department reconciled the proclaimed oversupply of teachers with its minister's separate claim that 50,000 classrooms were required to meet immediate needs, and 35,000 were needed to accommodate the 1.8 million additional six- to eighteen-year-olds who would flock to the schools by 2000, and with the Gauteng government's claim that it was short of 100 schools, is not clear. But this is a parenthetical argument and the question must be left open.

The second imbalance concerned funding. Measured in rands spent per schoolchild, some provinces were overfunded, and some were underfunded. The overfunded provincial education departments were in Gauteng, the Western Cape, the Free State and the Northern Cape. The underfunded departments were those of Eastern Cape, Northern Province, KwaZulu/Natal, Mpumulanga and North West. The divide roughly followed the one that separated the economically advanced provinces from those with greater numbers of lesser-developed inhabitants.

The government announced that it would bring funding parity to the nine provinces by 2000. One thing was clear, though: there wasn't going to be enough money to bring the underfunded five to the level of the overfunded four. There was only one way – cut the budgets of the overprivileged four. In bureaucracy's fondness for fancy language to adorn clumsy deeds, the exercise was to be known as 'top slicing'.

There was a tantalizing connection between the two issues – teachers' salaries are the biggest cost drain on the education budget – and the government yielded to the temptation to solve both problems at one foolhardy go. It opened the civil service retrenchment scheme to teachers. To get things going, it used a carrot and stick. The stick was a threat of 'redeployment', probably to remote rural schools. The carrot was the extravagant payouts, some even exceeding a million rands. It goes without saying that no-one enters the teaching profession with the expectation of becoming a cash millionaire in his or her working life, or even something approaching it. So 20,000 teachers gleefully applied for the retrenchment packages, and by October 1996, more than 17,000 had been granted. Hardest hit, of course, were Gauteng and the Western Cape – the latter losing about a third of its teachers.

Even commentators sympathetic to the government reacted angrily to what they called its great blunder. But there was a more sinister aspect to it. It is clear from statements by senior education officials that they knew that the teachers who would go would be the most experienced, who would be motivated by the biggest payouts and the greatest chances of re-employment elsewhere (the best were snapped up by private schools). The government also knew that about half of the country's teachers were deemed to have inadequate training, or none at all – and that these were the least likely to leave. The government, furthermore, never explained why it granted nearly three times the number of retrenchments that it needed to, or said at the beginning of the exercise it expected to. There is no other conclusion than that there was a stratagem, and it is perfectly transparent: the government saw an opportunity to undertake a massive affirmative action programme by promoting the lowly in the profession, and by eventually controlling the drafting of those who enter in the wake of the upwardly mobile. In this the government would simply copy its predecessor, which rewarded its voting constituency and bid for its future allegiance by bestowing civil service jobs, particularly in education, on the indigent and the inept along with the deserving.

Massification, restructuring, transformation and Africanization – all the clichés of the new order were brought together under one ideological and bureaucratic umbrella. It has been an exercise conceived in cynicism and short-sightedness that education in South Africa will not recover from in the next ten years, and which will send dull reverberations through the economy for even longer.

CENTRES OF YEARNING

The principle of 'top slicing' was earmarked also for the country's universities. Deep cuts will be inflicted on what are now known as the 'historically white' universities. These universities fought long battles under the banner of academic freedom to admit who they wanted and, to a great extent, defeated apartheid on their campuses long before it was vanquished from society at large. Ironically, they will now pay the highest price as resources are diverted to the 'historically black' universities, creations of apartheid and often disparagingly referred to as the bush universities.

The reassignment of resources has been couched in the terms of the call for the transformation and Africanization of tertiary education. Exchequer funding is one of the few levers of influence the government presently has on the universities. Having stated its intention to use it, the government feels that the universities themselves are not doing enough to transform and Africanize themselves.

The government is quite right, because no-one, not even the most fervent proponents of these goals, is quite sure what, in practice, they entail. Newspaper columns resound with thundering calls for transformation and Africanization in the universities. But they never say quite what these things are. The closest to something substantive is a Sasco (South African Students' Congress) suggested agenda. The list, replete with buzz-concepts, includes the 'governance structure' of universities and colleges, their 'democratization', the 'reconstruction of racist, sexist and generally problematic curricula', the alignment of institutions with national priorities as in producing graduates with the relevant skills for the RDP, and an improvement of student living conditions and staff working conditions.

Alongside this, the former vice-chancellor of Wits University, Professor Robert Charlton, nominated what he called the four daunting challenges faced by the country's institutions of higher learning. Reported by the Institute of Race Relations in its 1995/96 South Africa Survey, they are: shrinkage of resources as funds are diverted to other educational sectors, demand for places from inadequately prepared school leavers, growing numbers of students unable to pay fees or support themselves, and demands from students for 'democratization'.

The government has spoken firmly against the students' violent agitation on these issues, which has disrupted and even closed campuses. The government has left it abundantly clear, however, that its disagreement with the students is over methods, not goals. In compliance with this, the government has proposed greater involvement, via legislation, to hasten transformation.

One of the aims of transformation that is the most practical to implement is an increase in the number of black incumbents of senior academic and administrative posts. Early attempts at this at Wits have not, however, provided a propitious start – with controversies surrounding the credibility of candidates' curricula vitae, and a designated vice-chancellor, a South African who had risen to academic prominence in the USA, who had second thoughts about his appointment after it had been announced – and declined to take it up.

In the meanwhile, the government got to work and top sliced about R200 million off the budgets of the country's leading institutions. One of these universities' first forced economies was on student bursaries and loans . . . setting off a new cycle of strident demands for financial assistance.

In the face of this turbulence and uncertainty, the universities have experienced, unsurprisingly, an exodus of brain power as dispirited senior academics have taken up careers elsewhere. One among the near-household names of prominent liberal thinkers, Professor Charles van Onselen, wrote bitterly in *The Star* of one South African university that now spends more money on catering than it does on research, and another where unskilled manual workers earn more than junior lecturers.

The future of South Africa's universities does not call for deep divination – it is the same as that for hospitals and schools. The government will succeed, modestly, in its goal of greater opportunities for the masses through the extension and elevation of the previously underprivileged institutions . . . which will nevertheless not be able to provide candidates up to the requirements of globalization and world competition. The extension of opportunities, however, will be achieved at the expense of an overall levelling, and a decline of standards in the universities previously of the highest standing. This means an erosion of centres of excellence, and will open the way for the advent of private tertiary education, as in the case of schools. Once again, mechanisms of elitism will kick in and increasingly separate a shrinking class of the privileged from growing masses of the underdeveloped.

PART THREE

FUTURE OUTCOMES

CHAPTER TWELVE

ENDURING THE DELUGE

Daily life in future South Africa

Who controls the past controls the future. Who controls the present controls the past.

GEORGE ORWELL, 1949

Tuesday, 17 September 2002: 7.20 a.m.
It was late for the family still to be at breakfast. The electricity had failed four or five times during the night. Erwin Barnard had lain awake while his wife, Rita, and their children, Adrian and Lulu, slept. He had heard the electronic voice of the telephone answering machine in the study downstairs resetting itself each time. He heard, too, the muted chimes of the sound events written into the boot sector of Microsoft Pathways each time their computer repowered itself.

Electricity interruptions weren't frequent, but they weren't rare, either. Minor sabotage of suburban transformer units had started not long after the clashes in 1997 and 1998 between communities and the authorities over tariffs, non-payments and cut-offs. Individual consumers, and sometimes entire communities, would not pay their bills, and local councils would cut off their supply. There were protests and sporadic street battles, but the authorities soon gained the upper hand. Illogically, the defaulting consumers started sabotaging installations. Once these petty acts of destruction stopped making news, a hardened core of activists took their campaign for subsidized flat rates and debt write-offs into wealthy suburbs. The struggle of the poor would not advance until the rich shared their suffering, a spokesman for one of the community organizations had said.

As Erwin slipped back into sleep he forgot that the electronic alarm would now not go off at six. He was thinking, instead, that at the price of electricity these days it was almost a blessing when it got turned off. Electricity costs had soared because of the enormous political pressure to supply more townships and the myriad informal settlements that were springing up in urban areas. Existing consumers had to pay for this, just as paying customers – who accounted for about half of the electricity produced and supplied by the supply commission, Eskom – had to pay for the half that others didn't pay for . . . something an Eskom official on television had referred to roundaboutly as 'non-technical losses'. Eventually, it was the early light of the spring morning that woke him.

The mood at breakfast was subdued. The Barnards hadn't been in their townhouse long, and at times like this they missed their large dining-room, overlooking their private garden and pool. Rita was irritable because the power interruptions had scrambled a pre-timed e-mail transmission to her in the night. With Adrian and Lulu now thirteen and eleven, she had used her background in graphics and journalism to start an electronic DTP service. Clients – of whom she was getting an increasing number – would send her raw copy and data for house publications. She would write it up, edit it, and lay it out in electronic pages which would be e-mailed to the client, who would then distribute it on in-house terminals. From there, employees could print their own hard copies, if they wanted. Well, normally that's how it would work. Now she would have to get the lot re-sent at daytime rates. It was the pictures that made the transmission expensive.

Erwin hunched over a few printouts he had tagged from the

morning paper, which had come through OK before midnight. Normally, he would hold court over the news at breakfast – highlighting points of interest, comment on the day's issues, and challenge the others for their opinions. They would tease him, often, by rolling their eyes to the ceiling, or groaning when he began what they knew would be an expostulation on the state of the world. In reality, the children enjoyed the arguments and discussions over news events. Not today, though.

The issue that dominated the news didn't lend itself to interesting debate over breakfast. It was complicated. It had started with a Sunday report that the Malaysian-led consortium that had bought a stake in the South African communications parastatal, Telkom, was quietly canvassing international markets (local, too, but with less expectation of success) for a buyer for its share. The report said the consortium had become increasingly dismayed at its inability to initiate efficiency reforms from its minority platform and had accused its majority partners of 'timid management'. The consortium had apparently become disheartened at its failure to prod the utility corporation into a vibrant, profitable undertaking. That's what the Malaysians and Americans had thought they would be able to facilitate when their decision to buy in was made in the heady post-apartheid days.

The break-up of the ANC–Cosatu–SACP governing alliance two years ago, the formation of Anlap and the dramatic advances the new party had made since then had also led to the consortium becoming more cautious in its expectations for the utility's prospects and future operating environment.

The report went on to say that the consortium had told its principals that a 'contingency probability' of Anlap winning the 2004 election had to be reckoned with. If the principals wanted to liquidate the consortium's holding, it should be done before then – as the prospects of finding a buyer after an Anlap victory would 'diminish markedly'.

President Mbeki was furious. His minister of public enterprises had appeared on television's eight o'clock news on Sunday to make a gruff and scoffing dismissal of the report, and to deny there was any vestige of substance in it. The president himself had followed that up on Monday with a statement phrased in cold resolve, which revealed more than a hint of welcome for the opportunity the report had created for executive action. The report was a further and contemptible example of the determination in certain sections of the media to undermine nation building, President Mbeki's statement, released through the government news service to Sapa, said. The government could no longer allow the transformation of South Africa and the struggle of the poor for economic justice to be undermined by reactionary elements in the media. The government would now proceed with its Credo of Ethics and Code of Conduct for the media, which the government had reluctantly been contemplating for some time. No greater example than this of the necessity for such a code could or should be sought, the Mbeki statement said. Legislation for the creation of a national media council would be introduced as a priority when parliament reconvened, and the proposed council would begin drawing up the ethics and conduct code. President Mbeki gave the assurance that this would be done in a way that would not compromise the existence of a free and critical – but responsible – media, which was one of the pillars of South Africa's new democracy.

Sweet suffering mackerel, Erwin thought, what a rats' nest of ominous developments, bureaucrobabble and sophistry. What he found as curious as anything else was the language used. Mbeki had spoken of 'our journalists' – as in 'our journalists must be free to criticize us, when our leadership cadres justify that criticism, and can learn from it, but our nation needs to know that our journalists are with us in our struggle to transform South Africa'. In the same way, ever since the turbulence began on university campuses in the late nineties, Mbeki had admonished 'our students'. Erwin guessed that the unfamiliar employment of the pronoun was partly a ploy to create a sense of unity and to remind the recalcitrant of their higher purpose – but that it also reflected the African view of the indivisibility of the state, society, its elements, and their common undertaking.

The SABC had played its part in this affair. By this time the corporation had narrowed to broadcasting nigh-interminable sports, news in all the vernaculars, just slightly dated documentaries that it bought at a discount on the international television market, sitcoms that it got by the same means, and many, many studio-based current affairs shows and talk shows that were really vehicles for public information.

The latter dealt perpetually with mind-numbing topics that it was deemed the public should be informed on. When it came to government stories, the SABC was unfailingly on-side.

Last night's news had carried the Mbeki statement in full. This morning newscasters read long lists of organizations and prominent individuals that came out in support, apparently overnight, of Mbeki's intention to crack down on undemocratic reporting.

Newspapers like *The Star*, which Erwin had accessed electronically, were less concerned with the government's reaction to the original report, and more with the ramifications of privatization deals going into reverse . . . and the vein of anxiety that the Telkom consortium's views had opened up.

The Star and others like it – there was one that was available only through internet subscription – reckoned they were more or less effectively out of government reach. The world wide web was doing more for press freedom than the constitution.

Adrian and Lulu were ready for school. They piled into the lime-green Mitsubishi Amigo when Erwin pulled it out of the garage. At the start of several such trips they had talked about how the housing park they now lived in represented a return of the village concept. It was walled, like a medieval town, and guarded. There was only one gate where one could get in or out. There was a crèche. Some of the children of junior school-going age were being home educated, but this was a controversial practice, favoured only by a minority. There was a Depot & Agency, through which one could order household supplies like groceries and where one could leave items for outside services like dry cleaning and laundry. The trip to the corner café, so familiar in Erwin's youth, was now something well and truly of the past. People just didn't like leaving where they lived. Apart from going to work and school, there was little reason to – the housing park had lawns, a gym, a pool, two squash courts and two tennis courts.

As the three Barnards left the park in the Amigo, they drove past the manager's office and Erwin remembered he had to attend a residents' meeting there that night to validate a new sheaf of contracts between the park and others – like servicers of the Depot & Agency, gardeners, maintenance and a new refuse-removal proposal that had the novelty of the removers offering to pay for the contract while replacing the recyclers at the same time. One of the rules of the park, to maintain control of who came and went, was that residents had to use contracted service firms rather than hiring their own plumbers, painters, gardeners and the like. It was a security measure.

The park, comfortably located in the northern suburban belt of Johannesburg, was one of the first and most appealing of its kind. As an advance on the cluster-housing concept that had come to dominate the housing market in the early nineties, it had spawned many imitators, and would still many more. It was the way housing trends were going.

Erwin felt they were lucky to get it. More specifically, they were lucky to sell their regular, stand-alone house in order to get into the new, more secure, set-up – as much of a wrench as it was to leave all that space and privacy. Prices for homes like the one they had left had fallen to an all-time low, and they'd only got what they paid for it ten years before. It was only because of the effort they had put into the garden and outdoor living and entertainment areas that a sale had happened relatively easily . . . plus the fact that Vusi Khumalo had always wanted the place.

On Sundays around the braai, as the junior Khumalos joined the little Barnards in gay abandon in the pool and climbing the big willow, Vusi had often said – wielding the disarming charm with which he always lanced through social and racial delicacies – that as he and Erwin were at the same management level at JCN International, the Khumalos should now live like the Barnards. Well, that's the way it worked out. Except, you could say, the Khumalos now lived like the Barnards used to live.

Vusi and Erwin were both thirty-nine, and they were both marketing managers at JCN. The marketing portfolio had been divided between them: Erwin was designated 'marketing: sales' and Vusi was 'marketing: media and planning'. Erwin ran the sales force, and Vusi attended think-tanks and liaised with the ad agency. Vusi was hip to the difference – mainly that Erwin carried the responsibility for the marketing department's bottom line. He often joked that he was the post-apartheid equivalent of the token Afrikaans oomie. He was referring to a notorious apartheid-era stratagem. Indian traders established businesses in white towns by applying for their trading licences in the name and person, usually, of an elderly

Afrikaner . . . who would then spend his days sitting vacantly on a chair at the business, as its nominal owner, while the action swirled around him. Erwin often thought that Vusi was taking a lot more insidious stress than people realized.

Adrian and Lulu would be dropped at the mall. The private school they attended was on the top two floors of the office tower that rose above the shops. It was an unusual place for a school, sure, but it made sense from a number of perspectives. One of those was that office space was still greatly oversupplied and could be got for surprisingly low rentals.

They had stuck it out at their suburban state school for some years in the late nineties. It had quickly become a mixed proposition of children from widely differing social strata and backgrounds. Erwin and Rita had felt, though, that the schools were the crucibles of a new society and that opting out of the process would be to leave their small role in history unfilled. In the end, the nearby low-cost, high-density development (part of the 'densification' of the suburbs) had tipped the social . . . and the educational . . . quality scales at the school; and when the Aids-children issue became part of the mix, Erwin and Rita decided history could get stuffed.

So, school at the mall. Erwin didn't like the ring of it, but he had to admit it was the best option. For example, today, Lulu had to have her teeth seen to. It would be done there, while Adrian would start his homework in the library (but would probably play video games, what could you do?). Erwin had withdrawn from the medical aid fund he had initially been a member of. He preferred to build up his own fund. He paid his national health insurance, as he had to after resigning from the private fund, but he had never called on the government scheme. Afterwards, Adrian and Lulu would go home on the housing park's micro-bus that ran between the park and the mall four times a day.

Before they reached the mall, they had to get through an intersection they all hated. A concentration of beggars, window washers, poster men and hawkers hung around this crossing. As their numbers had grown, so had the competition among them, likewise the aggression. About six months ago a group of about five had stormed the Amigo. A fight broke out as they reached the vehicle. A knife flashed in a hand sticking from a ragged cuff. It went for the face of the washer, which was framed in the window his dirty rag was already wiping grime on to.

The incident had made a deep impression on the children, especially Lulu. Long after Erwin thought they had forgotten it, about two weeks ago, Lulu had said as they passed through the intersection: 'Dad, what was it that came out of the man's eye?'

Tuesday, 17 September 2002: 8.10 a.m.
Zama Mzilikaze leant his back against the corrugated tin sheet of his uncle Oscar's shanty. The tin was still cold but the early morning sun was starting to warm Zama. He was used to rising early, but not to the amount of sitting around he was doing lately. It seemed especially bad because he was only nineteen years old. If he had been back home now, where the Natal escarpment folded into gentle hills and long, deep valleys, he might have been on his way to the country school he occasionally attended; and that would have been after he had tended his father's few head of cattle, and had done some chores around the clan's homestead.

Actually, there had been too many chores to do around the kraal. That was a big part of his decision to leave two years ago. His mother was not his father's most important wife, and their mud-walled house was furthest from his father's. Yet the other grown-up sons, closer to his father, the induna of the kraal, had all left to live in the city. Their burden then fell on him. It wasn't fair.

He hadn't been going to school much – partly because of the chores, partly because his father wasn't there, anyway, during the week, and partly because nothing much happened at school.

He was eleven when the big election took place in 1994. He remembered that time well. There had been a lot of trouble at the school before the election, and after it there had been an air of expectation. Nobody ever said quite what they were waiting for, but everyone knew they were waiting. The months grew into years. Things stayed the same, and from time to time there was trouble, just as there had been before. Zama went to school sometimes, and sometimes he didn't.

When he was sixteen, the government had sent three new teachers to the school and two new classrooms were built. For the first time there was a desk for everyone. The new teachers said it was the law that everyone had to come to school every day, from Monday to Friday. Zama's mind spun as he grappled with his yearning and his ambitions. School every day, with only the young boys at the kraal to help him with his duties there. It wasn't an attractive thought. Especially when the really attractive thought was following the older boys to the city. Zama had been dreaming of that. It seemed the time had come to act.

His father was reluctant to give his blessing – but after having given it to his other sons he could not, in fairness, withhold it from Zama. It was only then that Zama revealed the secret he had been nurturing. He had a plan for showing himself not only equal to his brothers who had gone ahead of him, but eventually better than they were. He would not, he said, go to Durban as his brothers had. He would seek out ezinkulu, the big opportunities in Egoli – Johannesburg, the city of gold.

The announcement provoked some of the reaction that Zama had hoped for. His mother and other elders made perfunctory attempts to dissuade him, but he could tell they admired his boldness. Word of Zama's desires was sent to Uncle Oscar, and before long there was a reply: Zama would find a place to sleep in Uncle Oscar's house.

The city proved to be a place that was both thrilling and terrible to Zama. It was thrilling to be so close to the things he desired – cars, clothes and fashionable girls. It was not so easy to say exactly why the city was also terrible. What Zama could say, and what he had rapidly learned, was that greeting and befriending a stranger was not something that happened as freely and as easily as Zama was accustomed to. People seemed to be readier to regard one as an enemy than as a friend. Suspicion came before respect among new acquaintances. People were more concerned with what could be taken than with what could be given.

Zama's first venture into earning money came after he met Themba, who came from a place not far from the one Zama had left. Themba showed Zama the life of a tip man. The place of the tip was very busy. Enormous lorries would rumble through the gate, tip the great loads they carried, then roar away for more. They left little of value, though. Themba said that the 'recycle' took all the paper, tin and glass that used to provide an income for the tip people. In any event, Themba made it clear that he looked down on the people who scavenged on the tip itself. He and a group of others jealously protected their claim to a fenced-off portion of the tip where, in the late afternoons and on Saturdays and Sundays, the larnies would come in their cars pulling small trailers, and the small trucks they called bakkies. That, Themba said, was where they 'made business'.

Besides the branches, leaves and cut grass that formed the bulk of what the larnies dumped, they tipped goods that amazed Zama. There were chairs, tables, toys, bicycles and many other things that could be repaired and put into use again. That's what their business was.

There were a number of reasons why they didn't stick to it. No-one bought the decrepit pieces they lined up next to the road leading to the tip, and getting more than the occasional item back to Freedom Park, the shanty camp where they lived, proved impractical. When they did sell anything, the sale seldom gave them enough for food for a day or two. Zama's clothes became shabby, and although Uncle Oscar didn't say anything, Zama knew he was expected to contribute more food to the household than the bits he did.

The main reason they stopped going to the tip, however, was Ladypeace Rabotapi. She was the sort of woman that Zama both desired and feared. To him, she epitomized the attractions of city life. He was entranced by her glamour, but intimidated by her worldliness. There was also the fact that she was the girlfriend of Spokes Molapi to take into account before a country boy like Zama entertained any foolish thoughts. Spokes led a gang of high-rollers, and people said he got his name from the instrument he favoured for persuading others to adopt his point of view, or to get rid of 'problems'.

Zama could remember clearly that first time that Ladypeace spoke directly to him. He was sitting right where he was sitting now, morosely contemplating another pointless day at the tip with Themba. He watched Ladypeace pick her way through the debris in such a way as not to damage her white high-heeled shoes. She paused at the edge of the pitted surface that served as a road for those, like Uncle Oscar, who had vehicles. Then she turned to him and said that he and Themba were like kraal dogs who fed on what others threw away, and that neither of them would ever find a girl . . . certainly not one like her.

Zama burned with shame for many days. The truth of Ladypeace's words taunted him, and he never went back to the tip. Gradually, his shame turned to anger as the failure of his dream of coming to the city made itself apparent to him, accompanied by the realization that he couldn't go home with nothing to relate but humiliation and defeat. His anger deepened in the time that followed, as he moved through a succession of odd jobs. The more he encountered the larnies, whose cars he washed and whose gardens he tended, the more resentful of them he became. The black larnies and the white alike, all treated him with the same distance and disdain.

Once, things had appeared to change for the better. Uncle Oscar had got him work as a warehouse packer at the company for which Uncle Oscar was a driver. It was a real job and the weekly wage made Zama feel as if a great heaviness had been lifted from him. He threw himself into the work and, as Uncle Oscar had advised, feigned ignorance of the many schemes and subterfuges by other workers to get goods out of the warehouses without the knowledge of the bosses in the office block.

Just when everything seemed to be going along fine, it turned out it wasn't. The bosses called the workers into the courtyard one day and told them that there were 'too many problems' with the warehouse. They, the bosses, could not manage the warehouse any longer and their long discussions with the union representatives had not brought forth any plans that worked. A new company, that employed only operators of computers, would take over the warehouse. The existing staff would be paid off.

Zama felt the heaviness return, and the anger – only, now, both were greater. Then, one day, Zama's life changed in an hour. He was returning home through the maze of shanties from an exhilarating bout of the Zulu martial art of stick fighting. Learning the art was a rite of passage into manhood and here, in this life of broken dreams, it was something that Zama clung to.

He turned around the corner of a shanty home, heard a choked cry and saw Ladypeace Rabotapi in the grip of the man behind her. Ladypeace was being dragged towards the doorway of the shanty, in which another man stood, laughing. Ladypeace's skirt was rucked high on her hip and the white of her panty slashed across her dark flesh.

Zama swung the fighting stick with the knobbed end, which he was carrying in his right hand, in a practised arc as he accelerated two long strides into striking distance of Ladypeace's assailant. The blow felled the man. In another two quick steps Zama was before the second man, who stood as frozen as the expression on his face. The blow to his forehead dropped him, too. Neither man had uttered a sound. Zama surveyed their motionless bodies for just a moment, then swiftly struck a powerful second blow to the head of each, so that the matter would be ended there. When he raised his eyes to Ladypeace, she was already regaining her composure, smoothing down her skirt. When she had done that, she looked at him for a long moment before turning and walking towards the road.

Zama's heart was still pounding as Spokes Molapi's car pulled up, and Ladypeace got in. The discussion in the car quickly became animated. Zama saw Spokes erupt, and reach for the door to get out. Ladypeace caught his arm and spoke to him earnestly. Spokes listened. Ladypeace gestured towards Zama, and Spokes gazed at Zama while he listened to Ladypeace a little longer. Then the car sped off with a clatter of stones hitting its underside.

That's how Zama got into Spokes Molapi's gang.

Here he was now, letting the early morning sun warm him after the cold of the night in the tin home. The wall he was leaning against was still cold, but Zama no longer felt it. His mind was on other things.

After proving himself in Spokes's gang as a tough and loyal fighting man, and later having accompanied some of Spokes's men on a few raids on larnies' homes, Spokes had led him to believe he was ready for bigger things. This was to be the day that he would graduate into the top rank of men around Spokes, although Spokes had not told him what was in store.

When Spokes pulled up in his car, there were two other men with him.

Tuesday, 17 September 2002: 8.30 a.m.

Erwin was on his way to a downtown appointment at the new banking mega-headquarters. The headquarters had been part of a brave bid to revitalize the city centre, but it had not yet amounted to more than an island of development in a sea of decay. Erwin was driving easily, taking care to stay clear of the hawkers who spilled off the pavements and on to the edges of the street. He had plenty of time, and he had parking prearranged in the building's cavernous basements. In fact, if you didn't have parking, you couldn't go. That's the way it was.

It was time for the news. Erwin turned on the radio, catching the top story.

> The South African Chamber of Business has dismissed as 'unrealistic' a call by the African National Labour Party for a two-phase working week. A SACOB statement says the additional burden of costs and administration that Anlap's proposal would place on business would neutralize any benefits it may have. The proposal was nothing more than 'ideological pie in the sky', according to SACOB. Anlap's job-sharing plan was unveiled at a weekend workshop of its mass employment subcommittee, and is the first major initiative of its National Rescue Strategy, announced at the party's formation in May 2000. The mass employment subcommittee called on the government to legislate a forty-eight-hour working week in which every unionized job in the economy would be shared by two workers, each working a twenty-four-hour week. The legislation should include a minimum-wage provision to minimize loss of earnings to existing workers. According to the Anlap subcommittee, the job-sharing programme would reduce unemployment in South Africa to international norms. The increase in business's wage bills would be compensated by increased productivity in the longer working week, and by the benefits of near-full employment and a stable workforce.

The bulletin may be right, Erwin thought. It may be the first concrete policy proposal of the new party, but Anlap had been sending shock waves through the country since its inception on Workers' Day two years ago. The first great shock, of course, was the party's formation, which came along with the split of the ANC–Cosatu–SACP governing alliance. Since then the political initiative had very clearly shifted to the new party spearheaded by Cosatu and the SACP. It had the ANC on the defensive. And the ANC had plenty to be defensive about. It was vulnerable.

Its overall vulnerability was the result of the unchanged circumstances of the masses. The ANC under Mbeki had edged up its delivery on houses and education – but its efforts to publicize its achievements had seemed ever more like a propaganda exercise of statistics against an unmistakable impression that things had got worse, not better. Unemployment continued to grow as the economy failed to break out of the grip of jobless growth. While houses went up in patches, the homeless continued to sprawl in growing shanty camps on the peripheries of the country's cities. As central, provincial and local government sank deeper into a morass of declining skills, shrinking finances and endemic corruption and inefficiency, more and more people were ending up with less and less . . . despite the efforts of the government.

There had always been two South Africas, and they had always existed side by side. The new South Africa had, quite rightly and quite admirably, set out to embrace them in a single national identity. It had accelerated the inclusion of the rural, the poor, the homeless and the unemployed in a unified vision of South African society. But they were, in reality, separate entities with different interests and needs, and they required different methods of government. They were now worlds in collision.

It wasn't hard to see why Anlap's aggressive rhetoric had the appeal it did. That appeal was visibly translating into political support. Soon after Anlap's formation, the Pan-Africanist Congress had concluded a 'working arrangement' with the new party. Then, in a major blow for the ANC, the South African National Civic Organization, the hard-core leftover of the Mass Democratic Movement of the anti-apartheid struggle, known by its acronym SANCO, had sought and been granted 'permanent observer status' on all Anlap structures.

The truth was that there was a clear drift to socialism. It had looked so impossible in the Nineties, when the triumph of liberal democracy had seemed a full stop in history. Perhaps we were foolish, Erwin mused, to think then that nothing lay beyond that full stop. Whatever the outcome, Erwin reckoned, he wouldn't like to be in President Mbeki's shoes right now . . . nor in the time between now and the next election, which would have to be in early 2004 at the latest.

> . . . mass action in Johannesburg on Monday. A spokesman for the National Union of Jobless Workers said the union expected

40,000 unemployed people to join the march to ANC headquarters. The spokesman said the unemployed masses had lost patience with the government and the aim of the march was to put pressure on the government to accede to Anlap's two-phase working-week proposal. Police said the NUJW had not yet applied for a permit for the planned demonstration.

A union of the unemployed. It was almost a contradiction in terms, the way Erwin figured it. But if you thought about it, it had to come. The International Labour Organization had said a few months ago that workers without jobs were as much a part of a national economy as any other group, and could not be overlooked. It was true in a way, of course, but the ILO probably had to find a way of justifying what it had called its 'infrastructure assistance' to the NUJW. Cosatu had played a decisive role in helping the NUJW get on its feet, and in canvassing support for it. This in itself was unusual because, on the face of it, organized workers had competing interests with organized people who wanted the jobs. However, the overriding interest of Anlap in consolidating the support of unemployed voters had transcended the theoretical clash of interests.

Unions, at the best of times, Erwin thought, were a problematic counterweight in a free-enterprise economy. But this one, outside the structural limitations of the workplace, was something else altogether. The coalescence of the unemployed, numbering millions, into an organized force was any capitalist's, any economy's, and any government's nightmare come true.

. . . National Party's federal council says Mr F.W. de Klerk will not be a candidate for the leadership of the National Democratic Party at its founding congress in November. The NP's leader, Mr Hernus Kriel, will be the only candidate from NP ranks. Mr Kriel told our correspondent after the federal council meeting he hoped the NDP would retain Mr de Klerk's current NP status as 'ambassador at large' in recognition of Mr de Klerk's historic contribution to the realignment of South African politics. Mr Kriel said the NP's decision to disband before the forthcoming congress did not mean the end of the National Party's political role in South Africa. The principles of the party would be embodied in the NDP.

The confirmation that Mr Kriel will stand for the leadership of the new party brings the number of candidates to three. The others are the Democratic Party's Mr Tony Leon, who announced his candidacy in April, and the New South Africa Movement's Mr Roelf Meyer, who announced his shortly afterwards. The Inkatha Freedom Party has not yet announced its intentions with regard to the new party. Observers say although the IFP has participated in discussions on the formation of the NDP, it may yet decide to retain its identity and concentrate on regaining power in KwaZulu/Natal.

Boy, oh boy, Erwin thought. It took the arrival of Anlap to kick the existing opposition parties out of their rut. Even then, it was like watching dodgem cars as they swerved away from one another, then crashed into the inevitability of their merging, then swerved away again. Still, if there ever was any doubt that political activity to the right of the ANC was a side show, the gladiatorial entry of Anlap to the main tent had dispelled it.

How alike, Erwin and everyone else had thought, were the fates of de Klerk and Gorbachev. After a rise to prominence as agents of the inevitable, both had lapsed into irrelevance. Neither was carried forward by the events he had unleashed to reap their rewards. Perhaps the same was true for political parties. Perhaps the ANC's appointment with history was to bring about democracy in South Africa, then, after an interval, to be brushed aside by its consequences. It wouldn't be the first time the course of a revolution had run this way.

In recent years one had heard less and less from the National Party, particularly after de Klerk's great miscalculation in ousting Meyer and after that large swing of opposition voters away from the Nats to Meyer's group and the Democratic Party in the election at the end of 1998. Apart from the Meyer-ousting fiasco, one of the main reasons had been the outpouring of revulsion and horror at the exposure of the underside of National Party government in the hearings of the Truth and Reconciliation Commission. The loss of morale in the party and among its followers that went along with the revelations more or less sealed the NP's fate. At the NP's 1999 congress de Klerk had stepped down as leader, saying Hernus Kriel needed the authority of the leadership to forge a new alliance in opposition politics. Kriel had been uncontested as new leader because he was the only remaining Nationalist with any kind of power base.

The IFP had kept to form in its politics of permanent brinkmanship. It was just that it mattered less than before. Soon after the 1998 election, in which the IFP lost KwaZulu/Natal to the ANC, Buthelezi had left the stage of national politics to consolidate the IFP in its home province. Buthelezi's retreat from prominence, combined with his advancing age and declining enthusiasm, was accompanied by a winding down of the IFP.

What was most noticeable about the formation of the new opposition party and its prospective leadership, Erwin thought to himself, was that which its participants were leaving unsaid. The ambitions of attracting meaningful black support – even a potential black leader – had come to nothing. True enough, the new black elite, with its aspirations to Western ways, had been a potential recruiting field. That elite, however, was interested more in the rewards of free enterprise and liberal democracy than in ways of promoting and protecting those philosophies. When the new elite was interested in politics, it was canny enough to know where the power lay – and that certainly wasn't in opposition politics to the right of the government.

> . . . controversial housing scheme has been put on hold, according to a spokesman for the provincial government. The R72 million housing project for provincial ministers and senior officials was disclosed by the sole DP member of the legislature, Mrs Sylvia Delaney, who slammed the . . .

The patterns of politics repeat themselves. Erwin recalled a similar provincial government project some years ago, also unabashedly for top government and party members. Sooner or later the distinction between the party and the government becomes blurred. This had become very much more the case after Mandela. The patriarch's departure had taken with it his restraining and principled influence. The niceties of democratic behaviour had dimmed commensurately. To make things worse, Mbeki, who was equally principled but without the same pervasive influence, had terrible political pressures on him to reward the party faithful and corral the wavering with patronage. The pressures had been brought on by the looming split in the governing alliance (when it was looming, that is) and afterwards as Anlap had started huffing and puffing at the the ANC's house of straw.

> . . . the green paper will set out the government's proposals for formalizing private security services. At a press conference last night the minister of safety and security said the government accepted that the police could no longer combat crime alone. Private-sector security firms could form an effective bridge between communities and the police, if those firms were properly regulated. The concentration of private security services in affluent suburbs would allow the police to redeploy their resources to areas where they were presently lacking. The minister said the green paper would propose standards of training and capacity that security operators, who would be registered by the government, would have to comply with. Among the far-reaching provisions contained in the green paper will be limited powers of arrest and detention for registered firms. The detention provision would enable private operators to hold suspects, under certain conditions, until they could be absorbed by the currently overloaded justice system, according to the minister.

That's some admission to make, Erwin thought. It was another of those instances that left one undecided whether to be pleased the government had the good sense to concede, or to be disturbed at the underlying implication. Whatever. What it really entailed was another escalation in living costs – private services that were worth having would become much more expensive.

The growth in crime in recent years had provoked some communities to set up privately funded suburban police stations. Residents of a district would band together to rent business premises for the cash-strapped SA Police Service, and try to augment staffing with volunteers drawn from the residents. The stations, though, fell under SAPS management and control. That's where the system broke down. It merely tapped into the heart of the problem – the crisis of policing was more one of efficiency than resources. At least, that's what the experts said. Erwin had read just recently that the number of calls to the Johannesburg flying squad emergency number had increased from 2,000 to 3,000 a day in 1997 to the present 4,000 to 5,000. As unbelievable as it might seem, about 1,000 of the daily calls then were crank calls and 'only' about 700 were genuine emergencies. The balance was made up of unnecessary calls, like people seeking information. By now the crank calls had doubled along with the real ones. The flying squad then had about a dozen cars; now they had nearly three times that number, but the situation was still hopeless.

In the meantime the private security industry had burgeoned. No surprise there. But it had become chaotic. Where there was a quick buck to be made, standards fell. Subscribers to security firms had no guarantee of an effective service. Creating a parastatal police force was the logical step. And where subscription to a private firm had once been a security luxury for those who could afford it, it was now a costly necessity . . . and due to become even more so.

> A raid on a Port Elizabeth used-car dealership that police suspected of dealing in stolen vehicles has yielded an unexpected bonanza. Police found documents linking the dealership to a freight company and a prominent export business. A police spokesman said the dealership, the freight company and the export house conducted conventional business as a front for a car-theft syndicate. The syndicate bought and sold stolen vehicles through the dealership, and the freight company, working in tandem with the exporter, transported vehicles in pantechnicons and by cargo aircraft to neighbouring countries. From there luxury vehicles were sent to overseas syndicates. Police arrested staff and the managing directors of the three companies. Further arrests of customs officials working in cahoots with the syndicate are expected.

'Arrested the managing directors.' Huh. Those guys, no doubt, were members of the golf club and of the PTA. The increasing sophistication of crime, the rise in white-collar crime, and the encroachment of the syndicates was, in a way, worse than muggers in balaclavas. Because it didn't only blur the distinction between business and crime, it eroded the old-fashioned, visible difference between good and bad, between what you could believe in and what you couldn't. The respectable businessman had become a suspect notion. At the very least, 'respectable' and 'businessman' were words that no longer automatically went together. It was some criminologist who said on TV, Erwin recalled, that increasing employment and expanding the economy wouldn't necessarily reduce crime – because it would create more opportunities for dishonesty and institutional crime. Erwin had scoffed at the sophistry at the time. Maybe the criminologist had a point.

> A court date has been set for the civil action between two multinational corporations operating in South Africa, in what has become known as the Schreidberg kidnap case. The outcome of the case is expected to be a landmark in anti-crime insurance in South Africa. The action flows from the kidnapping of fourteen-year-old Stefan Schreidberg, son of Rador International senior executive Martin Schreidberg, in February. Rador International insured its executives and their families in South Africa. After Stefan was kidnapped while walking home from a regular Saturday afternoon soccer game, Rador International paid the ransom before the police were notified of the crime. Rador said afterwards it did not have the necessary confidence in the police and its first concern was the safety of the boy. Rador said it was imperative that international companies such as itself demonstrated that a priority was placed on the safety of their personnel, who took on greater risks in postings to South Africa. When Rador claimed the value of the ransom from its insurers, Amalgamated Life contested the claim – saying that paid ransoms fell outside the terms of the policy agreement between the two corporations. The case will be heard on 10 January 2003.

Erwin thought about his own family. Adrian was only a year younger than the Schreidberg boy. We did the right thing, he thought, moving into the housing park and selecting the school in the mall, even if it means our lives are lived in segmented locales, like hopping from one island of safety to another. The Barnard family insurance now also had a provision for kidnapping. Erwin would have to check the specifications. The outcome of the test case between Rador and Amalgamated would set a precedent, of course. He would have to consult with his broker after judgement was given.

It was a recent thing, kidnapping. Until two years ago it had been a form of crime that South Africa was free of – unlike other countries in similar circumstances, such as Brazil and India. It had to come, Erwin thought, because of two of the characteristics of crime: crime had fashions and trends like anything else; and it always, sooner or later, sought out the vulnerable. It targeted society's weak spots. We've been raping our children for so long, it was only a matter of time before we thought of stealing them from one another, he thought bitterly.

One could see the trends of crime in vehicle theft, for example. In the Seventies and Eighties your car would be stolen at night, or some other time when there was no-one around. Then came immobilizers and other anti-theft devices. That led to hi-jacking, whereby thieves had to steal your car while you were in it. Then came electronic tracking devices, so thieves had to steal you along with your car to prevent you activating the tracking alarm. Even so, hi-jacking became a tougher problem for criminals, and they had to look for new fields of endeavour.

Kidnapping was the obvious choice. It was the next point of vulnerability.

> A commission of inquiry will be set up to probe the terror attack on commuters at Tembisa railway station earlier this month, according to a spokesman for the minister of transport. Fourteen people died when unknown gunmen opened fire on a crowded platform shortly before 6 a.m. Three of the dead were crushed when they fell on to the tracks in front of an oncoming train in the pandemonium that broke out during the firing. Twenty-seven were wounded, and eleven are still in hospital. The ministry spokesman said the terms of the commission would include investigation of three other apparently motiveless attacks this year.

What's this all about, Erwin agonized? What was so vexing, so damnable, about this kind of violence was that there wasn't any discernible explanation for it.

True enough, it had happened in South Africa before. It happened in the first four years of the Nineties, the time between the decision to create a democracy and its realization. Erwin remembered the notorious drive-by shootings in the townships. At the time they, too, appeared to be without explanation. Later it turned out that it was a shadowy third force of state agents militating against black majority rule, hoping to tip the scales of a country suspended in uncertainty into anarchy. That would have forced the state to halt the political process, or so the perverse reasoning seemed to go.

In the Mandela era this sort of violence fell into abeyance. The sporadic exceptions were fitful right-wing attacks, and political clashes – usually in rural communities – where local politics were decided with machetes, stolen handguns and AK-47s.

Now the apparently motiveless violence was looking like making a comeback. Apart from the absence of a visible reason, the common characteristics were that the victims were always black, and the attacks always took place in poor workers' communities where there were high levels of unemployment.

So who was doing it, and why? Could it be right-wing extremists using black surrogates, with the same aim as before. It didn't seem likely. In fact it didn't make sense. There was no white state to intervene. Could it simply be symptomatic of a society destabilized by deprivation, poverty, unemployment and ignorance? Was it nothing more than an outgrowth of the phenomenal levels of personal violence, like rape, family murder and mindless assault? Could it be some form of factionalism, fought out on a social terrain far from Erwin's ability to grasp its reasons? Or was it something more sinister? Could it be extremists following the cruel dictum of revolution to begin by 'conscientizing the masses' – meaning that ordinary people had to be shocked out of their complacent acceptance of their lot, and that terror was the means of doing so? Did the extremists believe that sacrifices among their own had to be made for the greater good of the upliftment of the masses? If so, who were they? Whose undercover revolution was this, and what did it have in mind?

Was it possible that die-hard liberationists believed that by terrorizing and destabilizing Anlap's potential constituency they would, in effect, pave the way for Anlap to present itself as the saviour? Then again, did it matter? These incidents occurred, made headlines, and then life went on.

. . . in economic news: the receiver of revenue says the inflow of late individual tax returns has risen sharply in the last thirty days. This follows the successful prosecution in July of Roger Miller, chairman of the Citizens' Tax Reform Movement, CITREM. The organization, which campaigns for the lowering of individual taxes, launched a boycott of Pay As You Earn tax returns earlier this year. A spokesman for the receiver's office said more than half of the outstanding returns were expected to be sent in by the end of the year.

Four years ago attention was focused on the non-payment of rates and services, mostly in the townships and in disadvantaged communities. No-one was aware at the time, Erwin chuckled, that a middle-class revolt was already in its early stages. The true state of affairs was partly obscured by conditions in the government's revenue offices. They were badly understaffed, and clumsy management of affirmative action had brought skills levels down markedly. Behind the scenes, however, there was a massive underpayment of taxes, and disastrous undercollection by the receiver. Inevitably, it all came to light – and it was about then that CITREM came to the fore.

The organization argued that middle- and upper-bracket taxpayers were just not getting any value for their tax rands. There was little effective policing, and education and health services were rapidly being privatized. Local governments, usually dominated by the ANC, were reassigning resources to low-cost housing and other social upliftment priorities. The focus was necessarily shifted from the benefits and services that the middle and upper classes had taken for granted – suburban road maintenance, beautification, refuse removal, suburban parks, sports facilities, libraries and the like.

And so, what had started as a low-level civil disobedience manifestation – a rates boycott in upper-income Sandton, and a refusal to pay TV licences – had drifted upwards, and emerged as a resistance to paying tax. CITREM's first campaign had been to raise awareness that middle-income South Africans were among the most severely taxed classes in the world. CITREM made much of the fact that where the government had fallen down on collecting corporate taxes and customs and excise, the full force of government avarice had descended on the ones who couldn't get away – salary earners.

Now the chairman of the reform movement (a polite way of saying revolt, of course) had been tried and given a suspended sentence. It was meant to be a symbolic gesture, naturally, and the government had won this round. But the way Erwin saw it, it wouldn't make the underlying problem go away.

> . . . minister of finance. He said the report by the parliamentary finance committee that recommended the raising of VAT to 22 per cent was merely a working document. He said the government would take the impact on the economy, balanced against the urgency of accelerated upliftment, into account – as well as consult with all stakeholders – before what he described as 'the next increase in VAT'.

Well, there was obviously a connection between these last two reports. In the last five years, despite government promises and some well-meant attempts, the tax bureaucracy had remained a cumbersome mess. Erwin wondered what the result would be if the cost of collecting tax was compared with what was actually collected.

Over the last quarter of a century, as tax collection had become increasingly chaotic and inefficient, and as corruption and fraud had bitten deeper, successive governments had responded in the worst and most predictable way – they had sought new and higher taxes in bids to maintain their fiscal base. They did so until the stifling effect of taxes ranked as one of the economy's big three problems, along with crime and dismal productivity.

Sooner or later, Erwin reckoned, it was inevitable that the government would be forced into a simpler and more effective way of collecting taxes. That way was sales tax, VAT. This tax has two great virtues, particularly for a government in fiscal distress – it is collected by the economy's merchants rather than by the government's bureaucrats, and it embraces everyone, including the recalcitrants and the informal operators. The simple reason is that the tax is paid each time something is bought. It taxes the spending of money, as opposed to the earning of money.

Accordingly, the shift to VAT as the government's tax lifeboat began in the Mandela era. The ANC's first minister of finance, Trevor Manuel, engendered widespread goodwill with a sensible first budget, for 1997/98. The following year, the last of the ANC's first term of office, he exploited that goodwill by bumping up VAT by a modest 2 per cent, to 16 per cent. The good sense of the move was widely perceived and, despite the customary grumbling, it was widely supported.

President Mbeki liked what he saw. Armouring himself with a barrage of rhetoric about the dire consequences of failure to deliver to the masses, he kicked VAT up to 19 per cent. The only problem, of course, was that he didn't match the rise in VAT with a commensurate lowering of income taxes, indirect taxes and customs duties.

Now Anlap was claiming mastery of the upliftment agenda. The Erwin Barnards and their class were drifting further out of reckoning as an important constituency. The fight was on for a bigger, hence more important, constituency. It lay to the ANC's left, not its right. The Erwin Barnards would just have to squeal, and then pay.

What was it that Erwin's father used to say about 'Die wet van Transvaal . . .?'

> One of the country's leading independent book and multimedia chains, MediaWorld, has announced that it will close its retail stores on 31 December. Mr Les Wilson, the chief executive of the chain's holding company, Barret Industrial, told our economic staff sales had declined in the last twenty-four months to unsustainable levels. The holding company's board had recently decided to concentrate on its core business in the infrastructure development field.

Not the only one, Erwin thought. The pattern of South African business had undergone a distinct change in recent years. The top end of the retail market had narrowed and its base had widened. The action had unmistakably moved to the lower end of the market. That's where the growth was, because that was the point of entry by new consumers.

One could see the pattern almost everywhere. Here it was books. Elsewhere it was clothing, foodstuffs, furnishings, housing, and electrical and electronic goods. The upmarket retailers, at the apex of the retail pyramid, were in the pinch. The mass marketers, often with the same categories of goods, but cheaper and more uniform, were making headway. At the top of the pyramid there was room for only a few specialists . . . and then fewer than before. Erwin wondered why anyone should be surprised. This was Africa, not California, for crying in a bucket. Still, there were plenty who acted as if it were – or should be – otherwise.

Emigration was one of the things that had hit the top end hard. Not only were there now fewer consumers at the pinnacle of the pyramid, but a particular spending pattern had emigrated with those who had left. Now it was polony rather than salami.

Those consumers at the top end of the market who remained weren't in a spending frame of mind. Against increasing taxes and an escalating cost of living, they were consolidating. Additionally, they were wondering whether those on their block who had sold up and gone had perhaps not done the wise thing. This was not a time for expanding and entrenching lifestyles. There was an overall levelling of life in South Africa, Erwin could see, as could anyone who cared to look. Discounting the phenomenal growth of those effectively outside the economy, for those within it the old days of the gross disparities in society were going – and had been going for the last five or ten years. (From a political point of view, of course, it was too little, too late and too slow. But that was another matter.)

In the tragic case of the book and software chain, the great levelling had another dimension. It represented the dumbing down of South Africa. What was happening to Fables & Fancies had already happened to the big libraries, to the universities' research departments, to publishing, to television and radio, and to the film and entertainment industry. Kung-fu had always been bigger than opera in South Africa. It was just that the balance was now tipping horribly.

And now for the weather . . .

Forget it. That's enough bad news for now. Erwin flipped the radio to a music station.

Tuesday, 17 September 2002: 10.15 a.m.
Spokes, Zama and the two men with them loitered on the pavement at the intersection where the four-lane road led out of the city, to join

the arterial Jan Smuts Drive leading to the green suburbs and brown shanty camps beyond. They were inconspicuous in the bustling crowd. Behind them were the new four-storey residential blocks the government had put up on abandoned CBD land, meant for those who had jobs downtown and had lived in Soweto and elsewhere before. Spokes had explained that he liked this spot because, if something 'went wrong', they could run into the apartment blocks where there were always lots of people. More importantly, the police didn't particularly like going in there.

Zama was nervous, a condition exaggerated by the heavy weight of the dark handgun that Spokes had slipped into his overall pocket, with a significant and examining look into Zama's face. Spokes himself was alert. His eyes constantly scanned the oncoming flow of traffic, and the vehicles that halted at the intersection.

He had explained to Zama what they were after, and what Zama had to do about it. They wanted one of the popular new family vehicles, cross-bred between a station wagon and a micro-bus. When Spokes gave the word, Zama was to race to the driver's side. Using the gun, he had to get the driver's door open and the driver out of the driving seat, across to the passenger side, as quickly as possible. Zama had to follow him, keeping the gun to the driver's body, making way for the next man to leap into the driver's set. Spokes emphasized that it had to be a smooth motion, giving no opportunity for the vehicle's owner to activate an alarm or tracking device, if there was either of these.

Zama saw Spokes stiffen. He followed his gaze, and saw the lime-green Mitsubishi Amigo it had fixed on.

Erwin had completed his business and was heading out of the city. He rolled down his window and tossed out the vitamized gum he had been chewing. It wasn't a nice thing to do, Erwin thought, but then downtown was so dirty anyway.

When Spokes saw Erwin's hand flick through the open window, he grunted the signal. Zama's coiled nerves shot him from his standing position like a sprinter from the blocks.

Thursday, 17 September 2015: 5.40 p.m.

Nobody called Zama by that name any more. He was known as Zakes, a name far more befitting a warlord, which was what he saw himself as nowadays. Spokes had died in the big sickness, like so many others had. Three years after Spokes's death, Ladypeace had become sick, too. She had to go to the government clinic every week for a year. She still had to go once a month, but she wasn't sick any more.

Before Spokes died, he had entrusted the leadership of the gang to Zakes.

Lots of things had changed, Zakes thought as he leaned against the broken gate. One of them was that he was no longer in the shanty town. Freedom Park was ugly, filthy and, he had to admit, too dangerous. Too many young men, like he used to be, were too desperate.

There was something else, though. It was an animosity different to that of the youngbloods who would challenge him for his position. Sections of the youth didn't seem to have the same respect for a man of affairs, such as himself, as they did in the old days. Zakes could see that among some of the young, fear of the gang was being replaced by antagonism towards it. The youth was always hard to understand.

The house behind him was a real, brick house. Larnies used to live in it. Not the sort of larnies that Zakes and the gang would have bothered raiding, but larnies nevertheless. When a few of the houses had stood empty for a while, Zakes and some of the top men in the gang had moved in. The rest of the larnies had left soon after that.

Now he was lord of the district and no-one for several blocks, and even beyond, would cross him. (Except for those upstart kids.) The house was where he did 'business'. The set-up suited him. He didn't want to be watching his back all the time. Others did it for him.

Zakes had been in jail twice. The first time had been the result of carelessness. A man in his position shouldn't do time for assault. Anycase he was out after a few months as part of an early release for first-time offenders. The second time the sentence had been longer. Or, it could have been. With the connivance of a group of warders, Zakes and scores of others had simply walked out one fine day. That was the last time the law bothered him.

From inside the house, Ladypeace called.

Thursday, 17 September 2015: 9.20 p.m.
Erwin was alone in his study, putting books, compact discs and papers into two boxes. Into one box he was carelessly tossing those

he didn't want. Into the other he was carefully packing those he did. He paused and put his fingers to the scar on his temple, which his receding hairline was lately rendering visible.

He remembered how he had got the scar, thirteen years ago, when he had been hi-jacked leaving town after an appointment at the bank headquarters. He recalled how nervous the youngster with the gun had been. He couldn't have been more than twenty. He recalled, too, how frightened he had been when the jittery youngster, after staring at him for a while as they drove with the second man behind the wheel, suddenly made him strip off his shirt and shoes. When they reached the motorway, the driver, who appeared much more confident than his younger companion, had pulled to the side of the road with the engine running. He had taken the gun from the youngster, and in the same movement had hit Erwin viciously on the side of his head. He had heard the older man say something and laugh before they opened a rear door, and rolled him out onto the road.

Many times Erwin had told the story of how he had been robbed of the Amigo . . . and his shirt and shoes. His apparel had been an almost poignant postscript to the crime that said something about the way things were.

Erwin was in a reflective mood. This wasn't surprising. He and Rita were packing up for good. The children had been gone for some years already. Lulu had gone to university in Ireland, and Adrian to one in New Zealand. Adrian had taken a job with a multinational and had been given a well-paid posting in Jakarta. Erwin and Rita would join him there for a while, then move on to Lombok, sister island to Bali in the Indonesian archipelago. Erwin was fifty-two and Rita had just turned fifty. They had plans for a small export operation, and they were still young enough to catch the second wave of the Pacific Rim boom.

As he packed, certain items would evoke particular memories, and Erwin found himself reviewing their lives and the homeland they would leave behind. The Barnards' own lives had not changed radically since they had settled in the housing park, except that the park now had a fleet of four guarded shuttles that were available to ferry residents from island to island in the suburbs beyond the walls of the village. The changes were mainly inside their dwelling, which had become their cocoon. Entertainment was cabled in. The practice of hundreds of people sitting in a cinema to watch a new movie had become an archaic curiosity. Banking and shopping were done at the keyboard. The virtual supermarket was replacing the suburban grocer. Even routine medical diagnosis was done on the computer Interlink's touch pad, which read their subcutaneous chips.

They had never seriously considered moving, not even after Erwin's promotion. They would merely have moved to another, similar estate – and the new ones were very, very expensive. Beyond the estate, and beyond the suburbs, things had got out of hand. The suburbs were encircled by a malevolent orbit of population explosion, chaotic shanty camps, poverty and criminality.

Erwin's promotion had come after Anlap's election victory in 2004. The parent board had scrambled and Erwin and Vusi Khumalo had found themselves directors of the South African operation. After that, though, business had stood still. The parent company had its sights set elsewhere in the world and South Africa had drifted out of the reckoning. South African executives never came into consideration for overseas postings. They were not considered to have the right kind of track record, nor the right kind of experience in the right kind of operating environment.

The Khumalos had had to give up their suburban home-and-garden ideal when the densification project at the end of their block had degenerated and destabilized the district.

The country's politics had delivered moments of high drama, even melodrama, you could say, in late 2003 during the run-up to the general election in February 2004. Soon after the calling of the election there had been a second wave of desertions from the ANC to the greater political magnet of Anlap. Among those who moved were personalities who had once been luminous in the ANC. Several had once been cabinet ministers. Some were among those whose fortunes had mysteriously declined in the struggle for the party leadership and the presidency towards the end of the Mandela era. Names like Jay Naidoo, Winnie Madikizela-Mandela, Pallo Jordan, Peter Mokaba, Geraldine Fraser-Moleketi – all occasioned a gasp of surprise when they made the news. Bantu Holomisa had abandoned his own political efforts some time before, and had thrown in his lot with Anlap.

The really big shock, though, was when Cyril Ramaphosa and two other high-profile businessmen disclosed that they had been placed high on Anlap's list. Ramaphosa accompanied his move with a burst of rhetoric about how business could not survive unless there was genuine social upliftment. Erwin believed that Ramaphosa believed what he said. But the way Erwin figured it, Ramaphosa was a profoundly canny power player, and there probably was more to his decision than was apparent.

The ANC didn't take happily, or even gracefully, to losing power. It behaved as if the new South Africa had been entrusted to the ANC by a moral decree, and its violation was tantamount to a national betrayal. There were rumblings about 'intervention' – but the ANC was a party without an effective power base. The civil service, the police and the military lumbered on as if nothing of great significance had happened.

There was little to tell about what happened after Anlap's victory that would be a revelation. As things transpired, the influx of ANC 'conservatives' made scant difference to Anlap's socialist character. 'People's' parties invariably talk a lot and indulge in grandiose symbolic gestures. But they do little in the long run to improve the lot of the people in whose name they govern. Socialist governments, in time, consume more capital than they produce. And Anlap certainly did. So the poor got both poorer and more numerous. The very rich, while definitely not getting more numerous, got decidedly richer.

Nevertheless, the rousing oratory of the Anlap leaders, combined with the party's programmes – however chaotic and clumsily implemented – for public works projects to create jobs, township upgrading and rural school building, were enough to capture the popular imagination. The fervour ran sufficiently high to carry Anlap through another election victory in 2009.

Soon afterwards, right-wing extremists made their most concerted attempt ever for an Afrikaner mini-state. A well-armed group numbering nearly a thousand made a stand in a remote region of the Northern Cape. For some weeks there was sporadic violence associated with the bid, in the region itself and in the cities. Then a combination of government indifference, internal dissent among the separatists and disinterest from other Afrikaners consigned the secession attempt to obscurity. Erwin supposed some of them were still there, holding out in nowhere, against nothing.

It was not only the remote geography that defeated the Afrikaner secession attempt. It got lost, also, in the pattern of disintegration of the body politic. Central government's reach into the provinces became more tenuous as the years rolled on. Regions developed differing characters. The agricultural provinces of Free State, North West and Northern had Anlap legislatures. White farmers who remained on the land were in constant conflict with the authorities and unionized farm labour. The travails of the white farmers, combined with only a marginal increase in the number of black farmers who produced above a subsistence level, resulted in escalating food imports making ever-bigger demands on the country's balance of payments.

Mpumalanga, also under an Anlap administration, became irredeemably mired in official corruption. Despite this, its picturesque small towns and hamlets became a popular refuge for those who wanted to, and who could, escape city life.

In the Eastern Cape a long-lost tradition of black agriculture, crushed by colonialism in the late nineteenth and early twentieth centuries, showed signs of reviving . . . but not enough to make a difference to national, or even the province's, agricultural output. Eastern Cape industries clung tenaciously to modest profitability in the face of persistent labour conflict.

KwaZulu/Natal was the only province where the ANC maintained its outright majority. Local government, however, struggled under critical financial deficiencies – its resources, along with the province's, having been depleted by runaway population growth and the Aids epidemic.

In the provincial polls in Gauteng, Anlap emerged, as it did in most other places, as the biggest party – but not bigger than the ANC and NDP combined, and that's just what the two opposition parties did. From 2004, the country's heartland province was ruled by a liberal coalition, which gave Gauteng a better shot at things, politically speaking. However, clashes between the provincial government and central government were intense. In this protracted battle, the paucity of powers granted to the provinces in the democratic constitution of 1996 were starkly revealed, and the ANC lived to regret its pyrrhic victory in having negotiated a hollow form of federalism. In the end, though, it didn't really matter. The waves of crime, unemployment, population growth and homelessness that engulfed the province would have defeated any government and any ideology.

For these reasons there had been a substantial shift of economic activity to the Western Cape. The National Party there had survived the formation of the NDP in 2002, although it wasn't an NP that anyone from the turn of the century would have recognized. The group that had refused to go along with the formation of the NDP was in reality a collection of coloured ethnic nationalists, reinforced by surviving white nationalists who gave the breakaway party the organizational muscle it needed to outpace its rivals. The province had traditionally been unfamiliar territory to the ANC. Anlap found it equally difficult to penetrate. Consequently, the legislature was headed by an NP dominated by coloured leadership and backed by middle-class and working-class supporters. The NDP was in opposition.

Crime in the province was high, but contained to tolerable levels by the parastatal security sector. In many instances, the parastatal security providers had evolved into contracted local government law-enforcement agencies, reminiscent of the American system of city police. The moderate economic growth and social development the province enjoyed helped stabilize the Western Cape.

The new South Africa left the Northern Cape behind. The province sometimes considered this to be its principal appeal. With its low population density, isolated communities and arid open spaces, life continued there according to a timeless pattern. Anlap, the ANC, the NDP and a version of the Western Cape's NP all squabbled ineffectually over political control. Apart from the flurry over the failed Afrikaner succession bid in 2009, the province remained at peace. The rest of the country heard little from it and paid it little attention.

By the end of the first decade of the twenty-first century, the country was sagging to its knees.

It was then that the great turnaround began. It was imperceptible at first. A new generation of South Africans was emerging with a new way of looking at life, and a new vision of itself. The new generation outgrew the belief that it deserved a good life merely by virtue of protesting its absence. Once more, it seemed, South Africa would owe an historical debt to its children.

A new form of social anger was detectable. This time it was directed at criminality, ignorance, corruption and sloth. In the nascence of the new atmosphere the ANC and the NDP formed a national coalition in 2012. In the course of the following year it devised a business plan for national revival. The plan was presented, amid much publicity and supportive debate, to the UN and the World Bank.

Television images of African retrogression contrasted with Chinese and other Asian successes. The Third World, painful exceptions aside, was emergent. A new spirit of emulation was taking hold in South Africa. Anlap slipped into the role of culprit and obstacle.

In 2014 a revived and rejuvenated ANC won the general election, and the country embarked on the long journey to recovery.

The economy had followed a parallel path. At the end of the Mandela era growth had reached 4 per cent, meaningfully short of that government's ambitions. In the Mbeki years growth hovered around 3 per cent, sometimes gaining, sometimes slipping. Anlap's victory in 2004 knocked it back to zero. The public works programmes and development projects launched by Anlap re-stimulated growth to 2 per cent in 2007. However, there was too little influx of private foreign capital and too little creation of private domestic capital to replace the capital that Anlap expended. Anlap's projects dwindled and collapsed. The economy reverted to its apartheid pattern of shrinkage.

Anlap nationalized the banks, claiming it had been a fundamental tenet of liberation that the ANC had reneged on. Public control of capital was necessary for mass development, it argued. The results were predictable.

When the great sea change of attitudes began to manifest, the ANC/NDP revival plan was drawn up, and the ANC won the 2014 election, it was like starting all over again in 1994.

It seemed foolish, Erwin thought, to have lived through the last two decades and to leave now when things were changing. But he simply didn't have the enthusiasm for the long recovery. In any event, it would take up the rest of his and Rita's productive lives. What lay ahead belonged to someone else, to the new generation.

Perhaps Adrian and Lulu would return one day. One day.

Erwin reached into a deep shelf where a row of old books had spent years behind a row of newer additions. He pulled out a book with yellowed edges, and was struck by the vivid illustration on its cover. A row of faces in an ecstasy of . . . what was it? Exultation or anxiety? His eye travelled to the title above, *When Mandela Goes.* He smiled ruefully and flexed his arm to toss it into the throw-away box. Then he paused, shrugged, and placed it in the take-along box.

CHAPTER THIRTEEN

LESSONS FROM THE FUTURE

Defying the inevitable

. . . those who spent
Life without infamy and without praise.
They are mingled with that caitiff regiment
Of the angels, who rebelled not, yet avowed
To God no loyalty, on themselves intent.
Heaven chased them forth, lest their allegiance cloud
Its beauty, and the deep Hell refuses them,
For, beside such, the sinner would be proud.

DANTE, 1307

We live as if the future doesn't exist. But it does. It's with us in the present in an embryonic form. The seeds of the future are planted in the past, they incubate with us today, and they mature tomorrow.

It is a conventional wisdom to say that we don't know what the future holds, and that we don't have any control over it. But it is more true of the past to say that we have no control over what has happened. The continuum of events pauses with us in the present day, and by interceding judiciously and with foresight, we may exert a great deal of influence on what awaits us in the future.

GOODBYE TO ALL THIS

South Africa is transfixed by its present. Given the momentous events that have occurred, it is quite understandable. The country is assaying its achievement of democracy. The first democratic government is under daily scrutiny here and abroad. What is necessary now is to extend the horizons of that scrutiny. South Africa must assess all its probable futures and determine the one it wants. Then the present must be measured in terms of that selection. If the measure finds the present wanting, then action must be taken now.

What has gone before in this book is an illustration of the country's future if events continue to evolve in the manner they are. The picture that has been drawn, based on extrapolations from the present, is of South Africa's most likely future. But it is not inevitable.

South African society is being driven by great forces. If its leaders and citizens do not transform it now, it will transform itself. Then all in it will have to accept the results produced by these blind forces, referred to in this discussion as the silent dynamics.

NOT ALONE

South Africa's situation is not new. There are historical precedents of countries and nations in the grip of the forces that have taken hold of South Africa. Nor is South Africa's situation unique in today's world. There are other countries driven by similar dynamics. A fortunate few are solving the problems, and breaking free of the grasp of poverty, unbridled population growth, resource depletion, destabilizing urbanization, ignorance and crime. Others are showing tentative signs that they may begin to do the same.

So, if there is a way of evading the tentacles of the silent dynamics, and if South Africa is to defeat probability, the question, naturally, is how? This book is essentially about the problem, not its solution. Therefore, what follows in these remaining pages is meant only to highlight some of the avenues along which answers may be found.

NO, THE OTHER KENNEDY

Yale University's Paul Kennedy sees a paradigm in late eighteenth-century England for today's central global conflict, the clash between the haves and the have-nots. England's largely rural and ill-educated population was booming. At the same time, the Industrial Revolution was producing an elite founded on new technology and capital. The rural population migrated to the cities, to engender there harrowing conditions that threatened the stability of society. Kennedy draws a parallel with today's global imbalances, wherein the leading nations have industrialized and slowed population growth, while the world's heavily populated, impoverished countries lack the tools for advancement.

In England's case, effective social reforms, the democratization of education, the underclass's ability to elevate itself and the beneficial effects of supply and demand fended off disaster. The new technologies were able to provide employment and food. 'The challenges posed by one of these great forces for change was thus answered by the other force,' Kennedy says. England's experience demonstrated that a swift-growing population will not necessarily lead to lower per capita standards of living if its productivity is increasing at an equal or faster pace.

The lesson for South Africa, which replicates eighteenth-century England's social divisions, is clear. The lesson is also disturbing, as productivity, in real terms, is declining relative to the growth of the population.

Kennedy points to an important distinction in his example. The interaction of the forces in England's case took place within the borders of one country. Until recently the same disparities that existed there had been separated in the modern world by national boundaries, and even by continents. Globalization is now drawing the fates of nations together. This creates a new contact point for conflict, and challenges the world as a whole to achieve what England did in order to ensure stability and peace in the new century.

Once again, the parallels with South Africa loom large. Apartheid built a wall between the elite and the disadvantaged. Apartheid's demise has been the equivalent of globalization – the two classes have been brought into contact and drawn into a common fate. South Africa will have to meet the same challenges that the world does, and resolve the potential for social conflict if it is to avoid disaster in the opening years of the new millennium.

It is worth noting that Kennedy's opinion is that few, if any, contemporary political leaders are willing to face up to this – 'the greatest test for human society as it confronts the twenty-first century'. South Africa's political leaders have displayed no signs yet that they will make themselves an exception.

SUNTER SAYS

Clem Sunter, South Africa's best-known scenario strategist, whose thinking is schooled in the same intellectual framework as Kennedy's, has garnered acclaim for his 'high road, low road' scenarios for South Africa.

In terms of Sunter's description, South Africa has already passed its first great challenge in taking the high road. This was the achievement of a negotiated political settlement. It set the country up with the first set of conditions needed for stability and the pursuit of prosperity.

Sunter's view, and that of the international team of experts he has assembled, is that South Africa once again stands at a decisive moment. Once more, it is faced with a choice of a high road and a low road. The subject of the present choice is no longer political stability – it is economic growth. South Africa is faced with the challenge of translating its political gains into economic success. Failure to do so, according to Sunter, will reduce South Africa to a state where wealth is distributed rather than created, where authoritarian government becomes an inevitability, and where regional and social conflict will ultimately result in a wasteland.

Sunter is unequivocal on the priority of economic growth. A period of high growth must precede attempts to transform society through programmes of distribution and welfare. 'You have to earn the money before you spend it,' he says. He is not specific on precisely the level of growth that will ensure the high road, but he intimates that it needs to be in the 6 per cent-plus range shown by other countries that have sprung free of social decay.

Sunter recognizes that the stakes are high. He says South Africa's goal must be the creation of an entrepreneurial class with world-class aspirations . . . and that it must have the active co-operation of the unions. He makes the point about failure graphically: 'Both Mussolini and Hitler were elected by the unemployed to improve their lot.'

BREAKING THE CYCLE

There isn't an Ingredient X that can be interposed in the national mix, which will make a country turn from decline to growth. Kennedy makes much of what he calls the interconnectedness of the issues and dynamics that produce either success or failure. The variables that produce and accompany growth are complex and interrelated, and defy precise categorization and dissection.

In a seminal work titled *The Nature of Mass Poverty*, the Harvard economist John Kenneth Galbraith described impoverished rural communities where mineral companies built and maintained facilities such as schools and clinics while they undertook exploration in the communities' habitats. When the companies completed their work, they handed the facilities to the communities. Before long, the classrooms and clinics fell into disuse and disrepair. In this Galbraith saw the cyclical characteristic of poverty: the communities lacked the motivation to better their lot precisely because their poverty had deprived them of the will to succeed. Galbraith's example illustrates, too, that an outside agent – like a government, for example – cannot alone break the cycle of poverty. However, if the people who suffer the affliction cannot do it either, it makes our question of how South Africa can surmount Kennedy's great test of humanity, or how the country can embark on Sunter's next high road, an exceedingly difficult one to answer.

Yet it does happen. The successful developing countries of the world are the answer in practice. There is simply an indefinable moment when a shift in attitudes takes place, and individuals and whole nations take their fate into their hands – and construct their futures instead of waiting for them.

The worst manifestations of that decisive turn around are what has been referred to earlier as the Mozambique syndrome. In such cases a nation has to sink to its lowest level of survival before it discovers a workable desire for betterment.

It is not necessary, however, to wait that long.

MONKEY BUSINESS

A clue of great curiosity to the nature of social progress exists in the hundredth-monkey phenomenon, recounted by Cape Town psychiatrist Anthony Teggin, from the work of Ken Keyes. The Japanese monkey, *macaca fuscata*, was observed in the wild by scientists for a period of more than thirty years. An important element of the monkeys' diet was sand-encrusted sweet potatoes. In 1952 on the island of Koshima a young female monkey for the first time washed her sweet potato before eating it. Gradually other monkeys copied her. By the autumn of 1958 all the young monkeys and some of the adults had learned to wash their sweet potatoes. Other monkeys continued eating sandy sweet potatoes.

One day one more monkey – the exact number is not known, but convention has designated it the hundredth-monkey – learned to wash its sweet potato. By that evening almost every monkey in the tribe had taken to washing the sweet potatoes. The added energy of the hundredth-monkey somehow created a breakthrough.

Now comes the interesting part: from that time the colonies of monkeys on other islands across the sea and on the mainland of Takasakiyama also began to wash their sweet potatoes. Teggin concludes: 'It seems that when a certain critical number achieves an awareness, this new awareness may be communicated from mind to mind. Although the exact numbers may vary, the hundredth-monkey phenomenon means that there is a point at which, if only one more person tunes into a new consciousness, the collective thought field is altered so that this new awareness can reach and affect everyone.'

WANTED: 100 MONKEYS

What is instructive about this delightful anecdote is that the initiative began with the monkeys, not the scientists. For the purposes of our search for a South African answer: the impetus for South Africa's revival and salvation must come from its people, not its government. As long as the government provides the right environment, it's doing its job.

Professor Christof Heyns of the Centre for Human Rights at the University of Pretoria proposed transplanting the concept of the American Peace Corps into South Africa. Students and other youthful volunteers would work in holiday camps that would tackle building projects in disadvantaged communities. The symbolic value would be that communities would see that others care, and that problems can be solved. They would also benefit from the transfer of skills, according to Heyns.

That's a good monkey. Ninety-nine more needed. It's an example only, of course. In reality the country boasts many praiseworthy self-help initiatives. But even a cursory glance across the national board reveals that the hundredth monkey is not yet in sight.

CRIME AND ATTITUDES

Crime and corruption come readily into the reckoning of the argument that endemic social problems can be solved only by a change of attitudes.

Beefing up the police and renovating the justice system will help contain crime. But that's all. Proposals for new funding for law enforcement, metropolitan police forces and the like all have their place. They would all, however, be symptomatic measures and would not cure the underlying social sickness.

If the hundredth-monkey phenomenon were to work here, then it would have to be accompanied by powerful symbolism. The monkeys that must begin the effect are those sitting at the top of the social tree. Figures of authority must reform first. While politicians, bankers, school principals, policemen and civil servants are corrupt, there can be little hope that those lower on the social scale will attach value to honesty. While cabinet ministers waste millions with impunity, no-one can reasonably expect the factory worker to be diligent about conserving his company's resources.

SUCCESS STORIES

Just as there is no Ingredient X, there is no magic formula for economic success. The fruitless attempts of economists to develop a comprehensive theory that would bind the successful emerging economies of the last quarter of this century together in a neat and portable explanation demonstrate this very clearly. The failed bids to find a formula have included a major analytical study by the World Bank in the early years of the nineties. The patent appeal of such a formula, if one could be found, is that it could be applied to the laggards – and many of the world's most intractable human problems, and much of its suffering, would be over. But there isn't one.

There are, however, a number of characteristics that can be found among the high-growth achievers in Asia, recently in South America, and in the fastest-growing economy in the West – the Republic of Ireland's.

The first is social stability and political continuity. That doesn't mean full-blown democracy, but it can. In fact, in the majority of cases, particularly those in Asia, measures by conventional Western political yardsticks would find the subjects falling more than a little short. Commensurate with this fact is that individual rights and freedoms rank a lower priority than uniformity of purpose. In one of the most outstanding of the Asian successes, Malaysia, a popular singer was banned from government radio and television in 1996 for quipping 'Who's he?' at the mention of the prime minister's name. An official said the singer's commitment to Malaysia had become suspect and that 'such behaviour should not go unpunished'.

The successful emerging economies have, without exception, fervently embraced technology at all levels. Along with the recognition of technology as the means to prosperity, these countries have all extended themselves to pour maximum resources into education. India, for example, has come to the fore as an unexpected world contender in computer data processing services. A number of large

South African companies have their data processed in India.

While some of the countries have confounded free-market advocates with selective interventionist policies, they have all been what the World Bank describes as 'market friendly'. In addition, they have all opened their economic gateways for two-way traffic into and out of their economies. And they have all looked beyond their borders for business.

Their public sectors are invariably free, or substantially free, of corruption. With certain notable exceptions, like South Korea, there has been effective agreement between the public and private sectors – including the unions – on economic goals and methods. In Argentina union compliance was won and is maintained by strong-arm tactics, but it is there.

All have low personal taxes, usually averaging around 20 per cent, and low customs duties and trade tariffs. The low taxes have led to high compliance by taxpayers and collection is cheap and efficient.

Individual countries in these groups have undertaken economic processes that are interesting from a South African point of view. In a five-year period between 1989 and 1994 the government of Argentina transferred no less than one-third of the entire economy from public control into private hands. The country rode out the pain that came with the process. A former state oil company turned its losses into profits, but cut its workforce from 52,000 to 4,500 in doing so. The national result, though, was worth it. GDP more than doubled in this period and per capita incomes bloomed.

In its drive for technological emancipation, India recognized that the lifestyles of its majority were based on the land. Twenty-five years ago it began an intensive agricultural development programme. Before long, this vast country was self-sufficient in food. The agricultural programme had the dual effect of slowing migration to the cities. In its 1997/98 budget, the Indian government made dramatic across-the-board cuts in personal income taxes, corporate taxes and import duties.

Ireland has been able to maintain a steady wage-restraint policy and has matched personal tax cuts with far-reaching cutbacks in government spending.

GOING FOR GROWTH

One of the central ideas on which the discussion in this book has rested is that the balance between population growth and economic growth is the most important factor determining South Africa's future destination, whether prosperity or disaster. In a situation where there is any doubt about the prospects for economic growth, the government's highest duty becomes the curbing of population growth. This applies equally if there is economic growth, but not enough to outpace population growth. Such a situation means that some of the people are getting richer, while most of the people are getting poorer. This is a recipe for a perilous future.

The above equation would be relatively easy to deal with if it weren't for the fact, proven over and over again in developing countries, that the only effective curb on population growth is economic growth. Only in circumstances of mounting prosperity do emergent societies become motivated to limit births. There is no way around it: South Africa's survival depends on its ability to grow its economy.

GEARING UP

The central document in South Africa's economic life is the government's *Growth, Employment and Redistribution* strategy. In reality, GEAR is a feel-good document. It is strong on what must happen, but weak on how the fine goals can be realized.

The result is that few economists believe that the central target of 6.1 per cent growth by 2000 will be achieved. Nevertheless, of all of South Africa's deep-rooted problems, the economy is the one most amenable to executive action. All it will take is a little more boldness and a little more imagination.

STERN MEASURES

Early in 1997, the prominent American economist Joel Stern visited South Africa and discharged an observation of incisive simplicity: no economic growth until exchange controls, crime and high taxes go.

Leaving aside crime, which one can only hope will wither in the face of the beneficial consequences of action on the remaining two, the observation suggests a course of action that is so practical, and so self-evident, that it hardly requires explanation.

Exchange controls are the antithesis of the dominant modern trends in the world economy, globalization and liberalization. They are a barrier to two of the things the South African economy needs most – foreign investment and unfettered access to world markets. Certainly, money will leave the economy when controls go. But if that money were not matched by an inflow, then there wouldn't be an economy worth protecting anyway. Stern was definite on the subject: 'Never has a country which got rid of exchange control failed to benefit,' he told the *Sunday Independent*'s John Spira.

High taxes militate against growth and private endeavour, and foster evasion and fraud. Stern said South African rates averaged about 10 per cent higher than industrial nations and were a bar to attracting skills to the country. The world is replete with contemporary examples of how lower taxes result in larger flows of funds into the national *fiscus* as people work harder at the prospect of making more money, and evasion abates.

The only thing that is hard to understand about action on exchange controls and taxes, which could be effected in a week, is why the government didn't do it in its first months of office. If the government should find itself in a position, even belatedly, to take decisive action, it might just chuck in the wad of anti-trust legislation it has been fingering for ages. Nearly 80 per cent of the market capitalization of the Johannesburg Stock Exchange is controlled by five – yep, just five – corporations. This execrable state of affairs is a principal culprit in South Africa's hurtful price spiral, which has pushed the country into the top bracket of the world's most expensive places to live, eat, drive, dress, manufacture, stock and much else. It would be an opportunity for the government to show whose side it really is on.

Vigorous economic growth is the key to South Africa's salvation. Only through the creation of real prosperity can a future of social decay and political regression be avoided. Ultimately, this depends on the country's people discovering the zeal within themselves to take charge of the future in the present.

In the meantime, acts of great practical and symbolic value lie within the ambit of the government. It should be bold enough to make a monkey of itself. It might just be the hundredth.

NOTES ON SOURCES

The data that support the argument in this text are drawn mainly from my own files. They, in turn, are made up mainly of clippings from South African newspapers and periodicals. The publications I have drawn from most heavily are *The Citizen*, *The Economist* (British), *Finance Week*, *Financial Mail*, *Mail & Guardian*, *The Star*, *The Sunday Independent* and *The Sunday Times.* The main resource outside of my own collection has been the South African Institute of Race Relations. It has, to my mind, the best current affairs library in the country, under the skilled direction of Ellen Potter. The institute's regular publications, *Frontiers of Freedom* and *Fast Facts* – together with the it's irreplaceable, annual South Africa Survey – are indispensable to current affairs research. I am indebted to the institute's research staff. Its members are named below, and bear no responsibility whatsoever for the constructs I have placed on the factual material they supply.

In addition, the publications listed below have been important sources of information, and useful as background to the ideas that have been put forward.

Basil Davidson, *Africa in History.* Orion, London 1992.

Ian Emsley, *The Malaysian Experience of Affirmative Action.* Human & Rousseau and Tafelberg, Cape Town 1996.

Hermann Giliomee, 'Liberal and Populist Democracy in South

Africa: Challenges, New Threats to Liberalism'. Presidential address to the South African Institute of Race Relations, Johannesburg 1996.

E.J. Hobsbawm, *The Age of Revolution – Europe 1789–1848*, Weidenfeld and Nicolson, London 1962

Tom Lodge, *Black Politics in South Africa Since 1945.* Ravan, Johannesburg 1983.

John Kane-Berman, *South Africa's Silent Revolution.* South African Institute of Race Relations and Southern, Johannesburg 1990.

Paul Kennedy, *Preparing for the Twenty-first Century.* Harper Collins, London 1993.

Paul Kennedy, *The Rise and Fall of Great Powers.* Fontana, London 1989.

Arthur Keppel-Jones, *When Smuts Goes.* Shuter & Shooter, Pietermaritzburg 1947.

Martin Meredith, *South Africa's New Era : The 1994 Election*, Mandarin, London 1994.

Greg Mills (ed.), *South African Yearbook of International Affairs 1996.* The South African Institute of International Affairs, Johannesburg 1996.

National Productivity Institute, Proceedings of the World Productivity Assembly. Pretoria 1996.

Roger Omond, *The Apartheid Handbook.* Penguin, Harmandsworth 1985.

Lawrence Schlemmer, Quarterly Political Notes. South African Chamber of Business Parliamentary Information Centre, Cape Town (June – August 1996.)

Robert Schrire (ed.), *Wealth or Poverty? Critical Choices for South Africa.* Oxford University Press, Cape Town 1992.

Elizabeth Sidiropoulos, Anthea Jeffery, Shaun Mackay, Rory Gallocher, Herma Forgey and Cheryl Chipps, *South Africa Survey 1995/96.* South African Institute of Race Relations, Johannesburg 1996.

Alvin Toffler, *Future Shock.* Pan Books, London 1971.

Alvin Toffler, *The Third Wave.* Pan Books, London 1981.

Alvin Toffler, *Power Shift.* Bantam, New York 1991.

Bob Tucker & Bruce R. Scott (eds.), *South Africa: Prospects for Successful Transition.* Juta, Cape Town 1992.

Trade Union Research Project, *A User's Guide to the South African Economy*. Y Press, Durban 1994.

United Nations, Globalization and Liberalization: Development in the face of two powerful currents. New York & Geneva, 1996.

United Nations, Human Development Report 1994, Oxford University Press, New York 1994.

United Nations Conference on Trade and Development, Unctad Review 1995. New York 1995.

Minnie Venter (ed.), *Prospects for Progress: Critical Choices for Southern Africa.* Maskew Miller Longman, Cape Town 1994.

Anne V. Whyte, *Building a New South Africa: Environment, Reconstruction and Development.* International Development Research Centre, Ottawa 1995.

ACKNOWLEDGEMENTS

Many of the ideas that appear in this book arose, or were tested, in discussions with friends whose opinion I value – Peter Godwin, David Marcus, Kent McNamara and Anthony Teggin. Others stoically tolerated being test circuits for thoughts. They all contributed greatly, but the responsibility for what has been done with their ideas and opinions is mine alone. Rob Davies, Lena Farugia and Lynne McNamara read early drafts of the text and provided helpful guidance and encouragement. George Mazarakis, with his finely-honed senses of timing, pace and mood in good journalism, made valuable observations. Glenda Parker is a rare publishing executive. She had the vision to embrace this project, and act on it, within an afternoon. She and her lunch account kept up the spirits of those involved. Gavin Perrow provided first-line editing of a quality that is deeply reassuring to a writer. Jackie Kerr kept the finances on track, and remained bright even when they didn't.

From the start, Adele de Villiers believed in the worth of this project as much as I did. Through the long haul, her support was finessed and unwavering.